Adventures at Sea
in the Great Age of Sail

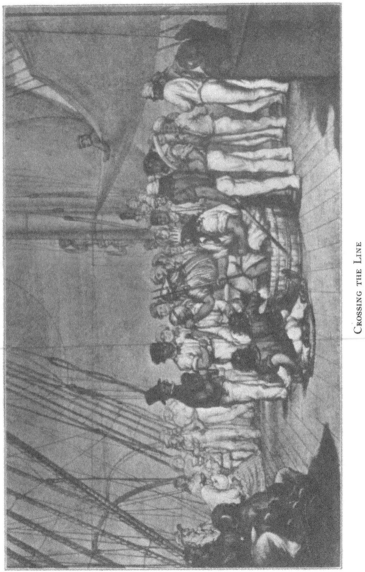

CROSSING THE LINE

From a colored lithograph in the Macpherson Collection

Adventures at Sea in the Great Age of Sail

Five Firsthand Narratives

With an Introduction by
CAPTAIN ELLIOT SNOW

Dover Publications, Inc., New York

This Dover edition, first published in 1986, is an unabridged republication of the work first published by The Marine Research Society, Salem, Mass., in 1925 under the title *The Sea, the Ship and the Sailor*.

Library of Congress Cataloging-in-Publication Data

Adventures at sea in the great age of sail.

Reprint. Originally published: The sea, the ship, and the sailor. Salem, Mass. : Marine Research Society, 1925.

Includes index.

1. Adventure and Adventurers. 2. Voyages and travels. I. Title.

G525.S44   1986   910.4′5   86-11559
ISBN-13: 978-0-486-25177-6 (pbk.)
ISBN-10: 0-486-25177-2 (pbk.)

Manufactured in the United States by Courier Corporation
25177207
www.doverpublications.com

PREFACE

THERE *needs no Apology in Behalf of Books of this Nature; they have, at all times, been favourably received, and never rejected, but upon plain and undeniable Conviction of Insincerity. They agreeably amuse, and usefully instruct; and are consequently relished by Readers of every sort. They are pleasing to those, who, at every turn, would be surprised with extraordinary Events, unexpected Accidents, and miraculous Deliverances; and acceptable to those, who, moving in a loftier Sphere, are desirous of converting all they know to Public Use; and these, regardless of what the former most admire, are particularly solicitous after Descriptions and Accounts of Persons, Places and Things.*

So wrote John Cockburn, in 1735, after returning from his wanderings in Spanish America; and it is safe to say that the spirit of adventurous exploration is as keen today as it ever was although little of the earth's surface is now unknown to curious mankind.

Two of the following narratives are here printed for the first time from journals recently discovered and now in the possession of the Peabody Museum, Salem, and Mr. Lawrence W. Jenkins, its Acting Director. John Bartlett, the sailor from Boston, in his voyage to the then, almost unknown Northwest Coast of North America, passed through many unusual experiences. He bartered with Indians along the Alaskan coast; narrowly escaped capture in the Pacific islands where

Captain Cook was killed twelve years before; spent considerable time in Chinese waters; killed sea lions in the desolate Kerguelen Islands in the Southern Indian Ocean; chased whales in the Mozambique Channel in company with Dunkirk whalers; and at last disappeared from sight while a "pressed" sailor in the British Navy. Captain Knights, of the Salem brig *Spy*, who wrote the other journal, was one of those master-mariners who sailed from that port a century ago in small vessels and bartered for beche-le-mer and tortoise shell with the savage islanders of the Pacific. His observations on native life in New Zealand and in the Fijis have unusual interest.

A scarce volume among American voyages is the "Narrative of the Sufferings and Adventures of Captain Charles H. Barnard in a Voyage Round the World during the years 1812, 1813, 1814, 1815 and 1816," New York, 1829. Captain Barnard's vessel was seized in the Falkland Islands by a shipwrecked crew of English seamen and he was soon after abandoned on an uninhabited island where he lived for nearly two years. Later, he tried Robinson Crusoe life on the island of Masafuera, off the Chilian coast, from which he was eventually rescued and brought home by way of China and the Cape of Good Hope. This volume may be found in the Library of Congress and two or three other libraries. The larger part of the Barnard narrative is here reprinted through the courtesy of Mr. Frank Wood, Curator of the Old Dartmouth Historical Society, New Bedford.

The adventures of John Nicol have been taken from a little-known volume published in 1822 in Edinburgh.

Nicol fought off the New England coast during the Revolution and was in the frigate *Surprise* when she captured the *Jason* commanded by Capt. John Manley of Marblehead. He afterwards sailed with Captain Portlock to the Sandwich Islands and the Northwest Coast of America. His account of experiences while steward of a ship carrying female convicts to New South Wales, is most entertaining.

William Mariner's account of his experiences while a captive in the Tonga Islands, in many respects may be compared with Herman Melville's classic story of life in Typee. It should be better known and is included as a fitting complement.

In the preparation of this volume a cordial spirit of coöperation has been shown by the officers of the Peabody Museum, Salem; the officials of the Harvard College Library; Mr. A. G. Macpherson of Tigh-na-Mara, Alverstoke, Hants; Mr. Charles C. Willoughby, Director of the Peabody Museum of Archæology and Ethnology, Cambridge; and Mr. Herbert Putnam, Librarian of Congress.

Especial thanks are due to Judge F. W. Howay of New Westminster, British Columbia, for his valuable annotations on Bartlett's "Journal"; and last, and also first, an expression of high appreciation belongs to Captain Elliot Snow, Construction Corps, United States Navy, for supplying a fitting Introduction to the following pages and also for his courteous helpfulness on several occasions.

CONTENTS

INTRODUCTION BY CAPT. ELLIOT SNOW, CON-
STRUCTION CORPS, UNITED STATES NAVY . . xiii

I. A NARRATIVE OF THE ADVENTURES OF CAPT.
CHARLES H. BARNARD OF NEW YORK,
DURING A VOYAGE ROUND THE WORLD
(1812-1816), WITH AN ACCOUNT OF HIS
ABANDONMENT AND SOLITARY LIFE FOR
TWO YEARS ON ONE OF THE FALKLAND
ISLANDS 1

II. THE ADVENTURES OF JOHN NICOL, MARI-
NER, DURING THIRTY YEARS AT SEA . . 105

III. A JOURNAL OF A VOYAGE IN THE BRIG "SPY,"
OF SALEM (1832-1834), JOHN B. KNIGHTS,
MASTER 168

IV. THE REMARKABLE TRANSACTIONS WHICH
TOOK PLACE AT THE TONGA ISLANDS, IN
THE SOUTH PACIFIC OCEAN, DURING THE
CAPTIVITY OF WILLIAM MARINER, ONE OF
THE SURVIVORS OF THE "PORT AU PRINCE,"
PRIVATEER, WHICH WAS DESTROYED BY
THE NATIVES 208

V. A NARRATIVE OF EVENTS IN THE LIFE OF
JOHN BARTLETT OF BOSTON, MASSACHU-
SETTS, IN THE YEARS 1790-1793, DURING
VOYAGES TO CANTON, THE NORTHWEST
COAST OF NORTH AMERICA, AND ELSE-
WHERE 287

ILLUSTRATIONS

CROSSING THE LINE . . . . *Frontispiece*
From a colored lithograph in the Macpherson Collection.

FACING PAGE

THE WRECK OF THE "ISABELLA" 6
From an engraving in Barnard's *Narrative of Sufferings and Adventures,* New York, 1829.

MAP OF A PART OF THE FALKLAND ISLANDS . . 7
From the original survey made in 1815 by Capt. Charles H. Barnard.

THE RETURN OF CAPTAIN BARNARD'S COMPANIONS 46
From an engraving in Barnard's *Narrative of Sufferings and Adventures,* New York, 1829.

ARRIVAL OF THE SHIP "MILLWOOD" AT MASSAFUERO 100
From an engraving in Barnard's *Narrative of Sufferings and Adventures,* New York, 1829.

VIEW OF THE ISLAND OF ST. HELENA 101
From a mezzotint by Edward Orme in the Macpherson Collection.

VIEW OF ST. GEORGE, GRENADA, W. I. 122
From a mezzotint by W. Daniel in the Macpherson Collection.

VIEW OF KARAKAKOOA BAY, OWYHEE 123
From the engraving by W. Byrne, in Cook's *Voyages,* London, 1784.

A MAN OF PRINCE WILLIAM'S SOUND 132
From the engraving by J. Basire, in Cook's *Voyages,* London, 1784.

FACING PAGE

WHAMPOA, CHINA . . . .
From an engraving by E. Duncan, in the Macpherson   133
Collection, after a painting by W. J. Huggins, show-
ing the view from Dane's Island looking towards
Canton.

THE ENTRANCE OF PORT JACKSON AND PART OF   148
THE TOWN OF SYDNEY, NEW SOUTH WALES   .
From an engraving in the Macpherson Collection, after
a drawing by Major Taylor, 48th Regiment, made in
1822.

VIEW OF LISBON FROM THE TAGUS 149
From an engraving in the Macpherson Collection, after
a drawing made in 1792 by Noel.

VIEW OF VALETTE, MALTA 164
From an engraving made in 1818, now in the Macpherson Collection.

THE SCHOONER "SPY," OF SALEM, MASS.   . . 168
From a copy of a watercolor in the possession of Stephen W. Phillips.

A MAORI VILLAGE IN NEW ZEALAND 176
From a photograph in the Peabody Museum of Archæology and Ethnology, Cambridge, Mass.

A NEW ZEALAND GIRL 177
From a photograph in the Peabody Museum, Salem,
Mass.

WILLIAM MARINER IN TONGA ISLAND COSTUME   226
From the engraving by Abel Bowen published in 1820.

A FIATOOKA OR MORAI, TONGA ISLANDS . . . 227
From an engraving by W. Ellis, in Cook's *Voyages*,
London, 1784.

VIEW AT ANAMOOKA, TONGA ISLANDS 244
From an engraving by W. Byrne, in Cook's *Voyages*,
London, 1784.

FACING PAGE

BOXING MATCH AT HAPAEE, TONGA ISLANDS . 245
From an engraving by I. Taylor, in Cook's *Voyages*,
London, 1784.

TONGA ISLAND GIRLS 276
From a photograph in the Peabody Museum of Arch-
ælogy and Ethnology, Cambridge, Mass.

A TONGA ISLAND HOUSE 277
From a photograph in the Peabody Museum of Arch-
ælogy and Ethnology, Cambridge, Mass.

MAP OF THE NORTHWEST COAST OF NORTH
AMERICA 288
From a Dutch map after the Vancouver survey, now in
the Harvard College Library.

PROSPECT OF BATAVIA, JAVA 289
From an engraving made in 1652 and now in the Macpherson Collection.

VIEW OF HABITATIONS IN NOOTKA SOUND . . . 302
From an engraving by S. Smith, in Cook's *Voyages*,
London, 1784.

INTERIOR OF A HOUSE IN NOOTKA SOUND . . . 303
From an engraving by W. Sharp, in Cook's *Voyages*,
London, 1784.

THE SNOW "GUSTAVUS" 312
From the drawing in Bartlett's Journal, now in the possession of Lawrence W. Jenkins.

HOUSE AND TOTEM POLE OF THE HAIDA INDIANS 312
From the drawing in Bartlett's Journal, now in the
possession of Lawrence W. Jenkins. Supposed to be
the earliest known representation of a totem pole.

HAWAIIAN ISLAND GIRLS 313
From a photograph in the Peabody Museum, Salem,
Mass.

MACAO, CHINA 318
From a Chinese painting in the Peabody Museum, Salem, Mass.

FACING PAGE

VIEW OF PORT LOUIS, ISLE OF FRANCE 322
From an engraving in the Macpherson Collection.

VIEW OF CHRISTMAS HARBOR, KERGUELEN LAND 323
From an engraving by Newton in Cook's *Voyages*,
London, 1784.

HOTTENTOTS DEVOURING THE ENTRAILS OF A
BULLOCK 334
From an engraving in Drake's *Collection of Voyages*,
London, 1770, in the Library of Congress.

INTRODUCTION

"THAT the Monarchs of *Great Britain* have a peculiar and sovereign Authority upon the Ocean, is a Right so ancient and undeniable, that it never was publickly disputed, but by *Hugo Grotius,* in his *Mare Liberum,* published in the year 1636, in Favour of the *Dutch* Fishery upon our Coasts; which Book was fully controverted by Mr. *Seldon's Mare Clausum,* wherein he proves this Sovereignty from the Laws of GOD and of Nature, besides an uninterrupted Fruition of it for so many Ages past, as that its beginning cannot be traced out."

So wrote William Mountaine in the Preface to his "Seaman's Vade-Mecum," published in London in 1778; and this doctrine, in its application, doubtless was very acceptable so far as the subjects of the King of Great Britain were concerned; but when his colonies in America took exception to over-seas government and revolted, at the close of their successful revolution, the new States, in perfecting their future relations with European countries, found themselves facing commercial isolation. The Navigation System of Great Britain automatically excluded American ships from trading in English ports and also with the English islands in the West Indies, where for a century and a half they had carried on a lucrative exchange of commodities. The French government granted only limited privileges of trade in the French West Indies; and Spain closed many of her ports to American vessels. The Dutch and Danish ports were open, however, and were the salvation of many an American merchant. It was a trying time for Yankee shipping and for the large number of seamen who had been released from service in the naval vessels and the many privateers.

Ship-owners had to find occupation for their ships and their seamen and having been deprived of their old triangular voyage to the West Indies and Europe, these enterprising merchants and sea captains turned to China and the Baltic and this trade grew rapidly. Much illicit trade existed, of course, and the losses by seizure were considerable, but the profits were large and warranted taking chances.

A few years later the European war became worldwide and notwithstanding the great losses by seizure, first by one combatant and then by another, Yankee ships and Yankee sailors prospered. English blockades and French decrees were alike evaded by the enterprising American ship-owners and their resourceful sea captains and maritime commerce grew marvelously.

The adaptability of the American master-mariner here emphasized has never been justly placed in doubt. When deprived of a known commercial advantage he has faced about, times without number, and by daring ventures into untried seas, has brought success out of seeming failure.

In this school of experience there was developed a type of trustworthy yet adventurous manhood that displayed with pride "The Stars and Stripes" in all parts of the world, — in the waters of the great Northwest; among the islands of the mid-Pacific; in the far

distant, uncharted and little-known waters of Poly-
nesia and Malaysia; along the coast of China, into the
"Spice Islands" and India, to the extremes of South
America and Africa.

It was from this type of men that our Nation has
drawn heavily, then and since, during every war. The
merchant marine has ever been a school of our Navy in
its larger meaning. This was largely so at the outset
and from it have sprung some of its renowned officers
and many gallant seamen.

In recent years Capt. John H. Sears, the Brewster
shipmaster, while writing of the men of the clipper ship
era, remarked "There are no young sea captains today
hailing from New England, of the same type as told of
in this book. Not because the breed is dead, but because the occasion for them in that line of the world's
work has passed. They are not gone, however, for they
have become captains of other industries in keeping
with the time. The records of such real men ought to
live."

Many passages in the true tales preserved in the following pages, will disclose to the thoughtful reader, the
real sources of our early maritime strength. These are
none other than the bold, fearless, resourceful, fair-
dealing sea captains and their well-disciplined crews.
More than once, too, the reader will have opportunity
to note the humane consideration of these shipmasters
for the men beholden to them and also their frankly
acknowledged dependence on Our Maker who rules
the land and the sea.

The foremost American writer on the clipper ship
era, which followed close on the heels of the epoch

dealt with in the following narratives, closes his account with substantially these words:—

"The commercial greatness of the United States rests upon the splendid qualities shown by her sailing ships and their captains. After all, the only real and rational sovereignty of the seas that exists or ever has existed, is maintained by the merchant marine whose ships and seamen contribute not only to the welfare and happiness of mankind, but also to the nation under whose flag they sailed."

These words are as true for the periods which preceded as for the times about which they were written.

The dangers fearlessly faced and the difficulties met and successfully overcome by our early New England mariners, cannot be visualized and certainly not appreciated, without the reading of accounts like those to be found in this book. Then, and only then, will the merit of the performances of these old-time shipmasters and the sterling worth of their characters be realized. The perils of the sea still exist and ever will — Nature has not changed her ways — but these are now better understood and man has changed his methods of facing them. Much of the glamour of the sea, its romance and particularly the incentive to adventure, has gone forever; cogent is the reason, therefore, for permanently recording these exploits. In the absence of real dangers, imaginary ones will always supply their place. It is well, therefore, for us to learn from and then to lean upon the experiences of our forebears on the sea as elsewhere.

Apart from this, by reading the following narratives one can learn much of the history and the ways of primitive man and easily perceive the benefits science has derived from the life-work of those who "go down to the sea in ships." Naval architecture, for instance, benefitted from the "Singapore fast boats" brought from the "Spice Islands." It is said that these craft, long and fine of underwater body, furnished the basis of the lines for the clipper ships of the following era.

The broad stretches of the Atlantic and Pacific "instead of being the two best defenders of the United States are in reality ocean thoroughfares on which hostile forces may be moved more cheaply, secretly and swiftly than on land." This fact is too little understood by the lay public at large. There are but two bars to our ocean highways on either side — our Navy and our Merchant Marine. These are complementary and have ever been so with any nation that aspires to real greatness. The ships and their masters and sailors of the navy and of commerce in the early days of our existence as a nation were fitting forebears of those that followed in the fifties and sixties; these in turn were worthy of their offspring of today. These, let it be hoped, will pass on their heritage with no lessened vigor to their successors of the future. Living tales of the sea, told by real sailors sailing real ships, make wholesome food for the imagination and cannot help but stimulate youth and old age alike, in the right direction.

"The right direction! Where does it lie?" No better answer can be given to this question than to quote the closing words of an Introduction recently written by Rear Admiral William Ledyard Rogers, United States Navy, Retired :—

"Our country to be truly prosperous and safe must create an adequate merchant fleet and preserve a strong navy."

The purpose of this book will be well served if it interests its readers and more so if they "perceive that the complete mariner is both seaman and warrior." The names of Capt. Charles H. Barnard of the brig *Nanina;* Capt. John B. Knights of the Salem brig *Spy;* John Bartlett of Boston, who sailed in the *Massachusetts;* John Nicol of Scotland and William Mariner of the *Port au Prince;* and all others like them who, though laying no claims to skill as authors, have written so well for posterity, "ought to live." Through this volume it will be so, at least in the memory of its readers. May their recurring thoughts of these events lead them to visualize the future of this Nation as locked up in the sea, the ship and its mariners.

ELLIOT SNOW,
Captain, Construction Corps, U. S. Navy.

Adventures at Sea
in the Great Age of Sail

A NARRATIVE OF THE ADVENTURES OF CAPT. CHARLES H. BARNARD OF NEW YORK, DURING A VOYAGE ROUND THE WORLD (1812-1816), WITH AN ACCOUNT OF HIS ABANDONMENT AND SOLITARY LIFE FOR TWO YEARS ON ONE OF THE FALKLAND ISLANDS.

THE brig *Nanina,* of one hundred and thirty-two tons burthen, Charles H. Barnard, master, sailed from New York the 6th of April, 1812, on a sealing voyage to the Falkland Islands. She was owned by John B. Murray & Son of New York and was completely fitted and also carried the frame of a shallop of twenty tons intended for use among the Islands. Captain Barnard proposed to spend the first season in procuring as many seal skins as possible and then to complete her lading with sea elephant oil and send her back to New York while he remained at the Falklands, with the shallop and a small crew, engaged in sealing, until the return of the brig or some other vessel to be sent out by the owners. On its arrival he intended to sail round the Horn and after visiting the usual resorts of the fur seals in the Pacific to proceed to Canton, dispose of the cargo there, and then return home.

With Captain Barnard sailed his father, Valentine Barnard (who was to command the brig on the return voyage to New York), Edmund Fanning, Bazilla Pease, Henry Ingham, mate, John Wines, carpenter, Havens Tenant, Jacob Green, a negro, who had sailed

on whaling voyages out of New Bedford, Harry Gilchrist, Andrew Lott, Thomas Hunter, William Seaman, steward, and John Spear, cook.

As the *Nanina* lay at her wharf ready for sea, news
came that Congress had passed a Bill laying an embargo on all vessels in the harbors and waters of the
United States and Captain Barnard promptly cast off
lines and sailed down the harbor to Sandy Hook where
the missing members of the crew came on board and on
the 12th of April, a course was set for the Cape de
Verd Islands to procure salt and fill up the water casks.
Bonavista was reached in thirty-five days and after restowing the hold and taking in a large supply of hogs,
goats, fowls and vegetables, the brig proceeded on her
voyage to the Falklands. While crossing the equator,
at longitude 18°, old father Neptune came saucily
aboard and was received with the usual formalities.
He was complimented with several bottles of the best
from the novices who were glad at so small a sacrifice
to escape the foam of his lather box and also save themselves a ducking.

Heavy gales from the south to west prevented making the Islands until September 7th, when the brig
came to anchor in Hooker's Harbor, New Island, in
four fathoms of water, and the yards and topmasts
were at once sent down and the next day the company
was employed in getting ashore the frame of the shallop. When launched she was called the *Young Nanina*.
As soon as fitted out, Captain Barnard went in her with
ten men to the Jason Islands, about thirty miles distant, where he left nine men with sealing apparatus
and stores sufficient for a stay of six weeks.

The shallop returned to New Island on January 3d, 1813, and Captain Barnard found that during his absence the ship *Hope,* of New York, Obed Chase, master, had come into the harbor bringing news of the declaration of war between the United States and Great Britain. This was bad news, for the Falklands, at that time, were frequently visited by English whalers to replenish their water casks and these vessels were generally commissioned as letters of marque. The men on the Jasons were at once recalled, leaving in stack the seal skins that they had collected, and the brig was re-rigged and taken into a less frequented harbor in the southern part of the English Maloon, one of the larger of the Falklands. This harbor was protected by several small islands and was surrounded by lofty hills. Here the brig was stripped for a year's stay as the prospects were good for obtaining a valuable cargo.

The shallop was then sent to the Jasons to bring away the skins that had been stacked there and meanwhile Captain Barnard went about in the ship's boat, with a few men, in search of seals on the nearby islands. Time was also passed in shooting geese and ducks which were found in great abundance and sometimes could be killed with clubs. There were also many wild hogs easily taken by the dog, so the supply of food was ample and good. In this manner the winter passed.

One morning early in April, the shallop was at anchor in Fox Bay, on the southeast side of the English Maloon, when the crew saw heavy columns of smoke rising to the eastward in the direction of the Anacan Islands. "We were at that time employed in examining the shores of the islands in the bay, in our pursuit of seal, of which we took several," relates Captain Barnard in his narrative. "As the columns of smoke continued to ascend in the same direction, I began to conjecture a variety of causes. Might they not proceed from hordes of the enemy, who might possibly use them as a decoy to secure us in their power? Did they arise from daring adventurers like ourselves, who were either preparing their food, or trying out the oil which they had collected? But such a supposition was improbable, as it is very rare that vessels touch at the Anacans. Occasionally the crew of a boat or a shallop belonging to a sealing vessel may land for a few hours in quest of seals; but never, except in case of shipwreck or contrary winds, are they known to remain in places so desolate. The fires, then, were possibly lighted by some unfortunate shipwrecked mariners, as signals of distress, who, without food and clothing, might be dragging out the last remains of life without a pitying hand to administer relief. I held a consultation with some of the party on the subject, and we determined immediately to go to the Anacans.

"These islands, which are three in number, viz., Eagle, George, and Barren, lie at the south-eastern entrance of Falkland Sound, and are separated from the south-western part of the Spanish Maloon by Jason Strait, which is from two to three miles wide. Eagle Island, the principal of them, is about ten miles long, and from two to three in breadth. George and Barren are from five to six miles long, and from one to two in width. They present nothing but darkness and desolation to the eye; their sole vegetable productions are a species of coarse, long grass, and scattered patches of tushook, which every where abounds upon all the islands on this coast. They are surrounded by numerous reefs and keys, which oppose a perpetual barrier to the approach of vessels; and woe to the unhappy mariner whom contending winds dash against this inhospitable region! for here he will find deliverance from the waves to be only a prelude to a more lingering and awful death.

"We now made sail from Fox Bay, with a fine breeze from N. W., and anchored the same day at Jack's Harbor, at the north-east end of Eagle Island, and despatched the crew in quest of seal. Strong gales, with heavy rain, from N. W. were now experienced, and several times we thought we heard the report of guns; but we could not be positive, as the sound might be occasioned by the breaking of the sea against the rocks from the opposite side of the island. It might be distant thunder, the last echoes of which were dying upon the waters. That they were signal guns of distress we had not the remotest doubt; and in this we were confirmed by the return of some of our party from the south, who had also listened to the report of guns; and this established the probability of the belief in question.

"We got under weigh, with a light breeze from W. S. W., and worked down towards the south-west part of the island, for a small harbor, called Shallop's Cove, where we intended leaving the shallop until we had searched the whole island for seal; in the mean time, the boat, with the sealing crew, was strictly examining the shores for the same purpose. At one, P. M., we hailed the discovery-boat, to come alongside, and at the same time perceived a flag-staff on the weather, or

opposite side of the island, which had the appearance of
a ship's topgallantmast. I was now convinced that the
smoke we had seen proceeded from fires made on this
island by the crew or survivors from some wrecked vessel; and, to strengthen this conviction, Mr. Fanning
informed me that, in coursing the shore, he had found
a new moccasin, and also a seal, which had been lately
killed and partly skinned.

"While we were at dinner, Tenant Havens, who was
at the helm, saw a man on a high part of the island,
coming towards us. We immediately repaired on deck;
and, in a few moments, eight or ten persons were observed on the beach, and as many more were rapidly
coming from the direction of the flag-staff towards the
same place; among the latter party, to our great surprise, we noticed a female, whose exertions and fleet-
ness were not surpassed by many of her male companions. Surveying the men, I saw with pleasure one
or two who wore the uniform of British marines. As
this immediately banished all apprehensions of their
being Spaniards, I began to devise the most effectual
means of aiding those unfortunates, whom I now conjectured to have belonged to some British man-of-war,
which had been cast away on this desolate island. Although they were enemies to my country, I apprehended no danger or loss from relieving them from their
perilous situation, as I felt assured that, by rendering
them this assistance, I should bind them to me by the
strongest ties of gratitude. To cheer those who had assembled on the beach with a prospect of relief, we
hoisted American colors, which they no sooner saw
than they manifested every symptom of the most ex-

THE WRECK OF THE "ISABELLA"

From an engraving in Barnard's *Narrative of Sufferings and Adventures*, New York, 1829

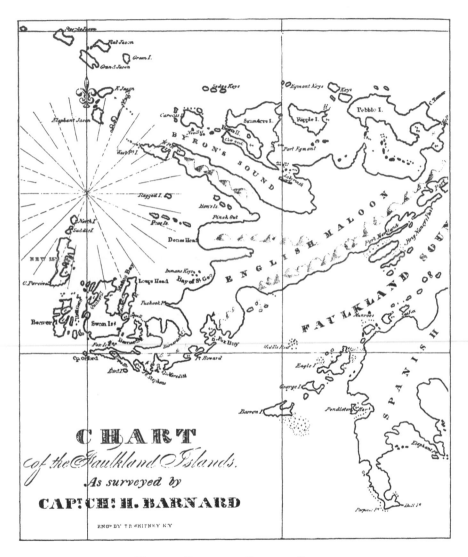

MAP OF A PART OF THE FALKLAND ISLANDS
From the original survey made in 1815 by Capt. Charles H. Barnard

travagant joy: they clasped their hands, they embraced, and apparently congratulated each other with as much ardor as though their deliverance were already effected. We stood close in shore, hailed, and eagerly inquired to what ship or nation they belonged. They replied that their ship was the *Isabella*, of London, which was wrecked on the island, on her passage from Port Jackson, New South Wales, to London. Our boat was instantly sent to bring some of them on board, and returned with seven or eight men and a sergeant of marines. The people on shore were so anxious to get into the boat, that the crew was compelled immediately to shove off, to prevent her from sinking; and so eager were some of them to get on board, that they followed the boat a distance through the water.

"Those who came on board informed us that they were wrecked on this place on the night of the 9th February, 1813, and that their situation had been very distressing. About a mile along the shore, I saw a number of persons standing together, with an English union jack flying over their heads; and, on inquiry, I was informed that the captain was among them. The boat was despatched for him; and he came off, accompanied by General Holt (formerly of the Irish patriots), and Captain Durie, of the seventy-third regiment, who gave me a more detailed account of their deplorable situation; that, as winter was approaching, in that inhospitable climate, their only shelter was temporary huts, formed of pieces of wreck and sails; that they found no other means of subsistence, but what few provisions they had saved from the ship; that they were almost denied the consolation of hope, for no other prospect presented itself than a painful, lingering death, as the termination of their sufferings.

"Yet, although they felt so acutely the horrors of their own situation, after being rescued from the jaws of this most dreadful of all deaths, they could traitorously deprive me of my vessel, and abandon me, as will appear in the sequel, to the same horrors, and thus prove how corrupt and abandoned human nature is, when the slave of its own passions. But my painful recollections have carried me from my subject.

"The captain, whose name was George Higton, further informed us, that, after his disaster, he repaired and fitted out the long-boat in the best manner their circumstances admitted, and had despatched her, about three months previously, in charge of Captain Brooks, a passenger, and George Davis, mate of the late ship, who were accompanied by Lieutenant London, and three seamen, an American, an Englishman, and a Spaniard; that there were yet on the island forty-seven persons, men, women, and children; that the boat was supplied with stores for three months, at a rate established by a committee soon after the ship was wrecked, viz., two pounds of bread and two pounds of salt provisions a man per week; and, in the event of their not attaining relief, it was left discretionary with Captain Brooks, either to return to the wreck, or attempt a passage to South America; but, as no accounts had been received of the boat since her departure, they had been compelled to abandon all expectation from that source.

"I was informed that the ship was only of one hundred and eighty tons and of course her boat was small. While conversing on board we continued tacking along shore but the wind was directly ahead and we didn't reach the anchorage until nine in the evening. We then went ashore to their encampment and the evening was spent in listening to accounts of the events previous and subsequent to their shipwreck. At the invitation of General Holt we lodged in one of his huts.

"During that evening I heard strange accounts of what had taken place at the time of the wreck and details, stranger still, of the lives of some of the shipwrecked. The night on which the ship struck was dark and gloomy, with no land in sight. She struck on the outer part of the reef and beat over without receiving any material injury, so that, if any discipline has been preserved, they could have anchored the ship and saved her. As it was, the ship slowly drifted across a channel more than a mile wide, with six fathoms of water, and at length drove upon a smooth, table rock at high water. The next morning she was lying nearly dry having sustained little or no injury. For six days the weather remained fine and there was a good opportunity to have hove her off; but unfortunately Captain Higton was so weak and irresolute in mind and also so attached to the pleasures of Bacchus, that nothing was done and on the seventh day after the ship had gone ashore, a gale came up and bilged her and then all hopes of release were at an end.

"Mary Ann Spencer, although one of the frail sisterhood, but now the selected companion of Mrs. Durie, informed me that a man named Mattinson, an ex-convict from Botany Bay, who had secreted himself on board until the vessel got to sea, after the ship struck, at the head of an intoxicated gang went about between

decks going through the rooms of the affrighted passengers, calling on them to hand out their bottles of
liquor. When he came to her he seized her glass and
dashed it on the deck, exclaiming, 'We shall have no
more use for glasses, for this is the last time, either on
sea or shore, that we shall ever drink.'

"Among the portraits furnished by Captain Durie
and his wife, a passenger named Sir Henry B. Hays,
Knight, claims a prominent position. He, too, was an
ex-convict who had been pardoned after spending fourteen years of his life at Botany Bay. I was informed
that the ancestor of this personage was a brewer in
Dublin. The son had rendered political services for
which he had been knighted and anxious to support
his new dignity he decided to marry and fixed his attention on a young and lovely Quakeress who was a
rich heiress. She was insensible, however, to his striking qualities and betrayed no desire to become Lady
Hays and at last forbade him her presence.

"Hays soon discovered that the fair Quakeress was
accustomed to visit relatives living a distance from her
home and on these journeys her carriage must pass
along a high road infrequently travelled. He then hired
a lonely cottage, in from this road, and determined to
terrify her into a pretended marriage. He persuaded
a boon companion to impersonate a clergyman and
learning of her next intended journey that way, with
two or three subordinate ruffians, he concealed himself
by the road over which she must pass. After patiently
waiting, the carriage containing the object of his de-
sires arrived at the place, when the horses were stopped,
the driver was pulled off the box and bound, and one

of the confederates took the reins. Sir Henry then entered the carriage and seated himself beside the terrified girl. Before she had recovered from her alarm, Hays pleaded her charms and his ardent love which had instigated him to this rashness, and told her of his determination to make her his wife that very night. Finding that tears and remonstrances were of no avail, she cried loudly for assistance, whereupon Hays ruthlessly gagged her and in that state carried her into the cottage. He then told her that a clergyman was waiting to perform the marriage ceremony and notwithstanding her tears and pathetic entreaties to the pretended clergyman that he spare her and save her from the fate that threatened, the ceremony was gone through with, some of the subordinates standing as witnesses.

"After the imposter had pronounced them to be man and wife the agents retired leaving Hays alone with his trembling victim. He imagined that after he had succeeded in ruining her the unfortunate girl would feel herself so humbled that, regardless of all but the preservation of her honor, she would consent to a regular marriage. Accordingly Hays seized her in his arms, when she, perceiving his intentions, renewed her cries and nerved by terror and despair, her resistance was so obstinate that the ruffian was unable to gag her and so smother her shrieks which, after a time, fortunately reached the ears of a gentleman who chanced to be passing. Alarmed, he forced his way in and surprised the Knight in his attempt to ruin the girl.

"Hays was apprehended, tried, convicted, and sentenced to be hanged; but when under the gallows, with the rope round his neck, on account of former services, he was reprieved and his punishment commuted to transportation to Botany Bay for life. These events took place in 1800. At the time Captain Bligh was Governor at Port Jackson, Hays rendered such important services when the officers and men revolted, that Governor Bligh exerted his influence successfully with the Prince Regent and Hays was granted a pardon.

"The next morning we made a general survey of the huts and the small vessel they were building. The huts were erected on a high bluff, about a cable's length from the wreck. There were twelve or fourteen of these miserable shelters placed in the form of a square. The largest hut was the store house and contained what was left of the provisions, wine, etc., that had been saved from the ship. The sides of these shelters were built up with dry tushook or sods from the bog; the rafters were small spars or pieces of the wreck and these were covered with sails or skins of seals.

"While viewing the vessel they were building, I fell in with Captain Higton, who invited me to his hut where I saw his *chere amie*, who appeared perfectly at her ease. In a few minutes he told me that he suspected breakfast was waiting for me at Captain Durie's. After so delicate an intimation to weigh anchor, I of course retired.

"That morning was devoted to a discussion of how these unfortunate people might best be rescued from their horrible situation and finally it was agreed that the *Nanina* should be refitted and the entire party taken on board and carried to Buenos Ayres. Articles were drawn up but previous to signing I thought it advisable to inform them of the state of war existing between Great Britain and the United States, of which I was convinced they knew nothing. The disclosure did not appear to make any alterations in the minds of the crew or the passengers, except that Sir Henry Brown Hays endeavored to prevail on the others to compel us to take them directly to England.

"The shallop was now cleared of seal skins, which were left on the island, and we took on board Captain Durie and his family and Mary Ann Spencer, the attendant on Mrs. Durie, a woman in the meridian of life, of abandoned habits, and mistress to Lieutenant London, who had gone in the long-boat with Captain Brooks. We also took on board a drummer and his wife, eleven of the wrecked sailors and four of my seamen, for the purpose of rigging the brig and bringing her round.

"On the 9th of April we weighed anchor and put out into Falkland Sound, the wind blowing hard from the N. N. W. which continued for several days and at last compelled us to come to an anchorage. It was not until the 29th that the brig was reached. All hands were now employed in taking out our oil and in rigging and fitting out the vessel. The shallop was dispatched to the wreck and on the 19th of May we beat out of the harbor and worked along the shore of the Great Maloon, at last coming to anchor near New Island. At this season of the year severe gales may be expected and such was our lot. The cold was severe and there were frequent storms of hail and snow so that we were obliged to remain at anchor. It was one continuous gale from the 22d until the 3d of June.

"Being in want of fresh provisions, on the 10th, for the supply of the passengers and crew, I proceeded to Beaver, one of the adjacent islands, with four men, who had volunteered their services, viz., Jacob Green, one of my crew, and an American citizen, and Samuel Ansel, Joseph Albrook, and James Louder, British subjects, late of the *Isabella*. Having procured a sufficient number of wild hogs to load the boat, we departed, and about 10 o'clock, arrived at New Island Harbor, when we discovered, to our inexpressible surprise, that the vessel was gone! But where? We instantly landed, hauled up the boat, and awaited the approach of daylight in the most impatient and tormenting anxiety, but still cherishing a hope that we might discover a letter, which would inform us of the reason. But in vain did we search; for, although they might have deposited one in a bottle, and buried, or suspended it in some conspicuous place, yet, after a long and fruitless search, we were reluctantly compelled to abandon all expectation of finding any communication from the vessel. We were so confused and irritated, that we could hardly persuade ourselves that we had been thus barbarously deserted, until we were constrained, by the certainty of the fact, to turn our thoughts to ourselves, and to devise means for prolonging our existence.

"To be reduced to this deplorable and almost hopeless state of wretchedness, by the treachery and ingratitude of those for whose relief I had long been laboring, and who, by our unremitted exertions, were raised from the lowest depths of despair to a prospect of restoration to all the endearments of country and home, was dreadful in the extreme; and what was my return? To be betrayed and abandoned; and at the very time when I was actually engaged in providing subsistence for them, to cowardly avail themselves of my absence in procuring additions to their comfort, and plunge me into a situation at which humanity revolts, without scarcely any garments but those on our backs, — and those considerably worn,—to withstand, without shelter, the severity of a winter on this barren island, without stores or bread, or any thing that would answer as a substitute, and under the apprehension that the island would not afford game sufficient for us to exist upon. Wild hogs and game there were; but for the former we depended only on our faithful dog; and of the latter we had no prospect, as our ammunition was expended.

"While reflecting on these circumstances, it occurred to me that possibly the brig had gone into Beaver Island Harbor to take us off; and she could have entered it without being perceived by us, as we were engaged in hunting on the opposite side of it. The longer I meditated, the more improbable it appeared that the crew and passengers could have so entirely divested themselves of every spark of humanity, as to leave us exposed to all the horrors and sufferings we must necessarily endure in this inhospitable climate. The weather being moderate, we went to the lee side of Beaver Island, whereas yesterday we were on the weather side; and, cheered by the hope that we should find the brig there, we entered the harbor, preferring to be considered, and even treated, as prisoners of war, and deprived of all our property, to being abandoned here;

for, in that case, I would have nothing to cheer me, but every thing to fill me with the most gloomy forebodings. But, on our arrival at Beaver Island Harbor, we were fated to endure, alas! the almost insupportable anguish of neither finding the brig, nor discovering any trace that she had been in the harbor. Thus our last gleam of hope died away, like most of those favorite pursuits on which we place our hearts. Yet we trusted that Heaven had not abandoned us, poor, forlorn wretches, thus cruelly abandoned of men. We concluded, notwithstanding the dangers we must encounter, — and which, under any other circumstances, we should have deemed insurmountable in an open boat, on account of the sudden changes in the weather, and the great tide-rips which we must unavoidably pass, — that we would attempt to effect a passage to Eagle Island, where the wreck was, distant about eighty miles.

"The dread of remaining on these desolate islands, and a new but faint hope that possibly the pirates might have stopped there to take on board the brig what they could of the wreck and cargo, and have left a written communication, and some necessaries, for us, inspired us with courage to face the dangers of the attempt. We therefore lightened the boat by throwing over four hogs, in order to make the passage in her with more safety; and retained four, which, in addition to the provisions we could procure at places where we might stop, on account of bad weather, etc., would supply us during the passage, which we commenced at noon, taking our course by the safest routes. After rowing the greatest part of the night, we landed on Island Harbor, the east side of Swan Island, completely fatigued by our exertions at the oar. Having been unavoidably compelled to fast all the time of our passage to this place, our sufferings were great; and we were necessitated to pass the remainder of the night on the open beach. The weather was so excessively cold as to freeze that part of the beach which had been covered with the tide, to a considerable depth. Our clothes were wet; and the men frequently exclaimed that they must perish: this harrowed up my already-agitated feelings, since they looked to me for relief, although suffering equally with themselves. What a blessed thing it is, that captains and commanders are often supported, sometimes with almost superhuman fortitude, to soothe down the murmurs and complaints, and unite the jarring tempers and interests, of the men who are placed under them! It is a fortunate circumstance when an individual thus situated feels himself thus sustained, and still more fortunate when those whom he directs are willing to listen to and obey his instructions.

"The next morning, after considerable difficulty, we succeeded in kindling a fire, and cooking some of the pork for breakfast; which was the first food we had taken for the last twenty-four hours. After our meal, we launched the boat, and proceeded on our passage. The wind being ahead and fresh, the sail was consequently of no use: we rowed down for Barnard's Island against a heavy head sea, which frequently broke over the boat's bows; but, having a favorable tide, we soon got under the lee of Barnard's Island, being distant twelve miles. We avoided going round Cape Orford, from its being an inaccessible, iron-bound shore, almost the whole distance from the commencement of the cape to Port Stephens, extending ten or twelve miles, and lying open to the prevailing winds, which throw in a heavy sea, and at all times dangerous tide-rips; and there was no place within the whole space where we could land with safety, or haul the boat up so as to prevent her from being injured, if not dashed into pieces; forming altogether the most perilous cape in this part of the world.

"We might have avoided the dangers of Cape Orford, by hauling our boat over a neck of land, about two miles across, which would bring us into Port Stephens, without any dangerous places to pass, except Cape Meredith, where the distance from one landing to the other was but short, and the tide-rips not so great. Having effected this, we thought that, by waiting for a favorable day to pass the sound, we could prosecute the remainder of the passage to the wreck, liable only to sudden gales, frequently occurring at this inclement season of the year. We therefore proceeded directly towards the mouth of McCockling's Lagoon, which is headed near the Bay of Port Stephens, but separated by a strip of land about two miles wide, across which we intended to carry or drag the boat; but, the wind blowing fresh and ahead, we could not reach it, but put into a small bay about one mile this side of the lagoon; the sun being down, we hauled up the boat, and turned her over for a shelter. The night was very cold, with a light fall of snow.

"This bay, or cove, is formed at the mouth of a valley, which lies between the mountains, with a gentle ascent of about a mile, and then gently tapers off with a gradual descent, nearly the same distance. There we discovered that it was entered by water, which, we had no doubt, was the head of a lagoon that communicated with Port Stephens: we therefore decided to carry the boat across from thence, instead of proceeding to McCockling's Lagoon, as the distance from the two waters appeared to be less than at the latter place; and the saving of time and labor was very important to us: We therefore carried the oars, masts, sail, and other articles, across, which occupied us till night, which we passed in the same manner as the last. In the morning, we undertook the task — and a severe one it was — to get the boat to the water on the other side, and succeeded, after much fatigue and difficulty. We attempted to carry her, but were too much exhausted by our many privations to accomplish so much; about sunset, she was floating in her proper element.

"We proceeded down the lagoon; and, if our conjecture of its communicating with Port Stephens were correct, there could, notwithstanding the darkness of the night and the falling snow, be no danger in proceeding down the bay. After running about three or four miles from the entrance of it, we were much surprised at finding ourselves in an open sea. The wind blowing fresh and fair, we kept before it to make a landing, as we had seen land in the direction we were steering, previous to its becoming so hazy and dark; but, to my astonishment, I found that we had run more than twice the distance of the breadth of Port Stephens Bay, yet made no land; and the sea rose so as to break into the boat at times, which greatly alarmed us all. I began to fear and suspect that, in taking the boat across, we had mistaken the course, and that we were now running out to sea; and as, unfortunately, we had no compass, we could not ascertain the course we were steering, nor those we had steered in following the windings of the lagoon. All was conjecture. We were soon agreeably surprised to find breakers to the leeward. Our next care, on approaching the shore, which was lined with low, flat rocks that were bare at low water, was to effect a landing without staving the boat; which, after much difficulty, we accomplished. It being low water, we were forced to haul the boat a considerable distance to reach high-water mark, which, at full tides, was against a clay bank intermixed with sand, fifteen or twenty feet perpendicular. On account of the darkness of the night, we could not find a safer situation. We removed the snow, which had fallen to the depth of six or eight inches, and turned up the boat, with her gunwale against the bank, for shelter. The four men, not being provided with a change of dry clothes or stockings, suffered severely from the cold, as their clothing was worn threadbare, merely covering their nakedness, but affording very little warmth, or yielding much protection from the severity of the weather. As soon as the boat was turned up, the poor fellows crept under it. As it afforded but a slight shelter from the wind and snow, they took their only blanket, and wrapped their naked feet in it, weeping bitterly.

"If the authors of our extreme suffering could have beheld them for only a moment, it might, perhaps, have touched even their flinty hearts with pity; although they must have known the consequences that would ensue from their inhuman desertion. The dog lay down amongst them, alternately licking their feet and legs, appearing sensible of their distress, and desirous of relieving it. After changing my stockings, I made a hole with my knife in that part of the bank against which the boat rested, built a fire under it, by breaking up a few pieces of drift-wood which we had brought with us, suspended the pot by a string from the gunwale, and boiled some pork for our supper and breakfast; for we supposed it now to be near daylight. While satisfying the cravings of hunger with the half-boiled pork, we were dreadfully alarmed by hearing the tide rapidly approaching; as, in that case, we should be obliged to turn up the boat, and remain in her till daylight, and at the same time be exposed to the fury of the surf, which might dash the boat against the bank, and stave her to pieces; but these apprehensions were soon quieted, by observing that it was neap-tide, and would not reach us.

"On June the 17th, strong gales from the south, and severe cold, were endured. At daybreak, we crawled out from under the boat, and looked round, to ascertain, if possible, on what land we were; but all appeared strange, and our suspicions that we had, in our haste, hauled the boat to the wrong place, were confirmed; and, taking our departure in the dusk of the evening, without a compass to take the bearings of Port Stephens, and the courses we had steered, I was completely at a loss to tell where or on what island we landed. I set to work, and broke up the remainder of the wood for the purpose of cooking our breakfast of pork. As I knew that we should soon be in great want

of wood and water, and as the preparing of this meal
would consume the whole of both articles, I sent Jacob
Green and Samuel Ansel along shore in search of a
supply of both; but they returned, almost frozen, without having been so fortunate as to procure either. We
were now almost in a state of despair; but, as I knew
that despairing would not relieve us, after eating of the
parboiled pork, and melting some snow in the cooking-
pot for drink, I took Joseph Albrook with me, and went
along shore, in the other direction, for wood and water.
Having travelled about a mile, we came to a frozen
pond, and, on breaking the ice, we found the water both
fresh and good; we filled our boat-keg, and left it on
the beach, and continued to proceed along shore in
hopes to find some driftwood, when we fortunately fell
in with four sea-elephants. We immediately killed the
smallest with our clubs, cut off the blubber, and carried it to the boat for fuel. By this successful attempt
in procuring water, which we had almost despaired of,
and the means of continuing our fire, and knowing
that without these two indispensable articles we could
not long have existed, our spirits and hopes were renewed.

"Strong gales kept us close as possible under the
boat, over a small blubber fire, the smoke of which
turned the skin of our faces pretty much of a color. On
the 20th the gale subsided and we launched our boat
and rowed along the shore following this course for several days . The food supply by that time was beginning
to be serious. Three wild fowls had been killed with
stones and seven rooks or carron crows were killed
while they were feeding on the putrid carcass of a sea-

elephant which must have been dead for some time. On the 23d we fortunately came upon a young elephant which we killed and this supplied us with food for some time. When we launched the boat and left this place of famine, I gave it the name of 'Pinch-gut Camp.'

"Slowly we made our way along the coast. When the sea-elephant meat gave out, for lack of something better, we fed upon the roots of the tushook grass but these occasioned vomiting and dizziness, particularly with Lunder and Green who were reduced to the greatest extremity. Fortunately we came upon a seal and not long after killed three geese and two foxes. The flesh of the latter was so strong that nothing but extreme hunger could force it down.

"The weather having moderated, and appearing settled, on the 25th July we launched the boat, and proceeded for, and landed on, that part of Swan Island nearest to, and in full view of, the harbor of New Island, as it was our intention to pass the remainder of the winter there, it being a good place to procure hogs, and only about one mile from the place which we had chosen for our camp was a small seal-rookery. This rookery was formed among a great number of loose rocks, that had fallen from the adjacent cliffs. The tops of these high cliffs project far beyond the base, having the terrifying appearance of being on the point of falling, and crushing into atoms any of us who might be passing beneath, or any where within the range of the rocky fragments. Among these broken masses, the seals, on being disturbed, seek for safety, and disappear in the caverns below; one of us then crawled in after them, and, when near enough to reach them with a boat-hook, dragged them from their concealment, and they were immediately despatched by a blow on the head, and skinned; this was performed as expeditiously as possible, from the threatening appearance of the overhanging cliffs.

"The men's clothing, which was in a very indifferent state when they left the brig, was now so far worn out, that it was falling from their backs; and, as food and clothing were indispensable to the preservation of our lives, we so arranged as to have two departments for procuring these, in full activity at the same time. A strict lookout was to be likewise kept up for any boat or vessel that might be approaching or passing New Island Harbor. Indeed, no kind of craft could enter without our immediate notice, it being only seven miles distant, and open to our full view; for, though often deceived by Hope, she yet flattered us, by representing that perhaps the shallop would return to the harbor to search for us. Our duties and employments were therefore so ordered, that one should cook, and at the same time keep watch, as the harbor, its entrance, and all its parts, were fully exposed to his view from the place where he had his fire. Two, with the dog, were to procure provisions; and the other two to procure fur-seals, to make clothing of their skins.

"The wild hogs had become very scarce and shy on this part of the island, the most of them resorting to the other end; and, consequently, to obtain food, we were obliged to follow them to their haunts, and had to travel seven or eight miles through the wintry storms and frosts. After killing our game, we returned to the camp, carrying it on our backs; having to pass over hills, across valleys, floundering through high snow-banks, wading deep creeks or runs of water; and neither our feet nor legs were a single moment dry. On these hunting excursions, what did we not endure? These hogs, in size, appearance, and habits, resemble the common or domestic hogs of the United States; the old boars are large, and generally fierce, sometimes inflicting severe wounds on our dog; they are very thin, and run fast; their flesh is sweet, but lean, not having an ounce of fat on their carcass, and has more the flavor of veal than of common pork. It is a very light diet, easy of digestion, which leaves a vacancy in the stomach that gives rise to unpleasant feelings, which it requires another meal to remove.

"When obliged to bring hogs from the other end of the island, we made them light enough for a single man to carry, by taking out all the entrails except the liver, cutting off the head, and leaving the whole of these behind. We tied the fore and hinder legs together, put our head between them, and by this management the hog laid firmly on the shoulders, and we then commenced our march for the camp. Such were the arduous and severe duties of the swine-hunter. The other two were in close attendance on the rookery, and more than fifty seals were obtained.

"We daily exchanged duties, so that each man performed his full share of all the labors. The seal-skins were prepared by us, in our best manner, for clothing; first, by drying, and then rubbing them until they were limber; they were then made up into full suits, consisting of jacket, trousers, vest, and cap; to sew them, we were fortunate enough to have sail-needles and a ball of twine; and when that was expended, we took a cloth out of our mainsail, which was new, light duck, ravelled it, and thus procured a good substitute for twine. When the suits were completed and worn, the men found them so comfortable, in comparison with their old ones, that I was induced, after a while, to try a suit myself; although I had other clothes sufficient to make necessary changes, having always been accustomed, in every excursion in the boat, to carry with me a requisite supply.

"The seals we particularly valued, not only on account of their skins, but also for their blubber, which we used as fuel: when destitute of it, we had recourse to the dry tushook-grass, which having little substance, we could not keep up a fire with it that would more than parboil our pork, which caused it to be very unpalatable. During our stay at this place, which we called 'Rat Camp,' we were intolerably plundered and annoyed by the almost incredible number of rats with which it was infested. To prevent their ruinous and extensive depredations on our provisions, when we were so rich as to have much on hand, we were compelled to adopt several plans to prevent their piracies; but, in general, their sagacity in committing their felonies was greater than ours in preventing them. At length we made trial of raising a pair of shears, by lashing three oars together, and, with the boat's painter, hoisting the provisions as high as the shears would permit; we then greased the oars with seal's blubber, and this prevented the rats from mounting to the top of the shears, descending the rope, and nearly destroying in the course of the night a whole hog or whatever part was suspended.

"One day, while performing our customary tour in pursuit of necessaries, we fell in with a very large, old sea-lion, asleep, at a distance from the shore. We were desirous to kill him, to have his blubber for fuel, and his skin for moccasins; but we were without our lance, which, owing to the great difficulty in landing and getting our things into the boat, we had unfortunately left behind at Hook Camp. We thought it impossible to kill him without the lance; yet, as his skin and blubber would be so valuable to us, and his being asleep so far from the shore seemed almost to promise success to my attack, after lashing a skinning-knife firmly to the end of my club, I directed the men to provide themselves with as many stones as they could carry in their caps and pockets. We then reconnoitred him. My plan of attack was, to stab him under one of his fore-flippers, being the nearest to his heart; and, if the knife were only long enough to reach it, we might succeed in killing him. The moment I made the assault, the others were to throw stones at his eyes, and blind him, so that he should not be able to see his way to the water; and this would afford me an opportunity to repeat the stabs. Accordingly, I very cautiously approached him; and, when I was sufficiently near him, being still asleep, I gave him a deep stab under one of his fore-flippers; but the knife was not long enough to reach the seat of life; and, on receiving the wound, he furiously sprang up, and dashed about, bit and rooted up the tushooks from pain and madness, and attempted to fight his way to the water; but the stones were so effectually thrown against his eyes, that he could neither see the water, nor in what direction we were. I repeated the thrusts, until, having fallen from loss of blood, we despatched him, and took off his skin and blubber.

"The killing of an old sea-lion without a lance, may appear almost incredible to those who have seen or attacked one of the largest size, and witnessed his desperate and determined manner of defence and attack. A blow on the head has little or no effect, even if a man has a fair opportunity to inflict it, which very seldom occurs, unless accompanied with great danger. The sea- resembles the land-lion in the head, shoulders, and breast; there is a difference in the mouth, their jaw-bones being larger, and their teeth nearly double the size; their neck and breast are covered with a mane, about four or five inches in length; their skin is very thick, particularly on the neck and shoulders. I have measured skins that were, on these parts, an inch thick. They have heavy and clumsy bodies, which generally weigh from 500 to 700 lbs.

"Having now resigned all hope of being sought for by either the shallop or brig, we decided to return to New Island, as whaling ships sometimes put in there for water. We therefore left Beaver, and crossed over to New Island. Having hauled up the boat, and made the usual preparations, I told the men that it was about the season when the albatross began to lay her eggs, and that they had better go up to the rookery, and see if the birds had commenced; they accordingly went, and found five or six eggs. Having lost the run or account of time, I concluded, from the circumstance of finding eggs, that it was now about the 10th of October; and, as the albatross begins laying in the first week of that month, I consequently began to reckon from this period as the 10th.

"The weather continuing pleasant, each man was provided with a seal-skin bag, and repaired to the rookery to collect eggs from the nests of the albatrosses; and, as they never leave their eggs from the time they begin to cover them until they are hatched, they soon become unfit to eat. Every one obtained and carried to the boat two loads of these fresh eggs, which afforded us a noble feast. This bird never leaves her young until they are half-grown; for the rooks are always upon the alert, watching for an opportunity to dive down on the nest, break the eggs, or kill and devour the young. The albatross is almost as large again as a goose, and their eggs are of a proportionate size; their wings, when extended, measure, from tip to tip, thirteen or fourteen feet; their bills are large and strong; they bite severely, and desperately wound the hands of those who disturb their nests.

"I proposed to some of the men to go down to Sea-Lion Point, at the south end, for a hair seal-skin, to make moccasins of, as they were more lasting than those made of the fur seal-skin. Green and Louder said it was their turn to go for vines; Albrook, that it was his cook day; and Ansel, that he wanted to mend his trousers. I went under the boat, and, having sharpened my knife, took my club, and called the dog, but he did not come. I inquired where he was; Louder replied, that he supposed the dog had followed Green and Albrook, who had gone for vines. As they had taken an opposite direction to that which I intended, I resolved to wait for their return. Ansel then sprung up from where he was sitting, and said, 'Captain Barnard, I will go with you.' I replied, 'If you will go, we ought to have the dog, to hunt the seals in the tushooks.' 'Or, if there is any there,' said he, 'I will hunt them up.' I agreed to his proposal, and set off. We passed round the mountain which makes the southwest part of Hooker's Harbor, and then descended, engaged in conversation, to cross the valley. This valley is full of tushooks, which are higher than a man's head, and through which, as we walked, we continued our conversation, although we could not discern each other. After I had got out of the valley, upon the plain, I stood still, waited for and expected every moment to see Sam make his appearance from the tushooks; but, as he did not come, I called, and, after waiting several minutes, I called again, as loud as I could, but no answer was returned. A suspicion now darted through my mind, that he had returned to the boat, and that they were all acting upon some preconcerted plan. Their first declining to accompany me, the absence of my dog, the clandestine disappearance of Ansel, — all added strength to the suspicion that some improper scheme was in agitation, the knowledge of which had been withheld from me.

"I returned through the tushooks, and proceeded with expedition towards our camp. Having gone about a mile, and being half way round the mountain, I perceived the boat running out of the harbor, before the wind. To attract their notice, I put my hat on the club, and waved to them; but they took no notice of it. I then hastened to the place where we had been living, to ascertain if they had left my clothes, and some other articles, which would be trifles in any other situation, but of great importance to me now, but more particularly if they had left fire and my dog. But I cannot describe my sensations when, on arriving in sight of the camp, I neither observed the dog nor any smoke. I endeavored to kindle a fire from the ashes of the vines, which had been used as fuel for cooking; but, on opening them, to my great dismay, I did not discover a spark of fire; yet, notwithstanding this disheartening obstacle, I placed on them some dry straw, which, after emitting a light smoke, kindled at last into a blaze. Thus I surmounted one of the most serious difficulties in which their inhuman desertion had involved me.

"Examining whether they had deprived me of all my little stock, I found that, in addition to the irreparable loss of my dog, they had taken my bag, containing an old jacket and trousers, a blanket, and rug, the remains of an old shirt, part of which I had torn off and burnt into tinder, and a powder-horn to preserve it dry for use, in case of losing our fire. They had also deprived me of my fowling-piece, and three or four charges of powder, which I had carefully preserved as a last resource to procure fire, when all other means should fail; also my fur seal-skins, which I had laid by for the purpose of making clothes; a great coat, two sail-needles, and all my tinder. By thus depriving me of every necessary article, it appeared evident that they expected I could not survive long, if destitute of every thing, and that they wished my existence at an end.

"I gazed at the boat, whose sail was yet in sight, and said, 'Go, then, for you are all bad fellows;' although I never suspected Green, Albrook, or Louder, of plan-

ning the desertion, but I considered the hardened villain Ansel as the author of it, who had instigated the
others to carry it into execution. I now found that I
must depend altogether upon my own resources and
exertions to procure food, clothing, and shelter. If they
had only left my dog, I could provide for myself as well
as when we were together; therefore I did not so much
regret their departure and knavery as might be supposed, as their barbarous hearts, if they had continued
here, might have united against me, and used me much
worse than robbing and deserting me. The first thing
to which I attended, was the preservation of my fire,
which, if lost, I could not regain. I had torn off one of
my shirt sleeves, burnt it to tinder, and, after enclosing
it in a stocking tied in a bag, had placed it in the dry
tushooks; but, on looking for it, I discovered that they
had taken my last flint. On leaving the vessel, I took
with me a small bag, in which were flints, needles, palm,
and twine; all of these, except the bag, — for which
they had no use, having seal-skin ones of their own, —
they had stolen. To preserve my fire, I used a piece of
tushook, which is a light and chaffy substance, being
equally composed of straw and turf, and retaining fire
several hours after it is kindled. This was of great
service to me during the night, and in my absence to
the rookery for eggs, or to the hills for vines. The fear
of losing my fire caused me more uneasiness than any
thing else, as my tinder, from the want of a flint, was
useless. I made a tushook house; placed the very few
articles they had left me in it; prepared several dry tushook bogs for replenishing the fire; laid myself down in
the tushook hovel, and prayed to God to direct and in-

spire me with fortitude to submit with patience to this doubly afflictive trial.

"During the pleasant weather, I commenced making a more comfortable shelter. This I completed tolerably well. Here I was to pass the night, and to be sheltered from the cold rain storms, which are very prevalent in those islands throughout the year. December, January, and February, being the summer months, are the only ones that may be considered pleasant; but even these summer months are not warmer or more serene than October and November are in the climate of New York. I recollected that I had seen, at some distance down the beach, about low-water mark, the remains of an old tin pot, without a bottom, which we had formerly used in the boat as a bailer, but, having become unserviceable, it had been thrown away. At low water, I searched for and found it. I turned up the sides and end, and converted it into a pan, to cook my eggs. I wished to erect a signal pole, and, for that purpose, I chose a small tree that we had brought to this island for the purpose of making clubs, which had become scarce among us, having been broken over the heads of the old bears and hair-seals. This small sapling, including the root, was about twelve feet long, and about the thickness of a man's arm. I lashed a strip of board, as a topmast, to the end of it, to which I affixed several strips of seal-skins, as signals. I then dug a hole on the top of a small rise of ground that was near my hut, and erected the pole, and on it cut my name and date. The first thing that I did, every morning, was to cut a notch in the pole, as a record of days; and, as I had lost Sunday, I appointed one, by calling the day on which I was left on this barren island, Friday. October the 14th, being my Sunday, I did no work, except cooking my eggs, and walking on the small hillock where I had erected my signal and register pole. To denote Sunday, I cut a longer mark than for the other days of the week.

"After completing my arrangements about the fire, and other concerns, I went to the rookery, and brought to my hut, during the day, four loads of eggs; and it was my intention to collect and bring home the same quantity every day, as long as the eggs continued good. After bringing them to my hut, I arranged them, in small parcels, on their ends, in the tushook, covered them well with tushook straw, and over that a thick layer of bogs of the same material. This was done to prevent the rooks from sucking the eggs, of which they are very fond. When employed in securing eggs, there were always twenty or thirty rooks flying over my head, while others were sitting on the ground, and watching my movements; and, the instant that I left the place, they would commence digging with their bills and talons for the eggs, which sometimes they would get, notwithstanding all my precautions. This would anger me, and I have sometimes employed myself the whole day in throwing stones at them, to prevent them from their attempts. They were so bold as to fly at my head, and with such force as to strike off my cap, and cause a severe headache.

"Until the 20th, I was employed in procuring eggs, which were my only food, and going every other day for a back-load of vines, for fuel. Having now procured a large stock of eggs, and secured them, I desisted from going to the rookery, as all the eggs were becoming spoiled.

"While on the hills gathering vines, I came to a spot where they appeared to be very plentiful for some distance round. I threw down my club and the seal-skin string that tied them, and began to throw them down by the club and string, and gathered them in my arms; when enough was obtained for a load, I bound them into a bundle, by means of the string, and looked for the club, to pass it through the string, and carry the bundle like a wallet. How surprised was I to find that it had disappeared from the place where it laid! I searched all round, and, not finding it, I began to think that the island, or at least this part of it, was the residence of some invisible beings, and that I was not the only proprietor. But, however mysterious I might consider the loss of my club, it did not much alarm me, as I was not inclined to superstition; so I took my bundle on my back, and returned home, kindled a fire, cooked some eggs for supper, and turned in.

"As I was meditating on the severity of my lot, cut off from all intercourse with my fellow-men, and doomed, perhaps, never again to see a human being, my thoughts, at one time, wandered to the unaccountable manner in which I had lost my club; at another, to my country, family, and friends; but my train of reflection was suddenly interrupted by a loud and near noise, resembling that of a cat when irritated, or in great pain. I was startled; but, soon recovering from my surprise, I thought that now I should discover a clew to a knowledge of the unseen beings who had appropriated my club. Going out from my shelter (for it was hardly commodious enough to be distinguished by the name of hut) and looking round to discover whence the strange noise proceeded, I saw an owl standing on the tushook that formed one part of my shelter; he was of a large size, and had a most frightful look. I advanced towards him with my club; but he was so intent on hooting that he took no notice of my approach. I gave him a severe blow with the club, which he immediately seized, and held in his talons, until I crushed his head with a stone. I then returned to bed, and, notwithstanding the alarm, slept soundly the remainder of the night.

"The day being very fine, on the 22d of October I was employed in doing a number of light jobs about my habitation; cut out of dry seal-skins a suit of clothing, and dressed them by rubbing them with a soft stone, of coarse grit, and afterwards rubbing them by hand, in the same way as clothes are washed, until they became as pliable as washed leather.

"The spring being advanced, and the weather more pleasant, the small birds singing, and flying, in great numbers, from one tushook to another, the music of their notes and airy gambols forcibly recalled to mind similar days and scenes, which, in childhood, I had enjoyed in my own country. But, delightful as are such associations to the mind in the possession of every comfort, they by no means feed the imagination of such unfortunates as myself. There is too much painful reality to keep alive the attention upon its own cares and reflections; and, if they ever occur at all, it is only to increase the wretchedness of the sufferer, by contrasting with his own miseries the blessings possessed by others.

"In the afternoon, I went to Fairy Hill, and to the same place from which unseen hands had conveyed away my club, for more vines. I hoped that the other club had been returned, by this time, to the place from which it had been taken, unless I had, while deeply engaged in thought, — which was almost always the case, — mislaid it myself. The one I now had was smaller, and had been lost in the tushooks by one of the brig's crew, and I had lately found it. On arriving at the mysterious spot, I laid down the club and string, much in the same manner as I did before, and went about gathering vines, frequently looking round to see if any thing was in sight that could carry away the club; but nothing then appeared. Having strolled round to the distance of about five or six rods, I returned with an armful of vines, and, behold, the club was gone! I searched in every direction, as far as a few minutes would permit, without seeing it. With the string and the few vines I had gathered, I made the best of my way from this place, which I now began to believe was the residence of some evil genius, who thus punished me for invading his retreat. Descending the hill, my attention was caught by a great number of rooks, some flying high in the air, others lower, when, to my great surprise, I discovered that one of them had my club in his claws; his talons grasped the larger end, and hooked under the iron ring, that is always put round seal-clubs to prevent them from brooming, or splitting against the rocks. The mystery was now cleared up, and the thoughts of having supernatural beings for neighbors, who, in the course of time, might condescend to become familiar, and 'disclose secrets of the invisible world,' were at an end; and an act which I deemed worthy of a spirit or enchanter, was the work of a villainous bird. I must admit that I felt rather chagrined at the inferiority of the real to my imaginary agent. It is strange that we are more prone to account for singular events from supernatural than mere physical causes; the reason may be, that the mind is fond of having sufficient food to keep alive the imagination, and, perhaps, find sensible demonstrations and arguments for the truth of an after life. But my most important concern now was, to regain the club: I gathered some stones, and pelted the thief heartily, until he was compelled to drop it.

"October the 25th, 1813, being the day of my nativity, and that on which I completed my 32d year, gave rise to many melancholy reflections. Memory recalled the table, covered with plenty, at which I used to sit, surrounded by my family and friends, but more particularly so on the last anniversary. But what a contrast! from substantial and delicate fare, with social mirth, and good wishes crowning the board, to my being now alone, destitute even of a crumb of bread, or smiling friends, to cheer and animate me; but memory became too painful, and, to divert my thoughts, if possible, into another channel, I repaired to the shore. In walking along, I tried several stones on my steel, and fortunately found one that produced fire enough to communicate with the tinder; this was a valuable acquisition, as the continual dread of losing my fire was, in a great degree, removed. I now began building a stone wall around the cooking-place, which was an arduous undertaking, as the stones were to be brought from a considerable distance.

"I made a discovery that promised to be of the greatest utility to me while I remained here. The north side of the harbor is formed by a high hill, which is covered, about half way up, with tushooks; those which formerly grew there had been burnt, and the fire had penetrated the bog or moor, into which it had made large and deep holes. I observed that the sides of some of these hills had caved in, and was of the substance of turf; but it had a greater resemblance to the peat which I had seen in Wales. I gathered some, and found, on trial, that it made a hot fire. Having made this gratifying experiment, I returned, and filled a large seal-skin bag, which I brought home; and, when broken into pieces about the size of a man's fist, I found that it took fire quicker, and threw off almost as much heat as coal. I could hardly believe in my good fortune, or realize the fact that it was in my power to have a good fire, until I had cooked some eggs. 'Now,' said I, 'there is no danger of my perishing next winter, from the want of fuel to make good fires to warm me, and cook whatever food it shall please Providence to provide me with.'

"I now determined to work steadily at building a stone house, with a fireplace, and endeavor to get a sufficient number of seal-skins to cover the roof. This I thought might be accomplished in the course of a summer, and I should be prepared to meet the severity of the next winter, with more comfort and security than the last.

"I began to feel so very solitary, and time moved so

slowly on leaden wings, that, bad as they were, I wished for the return of the men. Company, even were it that of a savage, like Crusoe's Friday, or that of my poor, faithful dog, would have been a great comfort to me, as it would sometimes amuse my attention, and prevent my thoughts from dwelling so continually on my forlorn situation and distant home. In this solitary state, agitated by hopes and fears, wishes and anticipations, I continued performing my customary daily labor.

"On the 3d of December, when the Macaroni penguins had collected in the rookery, and stowed themselves as closely as they could between the albatrosses, where thousands repair, every year, to deposit their eggs, I found that they were laying them in great abundance; I therefore commenced gathering and carrying them to the hut, where I placed them on their ends, and, at the expiration of six days, turned them, which was done to prevent the yolk from settling through the white and spoiling the egg. It was a curious and interesting sight, to observe those sea-birds landing on a flat, shelving rock, at the mouth of a gulley leading to the rookery, upon which, being on the weather side of the island, the sea breaks with tremendous violence. The penguins come from the sea in such immense flocks, as almost to cover the surface of the water to a considerable extent; but, on drawing near to this rock, their only landing-place, they discover their mortal and rapacious enemies the sea-lions, swimming outside of the surf, and awaiting their arrival, to seize and devour them. When a small flock of penguins discover the lions, they sheer off, and wait for the arrival of other and larger flocks, when,—as the few must be sacrificed for the preservation of the many,—they rush swiftly towards the rock, spring out of the water, and, making directly for the landing, meet the lions, where many lose their lives by falling into their mouths. I have often seen the lions swimming with their heads above water, and with their rapacious jaws distended, among those poor, defenceless little birds, dealing destruction, and enclosing within a living tomb all that were within the deadly circle; for the penguins, in the crowd and confusion, are forced into the jaws of their destroyers. As soon as the surviving birds have passed this formidable line of enemies, they enter the surf, which throws them, by thousands, on the shore so violently, that many are wounded and disabled, which fall a prey to the rooks, who are ready to take advantage of their disaster; these land enemies follow them as far as the rookery, seizing upon the wounded, or any that fall off from the main body. These penguins are the smallest of this species of birds, being only about twenty inches in height; their legs being placed near the extremity of the body, they stand and walk erect; their heads are ornamented with a topknot, composed of long red and yellow feathers; they have white bellies and black backs; their feathers are short, thick, and placed close together, like those of the loon, common on the coast of North America.

"There was a strong gale from the S. S. W., accompanied by showers of hail, on the 8th of December. The tide was remarkably low, far beyond common low-water mark. I walked out to almost where the brig had lain at anchor, but nothing but the sky and ocean

met my inquisitive view. I was now employed at the
walls of the house, which were about nine feet by sev-
en, and more than three feet thick. While at work, I
was surprised at hearing a loud crack, like that of the
breaking of a board; I looked towards my signal and
register pole, and saw that it was broken, with nothing
in sight that could have done it. This, to me, was really
unaccountable. I went to examine it, when I found beside it a large shag, lying dead, which had been flying
down the valley, to go a-fishing in the harbor, as many
of them do every morning. They fly with great rapidity, and cause a whistling in the air, like a cannon-ball
passing near at hand. This one, in his flight, came with
such force against the top-mast, which I had lashed to
the head of the pole, as to carry it away, and cause his
immediate death.

"On the 14th of December, I discovered a smoke rising from Beaver Island, which I knew was occasioned
by some persons setting fire to the tushooks, that being
the method here of making signals of distress, or when
various parties are sealing on different islands, and
wish to communicate, or convey information to one
another. For instance, two gangs may be out sealing,
only one of which has a boat; when the one has procured all the skins, they wish the boat or shallop to
come and take them and their fare off; for a signal to
that effect, they set fire to the tushooks.

"I will endeavor to describe the tushook: The bog on
its outside is soft and rotten and something resembling
decayed wood; on cutting or breaking into it, the inside is found to be firm, and not unlike Irish turf.
These bogs are of various sizes, from the dimensions

of a barrel to those of a tun-butt, and from three to four feet in height; they generally stand about three feet apart, leaving a space through which a man or a seal can pass without difficulty. The seals generally resort to them on coming in from the sea, where they pass several days at a time, in sleep and repose. On the top of the bog grows a long, coarse grass, bearing a resemblance to the flag-grass of the United States, but not quite so long or large, and standing about as tall as full-grown rye. In the spring, the grass shoots up from the centre of the bog, and grows rapidly during the short summer; but, on the approach of winter, it dies, forming a great quantity of dry straw, and falls around the bog. This, decaying, becomes, in my opinion, incorporated with the bog, and gradually adds to its size. I presume that the soil was originally wet or springy; that the tushook grass was its first growth or production, and that, annually growing and decaying for many ages, the bog was gradually formed from this decayed substance, which covers these savannas or prairies. If fire is kindled there, it will continue burning several days; and when it communicates to the bogs, or penetrates below the surface of the soil, which it most commonly does, it will burn several months, and make deep chasms or pits in the ground.

"I went to the top of the hill, which afforded a more distinct view, and there I could positively decide whether it was really smoke rising from Beaver Island, or only vapors from the sea. I had frequently been deceived by clouds passing over the tops of the hills, which, at times, had a very strong resemblance to heavy bodies of smoke rolling up from signal fires, and agitated me with hope and fear the greater part of a day.

"On arriving at the summit of the hill, I was satisfied, beyond all doubt, that I saw large columns of
smoke ascending from Beaver Island, and that it was,
most probably, a signal made to me by my runaway
companions; or, perhaps, the shallop was there; which
hope, notwithstanding the length of time since I was
abandoned, I still cherished.

"After remaining a considerable time on the hill, —
the wind blowing strongly from the westward, which
was directly against their coming to this island, who-
ever they might prove to be, — I descended, to wait,
with all the calmness I could command, for the coming of the next day, when I hoped that the wind would
change, and that I should have the happiness of seeing
them coming over to my island. But I could not so restrain my feelings as to patiently await the result; the
excitement was too great. I made a large turf fire, and
walked the beach the greater part of the night, as all
inclination for sleep was now banished.

"The weather being favorable on the following day,
I watched with the greatest anxiety for the appearance
of a boat or shallop, as I felt assured that it was the
crew of the one or the other that was on Beaver Island.
After a light breakfast, I made a large fire, the sight of
which I knew would astonish them, and then went to
my observatory on the hill, and concluded to remain
there until I saw them crossing, which I conjectured
would be in a short time. After continuing there several hours, and seeing nothing more than the large columns of smoke, which still continued rising, I fell
asleep, worn out and exhausted by watching, until I

was awakened by the rooks attempting to take the moccasins from my feet. I turned an anxious eye towards Beaver Island, but saw nothing to confirm my hopes. I returned down the hill, dispirited and heartsick, and, having taken some food, I continued on the lookout until every object was shrouded in darkness. Being now compelled to relinquish the expectation of seeing them this night, I retired to my bed of straw in a painful state of conjecture and uncertainty; and this day completed the ninth week that I had been left alone. The succeeding day was extremely propitious to cross from Beaver to this island. I was on the lookout the whole day, but nothing appeared afloat.

"Words cannot express my deep-toned anxiety. Day after day elapsed, and yet there was no arrival. They might have landed on the other end of the island; for, while engaged in cooking eggs, I heard a noise like the snapping of a gun; but, on looking round, I discovered nothing to excite my fears. In a short time, the noise was repeated, and again it sounded like the snapping of a gun. As Ansel and company had taken my fowling-piece, and a few charges of powder and slugs, and as it sometimes missed fire, I suspected that they were concealed in the tushooks that grew near, and were aiming the gun at me. I immediately started, and examined the tushooks very closely, but did not discover any indications of any one having lately been there. I finished cooking, and was eating my dinner, when the sound again startled me. I looked up, and observed, after a little investigation, that some shell spoons I had made, which were hanging near the wall, on a pin, were driven against it by the wind, which caused the noise.

"This was the invisible enemy who, I fancied, was plotting against my life; but I felt as much relief as though I had been preserved from the greatest impending evil. Thus, in the absence of real, imaginary dangers will always supply their place; and miserable indeed would that situation be, where there is no moral stimulus to awaken the mental powers, and make us feel our dependence on the great Being who made us.

"To banish or confirm my suspicions of the landing of the boat, and the secretion of the crew upon the island, I searched the shore narrowly at the south end, but returned home about the middle of the afternoon, without discovering the least sign of a living creature.

"While cooking some eggs, to my astonishment, I perceived the boat coming round a point of rocks, about half a mile distant; the men landed on the beach, at the mouth of the harbor, and in a few moments reëntered the boat, and shoved off. I attentively watched their manœuvres, and was prepared to meet them either as friends or enemies: they lay on their oars, in the middle of the harbor, apparently consulting what course they should pursue. After a few moments, they pulled in towards me, until within about twenty yards, and then ceased rowing, but did not speak. It was my boat, indeed, and my treacherous companions. The dog had recognized me, and wanted to jump out and swim to the shore, but was prevented by Ansel. Perceiving this, and imagining that they did not intend to land, I spoke, and asked them why they did not come on shore. James Louder replied, 'We wish to land, but are fearful that we have so offended you, that you do not want us to rejoin you. We have put a hog ashore

THE RETURN OF CAPTAIN BARNARD'S COMPANIONS

From an engraving in Barnard's *Narrative of Sufferings and Adventures*, New York, 1829

for you on the point, with some old newspapers that I
picked up at the wreck, as I had often heard you wish
that you had some books or papers to read.' I answered, 'Let my dog come ashore, and you may go
where you please with the boat; but, if you do not land
him and my gun, you may depend upon it that, if ever
a ship arrives, you will be made to repent of your late
infamous conduct.' Louder and Albrook said, 'We
wish to land and live with you again, and we hope that
you will forgive us.' I told them to come ashore, and
that I would not reflect on them on account of their
late proceedings. This declaration pleased them, and
they immediately began to pull in, when Ansel, who
had remained silent, ordered them to stop, and let him
speak, also. 'I hope,' said he, 'you will forgive me,
captain, as well as the others.' It struck me that Ansel would not feel himself at ease, conscious as he was
that I must consider him the instigator of the robbery
and desertion, unless, in addition to the general treaty
of peace, I made a particular one with him. I observed,
'You are four, and, if it is not your choice to land, let
my dog come, and you may go to any other place; I
can get my living alone as well as with company; and
last winter I instructed you how to get yours, and prevented you all from perishing. If you desire to remain
here, I am agreed, but do not wish to control you, neither shall I refer to what is past, unless you commence
the subject.' They now cheerfully landed and shook
hands with me. I told them I was glad that they had
got safely back, as I was afraid that they were lost.
They informed me that they had been to the wreck, but
that every useful article had been carried away or de-

stroyed. I had left two chests and one trunk, with clothes and books, on board the brig, and these I hoped had been landed, and left in one of the huts for me; for I did not suppose, even after their worse than piracy, that it was possible for them to commit the barbarous, and, to them, valueless robbery of these; but it appears they delighted to deprive me of what would not benefit them, but the want of which would increase my sufferings beyond description. Doubtless they coveted our deaths before the arrival of a vessel, that their unparalleled cruelty and inhumanity should not be pointed out as objects of scorn to the world.

"The truants, on their first landing, discovered my fire, and were much surprised and pleased, and inquired if I had found coal. I told them that the fears I had suffered from the dread of losing my fire, had led to the discovery of turf. I showed them the stock of eggs, and the potato vines that were just creeping from the ground. These sights, I presume, gave them more satisfaction than any they had seen since their departure. They had brought in the boat some trifling articles, that would be useful to us: there were a few pieces of canvas, which we raveled into thread; some old junk, which we converted into nettles about the size of common twine, and which, with the canvas thread, were intended for mending and making clothes; and some pieces of rags for tinder; — so that their runaway trip had its advantages; for, if they had not gone, I probably should not have discovered the invaluable turf; and solitude had suggested some improvements in clothing and shelter, and had taught me that I could depend upon myself to procure food, without the assistance of man or dog. By their failure, I was saved the disappointment of going to the wreck, which I was previously very anxious to do, in the hope of acquiring information of the crew, and secure some necessary articles; but, as every thing of value was gone or destroyed, I should have only lost that time in pursuit of that which could have been more advantageously employed on the island. They were now all convinced, particularly Louder, Albrook, and Green, of the propriety of having a superior who could direct their labors, and on whose judgment they could rely in unexpected difficulties and dangers.

"This being the time of year that the fur-seals have their young, we concluded to get as many of their skins as possible, and sew them together, and make blankets. We went to North Island, distant about four miles from our residence, and one from the north end of the island; it is inaccessible, except at one place, where the rocks had fallen from the cliffs. To these fallen rocks the seals resort, and in the hollows and cavities bring forth their young. Here Louder and Ansel volunteered to be left two days, and kill as many seals as they could. They were landed at considerable risk, as the sea was violently breaking against the shore. We left them a keg of water and proceeded for the north end of New Island; but, before reaching it, we observed a heavy swell, and the weather assuming a stormy appearance, I told the two that were with me, that we had better go back and take off the others, as I was fearful that, in case of a gale from the westward, there would be such a heavy rage of the sea as to dash them to pieces against the cliffs, which it was impossible for them to climb. We returned, and took them and five seals they had killed, in the boat, and made towards our place of residence.

"On the morning of December 23d, Ansel, Albrook and Green went in search of fur seals and Louder remained with me as it was his cook day. It was then that I learned from him that Sam Ansel had instigated the men to run away with the boat and that he was a bad man with an ungovernable temper, who would hesitate at nothing to accomplish his ends. After hearing Louder's story I resolved to bring the affair to an issue the next morning and after breakfast told Ansel that the time was arrived when I meant to have a full understanding with him and all hands. Sam appeared amazed and looking towards Green said 'Green, the villainous rascal has sold us.' Louder was beside me and I at once told Green and Albrook if they were disposed to join Sam, to go and stand by his side, but if not, to come over on mine. They at once advanced to my side and I never saw them move more quickly.

"As soon as Ansel saw the issue of the affair, all his courage left him and he ran about wringing his hands and crying 'What shall I do? What shall I do? They are all against me!' I was rather at a loss what arrangement to make respecting him and for the time accepted his promises of better behavior for the future; but later I discussed the situation with the others and found them all afraid of his savage temper so it was agreed that he should be taken to one of the adjoining islands and left there. It was agreed that I should propose a trip to Swan Island for hogs and while there Ansel should be sent down the shore for driftwood and

when some distance away the rest should shove off
and leave him. I cautioned them not to hurt him and
as it turned out everything happened just as it had
been planned. The men returned about eight o'clock
that evening and reported that Sam had come running back when he saw them pulling away and acted
as if he was frantic and took his knife and threatened
to kill himself. They told him not to do that but to
wait the arrival of a vessel when they would come over
and take him away; that they were sorry for him, but
his conduct had left them no choice, and they were
compelled to leave him.

"We now began to pass our time more agreeably and
a few days later the three men proposed to me to go to
the wreck, where they could pick up a number of small,
serviceable articles, such as some pieces of plank,
boards, old nails, and pieces of rope for oakum, to
mend our boat, which was very much out of repair. I
allowed them to depart immediately, and to take all the
hogs, which we supposed would afford a sufficient supply for the cruise, but leave the dog, as he could catch a
pig for me, if I should be necessitated. I particularly
charged them to get all the nails they could, and some
of the pieces of the sails, if not too rotten, that had been
used as coverings for the huts, and make a strict search
for any carpenters' tools that might have been thrown
away or lost.

"Accompanied by my best wishes, the boat departed
with a fine and pleasant breeze and was soon out of
sight. I was now a Robinson Crusoe again; but began
to be more reconciled to my hard fate, and determined,
with the divine aid, if it should be my destiny to con-

tinue here the remainder of my days, that I would in no case despair, but that, cheered by the recollection of having endeavored to perform the duties of my station, I would, with the calm surface of the ocean of eternity in view, say, 'God's will be done.' To this resolution I was enabled to adhere; and, when reduced almost to the last extremity by hunger and cold, I never despaired, but made greater exertions to persevere. Nothing, however severely it opposed my plans or comfort, could completely sink my spirits; which only occurred when I thought of my native country, my wife, and three helpless children, who were, perhaps, suffering from my absence or grieving for me as lost and numbered with the dead.

"The next morning, I took the dog, and went in quest of a pig, as my provisions were expended, which were only part of a hog (that the men insisted upon leaving, as I wished them to take all the stock in the boat) and on which the dog and myself had subsisted till now. After passing some tushooks, the dog was very anxious to get loose from the string by which I held him. I stopped, and, looking round, — for I was certain, from his impatience, that there were hogs near me, — I discovered, about fifty yards ahead, a sow, and seven or eight pigs, feeding on the long grass. The dog made for the sow; but she made her escape in the tushooks, which were so high and thick, that he could not hunt there. I chased one of the pigs, which was about half grown, and succeeded in capturing it in the chase, before it could gain the tushooks. I knocked it down, and was in the act of sticking it, when a large boar came out and rushed immediately at me; but, not being prepared to receive him, I gave him only a slight blow on the nose, which merely checked his force. He then made a pass at my legs, which I avoided. I caught hold of his ear with one hand, and, beating him over the head with my club, called to the dog, which immediately came and seized the boar by the other ear; but he still persisted in attacking me. The contest had continued some time, when, in making a blow at the head of the boar, it unfortunately fell upon the head of the dog, which instantly let go his hold and staggered to some distance. I now thought that, if the battle were continued, I should eventually be overpowered. I therefore prepared to retreat from the enraged beast; which was accomplished by springing on the top of a high tushook bog. From this I renewed the engagement, being better able to defend myself and repel his violent attempts to force his way upon me. There was a fair chance of using my club with advantage, by taking it in both hands and vigorously plying it, so that my assailant found that, by continuing the contest, he should acquire nothing more than a full allowance of hard blows: he slowly retreated along the tushooks, frequently stopping and looking back, his eyeballs glaring with fury and his teeth gnashing and foaming with rage. I remained on my station till the boar was out of sight, when I went to the dog, which had remained in one place, about thirty yards off, and hastily examined him, fearful that I had either struck out his only eye, or fractured his skull; but was glad to find that my fears were unfounded. After coaxing, and trying to make him understand that I did not mean to hurt him, he followed me to the pig I had killed. I took it on my back, and returned homeward, resolved not to go again alone hunting hogs.

"Having reached my hut, I examined the dog more particularly; but, although the blow was severe, yet I could not perceive that he had sustained any serious injury; at which I was very happy, for his loss would have been irretrievable to us and the most serious misfortune which could befall us here. This invaluable animal—which, I am sure, ranks among the first of his species, and which my companions frequently declared never had his equal—was, by this time, almost covered with scars, which he had received in his numerous conflicts with the old boars. These old fellows had immense tusks, projecting several inches from their jaws, with which they repeatedly ripped the dog's skin and flesh in a shocking manner; but he was regardless of wounds and never left his game until we arrived to his assistance. When we were drawing up around the two, the dog and his antagonist would be found looking directly in each other's eyes; and, as we cautiously closed in with raised clubs, the boar would take his eyes off from the dog's and bolt at us with the greatest fury, but never succeeded in injuring any of us; for, the moment that we drew the attention of the boar, the dog would spring on him, and the fight would last ten or fifteen minutes. Sometimes the dog's hold would be broken and he would be thrown to a considerable distance; but he always succeeded in seizing the boar again before he hurt any of us, and we all, at the same time, endeavored to give him a heavy blow on the small of the back, that being the place where it produced the greatest effect. In one of these encounters our brave dog lost an eye; in another, he received a blow that almost converted him into the neuter gender; but he never flinched, except at the time he lost his eye. The tusk of the boar penetrated so far into his head and so bewildered him, that he could not distinguish us from the boar; he was thus compelled to give up the contest, and the boar made good his retreat. No one can judge how serviceable he was to us; and we were the more sensible of it when he was wounded, for then we had but a very scanty subsistence, which consisted of fowl, which we luckily killed by throwing our clubs at them; but in this we did not often succeed. We would then go, at low water, to the rocky beach, and turn over the loose, flat stones, in whose beds we sometimes found a small fish about the size of an anchovy; and, after several hours, we could only procure enough just to support nature. But so great was our attachment to the dog, that we would not permit him to hunt and catch a hog for us, unless absolutely necessary, until his wounds were healed. To prevent, as far as possible, his engaging any of the old boars, we made a check-string of seal-skin, of about three fathoms in length, which we fastened round his neck. This hindered him, when he took the scent, from starting and leaving us so far behind, as to be severely wounded, or killed, before we could arrive to his assistance.

"About noon of the 26th of January, 1814, to my surprise, I discovered the boat standing directly into the harbor with a fair wind. As I thought they could not possibly have gone to the wreck, it now occurred to me that they had not been farther than to Swan Island, with Sam, and that he had regained some of his

former influence, and had persuaded them to take him
off and that he was now in the boat. I waited, with no
little uneasiness, for the boat to approach sufficiently
near to enable me to count, when I ascertained there
were only three. As my conjectures were very rapid, I
presumed that, although the weather had been remarkably fine since they left me, ʿ ʾmething had alarmed or
discouraged them from proc ːeding to the wreck, and
they had returned without accomplishing the purposes
of the cruise. But all my suspicions were erroneous.
On landing, they all ran to me; I held out both hands
to receive them, and they appeared almost as much
affected as if a ship had arrived to our relief. Although
they had been absent such a short time, yet they returned with a boat-load of such articles as they could
find, which they thought would be of any use.

"We now concluded to go to Sea-Dog Island for fur
seal-skins, on which there is but a small landing, which
is very difficult, even in fair weather. It lies about two
miles from Cape Orford, and about thirty from New
Island. We took in Ansel's proportion of the seal-
skins, which had been taken while he was with us, and
every article that belonged to him; intending to stop at
the place where he had been left, and leave him his
property, and see what situation he was in, and render
him every assistance in our power, excepting taking
him off, which was decidedly objected to by all hands,
considering that his motives for revenge were now
more powerful than ever.

"Previously to our departure, I wrote on a piece of
paper, that had been brought from the wreck, as follows:—'To the captain of any ship that may providen-

tially stop at this island. We beg leave to state to you, that there are five men of us, — two citizens of the United States, and three subjects of Great Britain, — who were left hereon; since which time we have been in a most deplorable and suffering condition, destitute of every necessary of life except what these barren islands afford. We are now gone to Dog Island to procure skins for clothing, to prevent, as far as possible, a renewal of our dreadful sufferings last winter, from the excessive cold, and frequent tremendous storms. If this falls into the hands of any one disposed to assist suffering humanity, we implore him to remain with his ship a few days, till our return, if possible, and take us from these desolate regions; but, if circumstances positively forbid his awaiting our return, we solicit, as the next greatest favor, to leave us some supplies of food and clothing; for we have long been strangers to these necessary articles, commonly used by man in a civilized state. We also request that information may be given to the American or British consul, at the first port where the ship may arrive; or, if an opportunity offers to write, to inform them of our dreadful situation; from which we entertain but faint hopes of being relieved, unless they should send a vessel for us.

(Signed)   CHARLES H. BARNARD.

JAMES LOUDER.

JOSEPH ALBROOK.

JACOB GREEN.'

"This paper I put on a horn, and hung it up at the door of the hut, so that, if any persons should land, it could not fail to meet their view.

"I told the men that, as it was not probable that any vessel would arrive this season, and as winter was approaching, it was advisable for us to go to work and finish our house. This was cheerfully assented to; we worked with so much cheerfulness and so faithfully, that in three days we completed the walls; which were from three to four feet thick, and five feet in height. But we had the most difficult part yet to accomplish, which was to make the roof, as we had not been able to procure drift-wood enough for the rafters; but we luckily substituted the ribs of a whale, which we found on the beach. After the top was prepared in the best manner which our scanty means permitted for thatching, we pulled the longest tushook straw we could find, and secured it with old rope-yarns, brought from the wreck, and succeeded in making a thatch resembling that with which farmers cover their barns.

"We completed the house; and, as our pork was expended, we concluded to go to Beaver Island, and endeavor to get a boat-load. As Ansel (whom, on a solemn promise of better conduct, we had taken from Swan Island) did not wish to accompany us, I directed him, while we were absent, to raise a bank of earth around the house, against the walls, of the same height, and let it slope off from the top, to the thickness of six or eight feet at the bottom, and then, with grass sods, cover the whole bank.

"We arrived at Beaver Island on the 21st, about noon, when the dog soon started a very large old boar, in the tushooks, that fought like a tiger, and, before we could enter fairly into the battle, they both fell into a large burnt pit, which we called a peat-hole. There the boar, having a great advantage, cut the dog severely. On our approaching the side of the pit, the boar leaped out, made a rush at us, and then ran away, which we were very glad of, as these old boars when attacked, seldom leave us but continue to fight, even though we avoid them, until they are killed. We got the dog out and found that he had received two severe cuts on the hinder parts, about six inches long and almost through to the bone, the divided flesh hanging down two or three inches from the wound. We took him to the boat, dressed and bound up his wounds. In consequence of this accident, it was pinching times with us; for our whole dependence was in killing a fowl with our clubs, and turning over the stones, at low water, for small fishes, when we sometimes found a little muscle or two; but these were very uncertain and very scanty resources. We continued to live in this meagre manner four days, keeping the dog confined, that, by remaining quiet, his wounds might heal the sooner.

"The dog having been kept quiet, his wounds were almost healed, and as our want of food was very pressing, I thought I could venture him against a small hog. After securing him with a string, we followed him: he soon took the scent, when he pulled so powerfully that the man who held the string was at times compelled to run. This was indeed a gratifying sight to us, as we were fearful that, by being so often wounded he would at length become shy and refuse to hunt. We soon came in sight of four or five hogs, feeding on the grass. We approached them as near as we could without being discovered and loosed the dog. From his long fast, and the recollection of his recent wounds, he was perfectly savage and appeared as if he wished, if possible, to tear them in pieces; he seized two, one of which proved to be fat, and made up for our long fast.

"The next morning we went towards New Island and arrived there about noon. We found Ansei well and that he had been very laborious. I was much pleased at his industry, considering it as a proof of his desire to obey my wishes and conciliate our good opinion. Our house was now completed to the extent of our materials; the roof proved to be perfectly tight and the chimney carried off the smoke well. Every man was now employed at his own private concerns, in dressing and sewing together pup-skins for blankets, making nettle-stuff to use in lieu of thread, &c. In one of my rambles near the place where we had built our shallop, I picked up an old adze, with the eye broken off. By heating it, I bent the upper part down, which formed an eye. I then supplied it with a handle and it answered in some respects the purposes of a hatchet and proved of great service to us.

"We had completed dressing and making up all our pup-skins into clothes and blankets. Our pork being all consumed, we all left this island (trusting to the letter on the horn to inform any person or persons who might come here while we were absent, of our situation and wishes) for Beaver Island, where we hunted two days. From Beaver, we went to Tea Island, in pursuit of fur-seals. Knowing of a large rookery there, we landed about sunset and the next morning we went to the place. The tide being out, we passed close along the water's edge until we were directly under the whole body of seals, which were lying in a deep gully between two high cliffs. I calculated that the number of seals was about three hundred, including small and great. Our approach awakened them, and they commenced their retreat towards the sea, which they invariably do when attacked. We felled the first one that approached us; but the whole body of them getting in motion, they came down upon us with such force that we could do little more than take care of ourselves. A large wig, or male seal, came down upon me, with a number of small ones, and, as I could not defend myself against them all at once, the old wig gave me a bite on the right knee, but luckily without inflicting any more injury than leaving the impression of his teeth in my leg and tearing off the lower part of the trousers. By reason of the rapidity with which they descended the gully, we only killed twenty-three large seals and thirty pups. We then skinned the pups and took the skins to the boat.

"We took a walk down to the south part of the island, distant about three miles from the boat, and observed that some of the high tushooks were much beaten down by the seals. We found, from the state of the ground, that the tushooks, which grew at some former period, had been burnt, and that the fire had penetrated the earth, in some places, to the depth of thirty or forty feet; the openings of the pits were from six to eight feet square, and greatly widened under ground. In many of these pits, we saw hair-seals and sea-lions, which had accidentally fallen in, some of which were dead and others dying. It was a distressing sight to behold the agonies of the poor animals that yet retained some remains of life, or had lately fallen in. We would have released them from their tortures by death, but we could not get down to them. We were obliged to walk here with great caution, for the tushook-grass had grown round those holes so thickly that they could not be perceived until the grass was pulled away. Our attention was now arrested by the loud and incessant barking of the dog, at a short distance; we went to the place; he was barking at an old lioness, who was lying motionless in the mud and water at the bottom of the pit, and her pup, who was moaning most lamentably over its dying mother. I was shocked by the agonies of these poor creatures; but more so when the poor little pup looked up to us, with tears streaming from its eyes, and seemingly imploring our assistance, and then renewing its efforts to aid the mother up to give it suck. We left this place, which, like the bridge in Mirza's vision, was full of deadly pitfalls, and returned to the boat. After dinner we took the boat's rope and went back to the tushooks; we made Louder fast to it and lowered him into the pit where the dying lioness and her young one were. He despatched the two suffering animals, which we then drew up, and set fire to the tushooks to prevent any more living creatures from being buried in them for the future.

"We dressed all the fur-skins and made them up into clothes and blankets; but we yet required more pup-skins, which we wanted to sew together and make bed-sacks, since we could now easily fill them with feathers, as the lowland geese had shed their quills and could not fly. I knew of only one place more to which the fur-seals resorted to bring forth their pups; this was on the windward side, and near to the south end of the island, where the cliffs were perpendicular and more than two hundred feet high. From their once arched and overhanging heads, large masses of rock had fallen, which were, by the descent, dashed into millions of fragments varying in magnitude from the size of a man's hand to a huge hill. Among these fragments the seals retired in great numbers.

"I informed the men of this place, where, if we could contrive any plan to get at the seals, we could provide ourselves with as many pup-skins as we should require; but we could not haul up the boat on the rocks, for there a landing could not be made, even in fine weather, without great danger as a heavy sea sets continually in and breaks against the rocks. Were a landing effected and any accident to happen to the boat, which it would be impossible, perhaps, to avoid, we must abandon all hopes of safety. Climbing the cliffs, or retreating along shore, was out of the question. The only way to get at the seals there, would be by fastening one of us to a line of sufficient length and lowering him down from the top of the cliffs; and thus one or two of the others could successively follow, by the same method. But another difficulty arose, which was, to procure a rope of sufficient length and strength for that purpose. I suggested that if we had our lance from Hook Camp, we could kill old sea-lions, cut their skins circularly into one entire piece and by knotting several of them together, make a line long enough to reach from the top of the cliffs to the bottom. I therefore proposed going for the lance; but they seemed rather fearful to attempt hauling the boat over the land, and unwilling to go so far from Beaver or Swan Island, on either of which our dog could procure us provisions.

I found that our past sufferings were fresh in their recollection and also our danger of perishing last winter
at the haul-over place, in our abortive attempt to reach
the wreck.

"I observed to them that the season, and of course
the weather, was exactly opposite to what it was then,
as we had now summer and long days and a great
plenty of birds which we could kill with our clubs;
that the lance would be of great use to us as long as we
remained on these islands as we should also want lions'
skins for moccasins; that if we did not go for it now,
while the boat was in tolerable condition, we could not
when she should become out of repair. With these con-
siderations they all agreed to go for it.

"The weather being fine and the sea smooth, on the
12th, we launched the boat and went round to the
windward side of the island, abreast of the seal rookery, to land Ansel and Louder, if it could be done with
safety. The rocks were covered with seals, and the sea
was dashing against them with great violence; we
waited for a smooth time, and then pulled in; Ansel
and Louder jumped out on a rock, on which we threw
them a piece of pork and instantly made off, as we saw
a heavy sea coming in; but we could not avoid its fury,
for it struck the boat, drove her against the rocks and
was near dashing her into atoms. By great exertions,
and the aid of Heaven, we escaped instant destruction.
If the boat had been dashed in pieces, the fate of those
on the rocks would have been dreadful, as they must
have perished at the feet of those perpendicular cliffs.
We rowed back to our residence fully determined not
to venture there again in the boat. We now collected

all our rope of hemp and skin, which, with the boat's painter, knotted together, made about fifty-five fathoms; and this we thought would reach from the top to the base of the cliffs.

"We arrived with our rope at the place, drove one of our strongest clubs into the ground, about thirty yards from the edge of the precipice, made the rope fast to it, and I directed Green and Albrook to sit down and hold on, to prevent it from starting. I then took the rope to the cliff, and, on looking down, discovered the two men almost directly under me. I threw down a stone, which caused them to look up, and at length they saw me. I called to them, and they to me; but the distance, combined with the roaring of the surf, and the bellowing of the seals, prevented our hearing or understanding one another. I threw down the rope, which reached to about thirty feet from the bottom; Louder climbed up to it, and in a few minutes I perceived him ascending by the rope, hand over hand, with his feet against the rocks, where, in some places, he could get a foot hold, and rest himself, and at length he arrived safely at the top. He related their success in catching seals; that he did not find much difficulty in coming up, and was willing to go down again, if one of us would accompany him. Green and Albrook refused to pass beyond the stake. Louder went down, and, when about half way, stopped to rest on a rock which projected from the side of the cliff. I directed him to remain there, and to order Sam to fasten four or five skins, which he could haul up with ease to his resting-place, and from thence I would draw them to the top of the cliff; and, when we had drawn them all up, that he should return to me, and assist in carrying the skins to the stake. All this was effected, and Green and Albrook were directed to carry the skins to the house, wash and peg them out, and, the next day, after they had completed that work, to return here and draw up more skins. We according-ly went down, and skinned the seals they had killed. At night, we laid down on the rocks, as close to the cliffs as possible, to guard against the incursions of the sea, which we should not have been able to do, if a gale of wind had risen from the west, which would have produced a heavy, raging sea.

"On the 14th, about noon, while skinning the seals, our attention was arrested by stones falling on the shore from the cliffs. Concluding that they were thrown down by Green and Albrook, I told Louder to go up and see, as they would not probably come in sight; he went up, and found them there, and we therefore decided to get all the skins up, and leave this danger-ous place. We succeeded in drawing them all up in the course of the afternoon, and, at night, arrived with our back-loads at the house, extremely fatigued. We cooked the last of our pork for supper, and crawled un-der the boat, to procure that rest and sleep of which we stood so much in need.

"While employed in pegging out the skins, two men, with the dog, went to the north end of the island in search of hogs, and succeeded in getting a very fine, large boar, which furnished the best meat we had eaten on the island. We were employed in dressing the small skins, and making them up into bed-sacks and blan-kets, and hunting occasionally at Beaver Island.

"When the boat departed for Beaver Island, on the

customary errand, Louder and myself remained at home. We were now much more comfortable than we had been at any time since we were abandoned; our house was warm and tight, and we had plenty of peat to burn. We brought the peat from different places, in hog-skin bags, two full ones of which were sufficient to keep up a good fire all the day and evening. The winter had now completely set in, and the cold snow and rain storms made it difficult to pick up enough for us to subsist upon while the boat was gone after hogs. Most of the birds had left the island, and geese and rooks were all that remained. I told Louder that we would twist some rope-yarns into a cord about the size of a cod-line, make a slip-knot in one end, lay it on the beach, and lead the other end into the door of the house; and, when the geese lit on the beach, which several flocks did every day to drink from a run of fresh water that emptied on the beach, that we would catch them by means of the noose. We toiled hard every day to procure something to eat; sometimes we were tolerably successful; at others, our luck was very indifferent. The evenings were passed by the fire, either in making lines for the snare, or twisting thread out of rope-yarns to make clothes.

"Having completed the snare, we took the slip-knot, which was made of finer line than the other part, and laid it open on the beach, having first greased it. In a few moments, a flock, consisting of the old goose and gander, and five young ones of the last year's brood, alighted on the beach; but, as they did not go toward the snare, I sent Louder round to a distance to drive them carefully toward it; this he did so well that I soon had the satisfaction of catching the gander by the legs, and drawing him up to the house, with the others following him almost to the door. I locked his wings, and let him run, and continued working the snare until we had taken six. The other had become shy, and, while trying for him, the boat appeared in sight. We conveyed the six geese into the house, and went down to meet those that were in the boat, as she was now close to the beach. On their landing, we were much surprised to see them look very melancholy, and not a single hog in the boat. On inquiring the cause of their appearing so dispirited, and being without game, they replied that they had not caught a hog since they had left home, and were nearly starved, as the most of their food had been the few little fishes that they could gather from under the stones along shore; that, on their first landing on Beaver Island, they discovered a hog near the beach; that the dog gave chase, and that they both ran into the tushooks. Some of the men followed them, and the others ran round to discern which way the hog and dog would go when they came out; the hog soon passed them on the other side; but, after waiting a short time for the appearance of the dog, as they supposed he had lost the scent, but would soon recover it, they all entered the patch, searching and calling for him; but he was neither heard nor seen. As it was near night, they went to the boat, and hauled her up for shelter, knowing that, if the dog was alive, he would certainly come there. But Green could not bear the idea of abandoning the search for the faithful animal as long as he could see, as he was fearful that he was either killed, or that his other eye was put out. While he stood on the top of a high bog, looking and calling for the dog, he thought he heard him whine; he listened attentively, and heard him again, apparently close to his feet. Pulling away the straw, he discovered a hole not larger than a hogshead top, but the pit below was large and deep. There was the poor dog, with his fore feet against the side, and the lower part of his body buried in the mud and water; but he could not get him out, which could only be done by lowering a man with the boat's painter, making the dog fast to it, and then drawing them both up. His comrades were down at the boat, out of sight and hearing, and he dared not leave the place, for fear that he could not find it again; he therefore determined, if his comrades did not return, to remain by the dog all night, and talk to and try to encourage him. However, Green's companions returned to search for him; one of them ran back, and brought the rope, made it fast to Albrook, lowered him, and he brought up the dog. I told them not to be discouraged, but to come up and see what we had got in the house; they were surprised to find that we had so many live geese, which were a pleasing sight to hungry men.

"On the 1st of November, 1814, we departed on an excursion to Swan Island, to hunt for hogs. After remaining here several days, while eating breakfast, I told Albrook that he and I would go to the top of the hills, and gather some balsam. On the tops of the high hills there are large, green bunches, growing in the form of a bee-hive, and varying from the size of a common hive to that of a hogshead; from these the warmth of the sun draws out a resinous gum, which is the best application to a bite or cut that I ever used anywhere.

"We had not proceeded far, before we heard Louder cry out, as he would have done if suddenly and severely hurt. I supposed that Louder was bitten by an old boar. We called to the dog, which was a short distance ahead, and ran as fast as we could. The dog, hearing Louder crying and screaming, passed us like an arrow. When we came to Louder, he was lying on the ground, rolling and crying, and the dog jumping round and over him as if he wished to know how he was hurt. Albrook, who was a little in advance of me, turned round, looked suddenly pale, and was near falling; but, clasping my hand, he began to cry. The first thought that struck me was, that they were both mad or crazy, and that it was occasioned by our diet. All that Albrook was enabled to say was, *'Two ships! two ships!'* I had not looked towards New Island since we had turned back, for my attention was fixed on Louder, who was still on the ground. I now looked, and saw indeed two ships, far off in the offing, apparently standing in for New Island. Louder, recovering himself, came to me, crying, and, taking my other hand, repeated, 'Two ships!' They both held me, and continued shedding tears, till I felt one trickling down my own cheek. I rallied myself, and said, 'Come, come, boys, do not let this glad sight overjoy you, for fear they may pass without stopping at New Island. We must go and watch them, and see where they anchor;' as I was almost certain they would anchor at some of these islands, from the direction we saw them in, as they had already passed the Jasons. In about three hours, we had the satisfaction of seeing them haul their wind round

North Island, and stand well over towards us, close on a wind, and then tack and stand in for New Island Harbor, out of our sight.

"About the middle of the afternoon, the tide being down, and the sea not breaking so violently against the shore, we got the boat down, took in the hogs, but left the wood and skins. I took out of my bag the only apology we all had for a shirt, from which I had torn the sleeves and tail to make tinder. On putting on this remnant, I observed, that, on this joyful occasion, I could afford to wear a shirt. We pulled up along shore, towards Quaker Harbor, in order to be so far to windward, that, in the morning, we could be able to lay across; but we run the boat so fast, that we were abreast of the windward part of Lock's Island an hour before sunset. We now made sail, to try if the boat would lay over, and found that she headed up for New Island; we kept the oars in operation, and by the assistance of the sail, reached the north end about dusk.

"Before arriving at the ships, as I was certain that they were English, I inquired of the two young men, when the captain should make the usual inquiries, of what country they were, what would be their answer. They replied, 'We shall say that we are Americans, and are determined never to say to the contrary.' This was the reply that I anticipated, as I had frequently heard them declare that they should always consider and call themselves Americans. They had learned from Green, the names of many of the streets in New York, and other local information, to be prepared to answer in case of being examined by a British man-of-war. I observed that, if the captain inquired of me, I should say

that they belonged to the English ship that was wrecked
on these islands, and would say nothing more concerning them. We were now rapidly nearing the ships, and,
at about six o'clock in the evening, we were on board of
the whale ship *Indispensable,* of London, William
Buckle, master; the other vessel was the *Asp,* John
Kenny, master, who (William Dunkin, the mate, told
me) was in the cabin with Captain Buckle. Mr. Dunkin requested me to go below, in the cabin; but I declined until I was invited by the captain. The mate informed me that war still continued between Great
Britain and the United States. Captains Buckle and
Kenny soon came on deck to see me, and I presume
they expected to behold a man whose outward appearance was something like their own. But, if they did,
they were disappointed; for they saw before them a
being who, from the inhumanity of their countrymen,
had more the appearance of a savage of the forest, than
a native of an enlightened and Christian country.

"The whole of my dress, with the exception of the
piece of old checked shirt, was composed of skins, and
my face was almost entirely covered with a beard eight
inches in length. I was reviewed with more attention
and astonishment than any of my fellow-sufferers,
whose beards, being very light and thin, their faces
were not so fully and richly ornamented as mine, and
of course did not furnish so perfect a Crusonian representation. The captain invited me down into the cabin,
and offered me some refreshments; but I declined, having no inclination for food, for all my feelings and
thoughts were engrossed by this sudden and unexpected change in our situation. A few hours ago, we were

banished, and debarred from all intercourse with the rest of mankind, and experienced the want of almost every necessary comfort; and now to be again restored, as it were, to the world, — though in a partial degree, I admit, but which I considered only as preparatory to my restoration to my country, family, and home,—was inexpressibly delightful.

"In the course of the conversation, Captain Buckle informed me that when he was on the coast of Peru, last voyage, one of our frigates was there and had captured all the English whalers, except his ship and one more. I asked him what American frigate had been round Cape Horn and captured the whalers and he said the *Essex,* and added very indifferently, 'but one of our frigates went round and captured her.' He then abruptly remarked that one of their frigates had taken the *Chesapeake.* With wounded feelings I asked 'What frigate?' He said, 'If you will look at that paper which is rolled up behind the glass, it will inform you.' I opened it and found that it was a large print representing the action between the *Shannon* and the *Chesapeake* in which the latter was depicted as being much larger than the *Shannon,* and suffering severely in every respect, while the *Shannon* was represented as trim as though she had just come fresh out of port.

"Captain Kenny broke the silence by observing that the *Essex* fought under great disadvantages; her main-topmast having been previously carried away; that their own frigate was assisted by a sloop-of-war; and that Captain Porter had behaved remarkably well and defended his ship bravely. But, continued he, 'Some of your frigates have taken some of ours in a crack, before they had time to look round them.' At this acknowledgment I felt highly elated but forbore inquiring about particulars.

"The next morning Captain Buckle fitted me out with a suit of clothing and after breakfast we went ashore with a number of men hunting hogs and geese. Several were employed in bringing down eggs from my stock and loading the boat. Men from the *Indispensable* brought peat from Green Island, as Captain Buckle preferred it for cabin use to coal, making almost as hot a fire and being much cleaner. A stock of water was also taken on board.

"On the 29th of November we got under way, with a stiff breeze from the N. W., and four days later at 10 A. M. saw Cape St. John's, the southeastern part of Staten Island. The ships bound round Cape Horn double it as close as possible.

"The day after Christmas we discovered a school of spermaceti whales and succeeded in killing two, getting them alongside, cutting their blubber up before night and setting the try-works in operation. The next morning we came upon another large school of whales and both ships gave chase, the wind blowing fresh with much sea. We succeeded in getting a very large one, calculated to be good for seventy barrels of oil, but the wind increasing, bringing in a heavy sea, we lost half of it before we could cut it up. We saw several columns of smoke rising from the island of St. Mary's and supposing them to be smugglers' signals we put away before the wind.

"As Captain Buckle intended to cruise for several months without going into port, when in latitude 16°, with the Cordilleras in sight from the deck, I determined to make the passage to shore in my boat, which had been brought along on deck, notwithstanding warnings that the Spaniards were a cruel people who might either murder or imprison me. Captain Buckle at last consenting and Louder and Albrook wishing to go with me, I took a copy of a chart of the coast and was provided with a compass, keg of water, some pieces of pork, a bag of bread and several bottles of porter. Captain Buckle also furnished me with letters to the Captain of the port of Callao and to Mr. Samuel Cozus, an American merchant at Lima, at the same time giving me $2.20, which was half of the money he had on board, and told me to choose from the slop-room as much clothing as I needed.

"When the boat was put overboard we were about forty-five miles from land and the next morning found us close in shore near steep cliffs. At the time the number of whales spouting and playing about us was so great that we were afraid, in their gambols, they would come in contact witht the boat and destroy us. We rowed along shore to the northward and towards night came to a rocky island, about two miles from the main land, where we hauled the boat up and spent the night. The next morning we heard fur seal calling their pups and after killing two and roasting them we ate heartily and then launched the boat and shaped a course up the coast before a fresh southerly breeze, which continued for several days and at length brought us to Callao, where we found an English ship, called the *Wildman,* landing two large steam engines to be employed in drawing the water out of the gold and silver mines at

Cosco. As part of the crew had deserted, Louder and Albrook decided to ship on board of her. Here I hired a house for which I was to pay five dollars per month rent. It was of the height and breadth of the door, about nine feet in length and the yard was only large enough to admit of a fireplace. After purchasing the most necessary articles of housekeeping, with a fishing line and hooks, I lived here for some weeks, but unfortunately not alone, for the place swarmed with fleas in such immense numbers that when I rose each morning from my bed on the floor, I was so covered with them that I appeared almost as though clothed in black.

"One morning I took my usual walk down to the harbor and discovered to my great joy that the English whale ship *Indispensable* had come in during the previous night and before long I had the satisfaction of taking my friend Captain Buckle by the hand. He was glad to see me and learning that my situation was very uncomfortable he at once offered me his ship as my home, which I gratefully accepted. That afternoon I got my clothes, gave away my furniture and left the fleas to eat the bugs, or the bugs the fleas, and went to the key where the *Indispensable's* boat was lying and soon was on board again. I found that they had been very fortunate in taking whales during the past three months and had filled up thirteen hundred barrels with oil, which two-thirds loaded the ship.

"We sailed from Callao on the 16th of May, 1815, in company with the English whale ships *Nimrod,* Captain Day, *Cyrus,* Captain Davy, and *Eliza,* Captain Walker, on a cruise off the Lobs Islands and Cape Francisco, near the Equator, and continued cruising there until the middle of June, and then ran over to the Gallipagoes Islands where boats were dispatched from each ship to the shore to procure terrapin and at night they returned loaded. While here I left the *Indispensable* and went on board the *Eliza,* as the season for whalers in that quarter was now over and Captains Walker and Buckle planned to part company and later make for the coast of Chili, as the whales were to be found there during the summer months.

"On the 20th of August, 1815, we made the Island of Massafuero. As I felt myself rather uncomfortable, from being so long confined on ship-board, and not having any active employment, to which I had been previously accustomed, I requested Captain Walker to land me on this island, where I judged that a large quantity of fur seal-skins could be procured; and, after the completion of his cargo, at his return I would again go on board, as he always touched here to procure supplies of wood and water. Captain Walker warmly remonstrated against my plan; but, finding that I was really desirous of carrying it into execution, he consented, and gave directions to make up a stock for me, consisting of a bag of bread, one of seed potatoes; several pieces of beef and pork; four terrapin; tea, sugar, chocolate; twelve bottles of rum; a pot for cooking, tin pot and spoon; a hatchet, shovel, fishing-lines and hooks; clubs, knives, steel, and lance; musket, powder, and shot; two duck frocks and trousers, a red cap, and a dog. I was thus fully equipped to recommence a Crusonian life, but under much more favorable circumstances than those in which I commenced and terminated my former one.

"There was on board a youth of about seventeen, born in the United States, who had been left on this coast by some of the whalers, and was taken on board, at his own request, by Captain Walker, at Lima, who, hearing of my intentions, came aft, and desired to accompany me. Captain Walker consented, and furnished him with clothes. Now my character was complete; I had obtained a Friday without encountering the least danger. At 4 P. M., being contiguous to a good landing, I was put on shore, with my suite, consisting of Friday and the dog, with all the stores, and took possession of the island, in my assumed title, as governor for the time being. The ship made sail and continued on her cruise; and now we gazed on her, not without wishful eyes, uncertain of the perils and sufferings we might encounter.

"We began to search about us at a short distance from the landing-place. The walls of several old huts were standing, which had been erected by former sealers, for their accommodation, during the time they remained on the island. We placed all our stores within one of these roofless huts, kindled a fire, prepared and took our supper, and lay down to sleep, with no other covering than the heavens. We slept but little, our repose being frequently interrupted by the attempts of several animals to possess themselves of part of our provisions; but they were constantly foiled in their attempts by the watchfulness of our dog, who kept a bright lookout for these villainous intruders, and sprang at them as soon as they appeared at the door; but they were too nimble, and avoided him. I could not, owing to the darkness of the night, discover what kind of animals they were, neither were there any tracks discernible in the morning that would enable us to decide to what species our nocturnal visitors belonged. They appeared, as well as they could be distinguished in the dark, to be about the size of a fox, with large, flaming eyes, that made a frightful appearance. As I had never heard of this island being infested by wild beasts, I conjectured that they were amphibious animals, most probably sea-foxes, that repaired to the shore at night to sleep, or for other purposes, and had been attracted to the hut by the smell of our provisions. Considering it injurious to our health to be exposed to the night air and heavy dews while sleeping, all my thoughts were at present centered on procuring a roof for the hut; but I soon found that thinking would not effect any thing towards that object; for we neither possessed, nor could we procure in the vicinity, a single article that would answer the purpose. There were, indeed, several collections of old, dry branches, the trunks of trees; but we could not apply them to the purpose, for they would not make a roof water or wind tight.

"I explored the surrounding rocks and precipices for a situation that would afford us more suitable lodgings than the ruined hut. In searching, I discovered, on the side of the adjacent cliff, a cave that would make a tolerable bed-room. Here we removed our bedding, and slept that night, and found that we had greatly gained in point of comfort. This cave was ten or fifteen feet above the level of the water, and fifty or sixty feet from the huts, and formed what is generally termed, by voyagers in these seas, a gulch; that is, a wide rent, or chasm, extending in the rocks through the whole depth, from top to bottom; it was from one hundred and fifty to two hundred feet wide at its mouth, and gradually contracted as it extended some distance, perhaps a mile and a half, through the rocks, with a moderate ascent to its head, which was at the base of a high and inaccessible cliff. The mouth extended to the sea, and formed the landing-place, which was a small, rocky beach, bounded on each side by a projecting head. This beach had a gentle ascent for about two hundred yards, when it was level for a short space, where the huts had been erected; and here, again, the rise commenced. The sides of the gulch were stupendous cliffs, whose dark summits seemed almost to reach the clouds; they were covered with a tolerably deep soil, which produced a variety of shrubs and trees of different appearances and magnitudes. During the winter months, — June, July, and August, — this gulch is the channel by which the accumulated water, occasioned by the heavy rains that fall on the mountains during that season, is discharged into the ocean. Then this mountain torrent carries along with it branches and trunks of trees, earth, and rocks, which are either left upon the level, or thrown up in large piles, in consequence of a tree or its branches coming in contact with a rock, by which its progress is arrested. During the summer months, no rain falls, and the channel is dry, and covered, in many places, with trees and various fragments, forced, by the violence of the waters, from the sides of the mountains and cliffs.

"I proceeded to look for a suitable piece of ground on which to plant potatoes. Having found one which I considered to be adapted to the purpose, I commenced preparing it, and, in two days, all the potatoes were in the ground. There were many goats on the mountains and precipitous cliffs; and, being desirous of ascertaining if they were well-flavored, I took my gun, and, attended by my man Friday and my dog Tiger, set out, and searched along shore to the westward for some gulch, or chasm, by which the resort of these animals could be found; for there was no possibility of gaining the tops of the cliffs in the vicinity of the huts. After travelling about two miles, we came to a level piece of land, of an oblong form, about three quarters of a mile long, and one quarter wide, running under the cliffs, and called, by sealers, the North west Plains. Here we discovered a number of goats, feeding. I stationed Friday at the entrance of the plain, to prevent the escape of the goats that way, while I proceeded to prevent their retreat at the opposite end. I had no apprehension that they would be able to make their escape before I had made some fair shots at them; for the rocks in the rear appeared to be almost as straight as an artificial wall. On our closing upon them, they made no motion towards either end, but fell back to the cliffs, which, to my surprise, they began to ascend, leaping from one small ledge and chasm to another. In this manner they continued to ascend until the last one gained the top, when they all bounded swiftly out of sight, without my having been able to get a single shot at them. I found, on reaching the westerly end of this plain, that it was abruptly terminated by a high, steep rock, which projected out into the sea, and effectually prevented any further advance along shore in that direction. Several sealing huts had been erected here, which were falling into ruins, although two of them, from appearances, had been recently occupied, and one of them contained several seamen's chests, in which were some fishing-lines.

"We now returned to our camp, where we arrived at night, both hungry and fatigued, and without having been so lucky as to make any addition to our stock of provisions. The next morning, I thought it absolutely necessary that we should, with as little delay as possible, ascertain if there were any sources that we could depend upon for a supply of food, when the stock we had brought from the ship should be exhausted. I therefore went to the seaside, and threw out a line; but, there being a strong wind, and a considerable swell, my line was so quickly driven ashore as not to afford an opportunity to a fish, if any were there, to take the hook. In clearing the line from the rocks, I drew up an eel, about five feet long, and of a proportionable thickness, sprinkled with faint red spots on a dark ground, resembling the speckled coats of adders which I had seen on Long Island. This appearance was not very prepossessing, nor calculated to stimulate the appetite of a person unaccustomed to the sight; he was very vicious, making several attempts to bite me; but, after he was dead, as I was rather doubtful of his genus, I examined him, and from his general formation, and the presence of gills and fins, I was convinced of his being an eel; I did not, however, think I could eat of him with much relish; but Friday, not regarding appearances, said he would try him, and he was taken to our roofless kitchen, and cooked. Friday fed heartily; I tasted of it, and, though not delicately flavored, it was palatable, and might have furnished a good, substantial meal.

"This night, I thought I had discovered the kind of quadruped that interrupted us the last night. No sooner had we retired to our cave to sleep, than a number of animals, attracted probably by the smell of the eel, assembled before the door of the hut. From their motions and discordant notes, I was certain they were cats. I set the dog at them, when they took to flight. The next morning, I selected, from the piles of broken wood formed by the torrent before described, three logs suitable for the construction of a catamaran, to go a-fishing on, at a short distance from the shore, just without the breakers. The wood was light and dry, which was an advantage. While engaged among the logs, I disturbed a large cat, perfectly resembling the common or domestic one; she was apparently in good case, and immediately exerted all her speed to gain the cliff. I conjectured that cats had been left here by those who had erected the huts, the ruins of which were still remaining. I carried the logs to the sea-side, and commenced constructing the catamaran, by placing the longest piece in the middle, and the two shorter at the sides. I banded it with the small ropes which I had found in the hut on the plains, and shaped the ends of the outer pieces for the bow. Having launched it, I equipped Friday with the shovel for a paddle, a line and bag, and shoved her off, ordering him to go no farther than a few yards from the shore, and, while fishing, to keep his feet and legs out of the water, for fear of the sharks. Soon after taking his station, he began to catch fine large fish, and very fast; his success, and the calmness of the water, induced me to throw out my line from the rocks, when I also caught a number, in a short time.

"Friday, notwithstanding my repeated cautions, continuing to fish, with his feet and legs suspended in the sea. I directed him to come on shore, as we had fish enough; but so eager was he to continue his sport, that he remained engaged in it much longer than I desired. This, together with his exposing himself to the attacks of sharks, vexed me; and, as I found that, in still weather, a sufficient supply of fish could be procured by throwing a line from the rocks, when he reached the shore, I cut the bands of the catamaran, and let it go adrift; upon which Friday dryly observed, 'Alpha and Omega, the beginning and the end! the catamaran is begun, completed, and destroyed, in one day.' Having now, to my great satisfaction, realized a source upon which we could rely for a supply of good and nutritious food, which, though not various, was fully adequate to our comfortable subsistence, I felt much more at ease. While engaged in cleaning the fish on some flat rocks, a short distance below high-water mark, large eels, like the one I caught, would protrude their heads and necks to a considerable distance from the water, to seize upon the entrails of the fish; they were so voracious and intent upon their object, that they projected their heads so far over the rocks as to present a fair mark to the knife, which I applied with so much effect, that several were beheaded. There, when the weather was such as to prevent us from fishing from the rocks, by placing bait on the stones, we could easily and quickly procure food sufficient for the day. We had, for several successive days, prepared our meals of fish only, as the small quantity of pork remaining was held in reserve for cooking our finny fare. The terrapin were secured in one of the huts, that, in case a long succession of inclement weather, or other causes, should prevent us from seeking for supplies from the ocean or on the land, we might have a fresh stock in reserve.

"Being ardently desirous to embellish our hut with one of the bearded gentry, living or dead, I one day took my gun, and accompanied by Friday and Tiger, again sallied forth in pursuit of goats. We rambled along shore to the eastward in search of a split or gulch, by which we might ascend to the tops of the mountains. If I could effect this, I felt almost assured that I should be able to shoot one or more of them. Now we clambered over heaps of loose stones, lying directly under the heads of the frowning cliffs, from which, in all probability, they had been detached; then, for a short distance, we walked or slid over the glassy rocks; for the whole shore was diversified by these, lying singly, or thrown into misshapen heaps. Having waded along this tiresome and harassing road for about two miles, we arrived at a gulch, or valley, which bore a striking resemblance to the valley in St. Helena, in which Jamestown is situated; and that which I occupied corresponded in appearance, course, and distance, with Lemon Valley. Indeed, I had often been struck with the marked resemblance of the cliffs, when viewed from the shore, to those of St. Helena, not only in generals, but also in particulars, with the single exception that the summits of the mountains of St. Helena are not so well wooded as those on the island of Massafuero.

"We entered the gulch, and commenced the difficult and dangerous task of ascending it; but, by perseverance, we succeeded, and safely gained the summit. It was a small plain which, it was very evident, had once been entirely covered with trees, as the few now standing were scorched, and the trunks of some of them partially consumed. From these marks, and there being no underwood, it was conclusive that fire had once raged here, kindled either by accident or design. This beautiful little plain was now covered with a rich growth of young and tender grass, on which a large flock of goats were feeding: I approached them with great caution, and succeeded in getting within gunshot undiscovered, when I fired at and killed a fine she-goat. Thus having effected the primary object of my ascent, I had leisure to view and contemplate, from this elevated region, the prospect it afforded. The surrounding ocean, with its roaring billows, appeared to be at an immense distance, and in a state of soothing tranquility; its rolling waves appeared like silver dots on its surface; and its roaring surge could not be heard so high.

"We now descended the rocky mountain with the goat, which was a dangerous performance, as by one misstep we might lose our footing, when we should be precipitated on the rocks below, and be inevitably dashed to pieces; we therefore groped along with all possible caution, and succeeded in winding our way to the bottom without accident. Now that the most difficult part was performed, I gave the goat to Friday to carry; but I soon found that he was not equal to the labor of carrying it along this rough and rocky shore. I retook it; it was near night, and both of us were excessively exhausted with hunger and fatigue. When we got home, we were fully resolved not to ascend any of the precipitous mountains again in pursuit of goats, however grateful their flesh might be to our taste and appetites. We dressed our game, and prepared a part of it for supper; it was excellent, and our abstinence since morning, together with our exercise in the mountain air, had excited a keen appetite, which we allayed by making a hearty supper. We then retired to our cave to sleep. This cave was about seven feet across; the dog slept at the mouth, as the advance guard, I was in the centre, and Friday in the rear. The dog, several times through the night, ran down, barking, to the hut, to drive away the cats, which were attempting to partake of our game.

"At some former period, cabbages had been introduced into the island, and, running up to seed, were carried by the winds to different and distant parts of it, and were very plentiful until the goats acquired a relish for them. None were now to be found, except in some small crevice or ledge, too narrow for one of these mountaineers to plant his feet. Having observed some sprouts growing in such situations, I sent Friday with the boat-hook, to pull them down, which he did, and procured a considerable quantity, which, cooked with some goat's meat, furnished a delicious repast.

"The days passed so uniformly alike, that nothing occurred to excite particular attention. When the weather was favorable, we attended to the fishing, and to cleaning out and watching the growth of the potato

vines, which were in a flourishing state. I had observed, for a long time, that the goats frequently descended from the cliffs on the western side of the gulch,
and proceeded leisurely down, directing their course
to any little ridge or level, where a small patch of grass
or cabbages grew. When they arrived at the gulch,
they would cross it, spread themselves on the other
side, and slowly ascend it, seeking for a few blades of
grass, which, perhaps, they preferred to what grew on
the levels at the top; or prompted by their fondness for
roving among rocks and precipices, inaccessible to all
other animals but those of their own species. I made
several attempts to shoot them during the time of their
descending and climbing up the gulch; but, before I
could get within the proper distance, they invariably
took the alarm, bounded up the cliffs, and were immediately out of sight. As they generally crossed the
gulch at one place, I resolved, as soon as they were
again discernible on the cliffs, I would conceal myself
near their crossing-place, and patiently await their arrival.

"One day, observing them apparently inclined to descend, I placed myself in ambush, and, at length, had
the satisfaction to observe a fine buck within shot. I
fired, and wounded him; he sprung for, and ascended
the rocks to some distance, and entered a cavern which
I could ascend to. I reloaded my piece, and, on looking into the cave, I perceived that he was s e v e r e l y
wounded; and, after securing myself in such a manner
that, if he made a rush, he could not throw me off the
rocks, I fired, and he fell. The report of the gun and its
echo in the cavern were deafening, and almost terrific.

The buck was large and fat, and afforded good meat.

"While Friday and myself were engaged, the next day, in skinning the goat, we were surprised and alarmed by a ship coming round the southeast head, which terminates that side of the gulch. She was almost within hail before she was directly opposite to the landing. Our view of the ocean was so contracted by the proximity of the two projecting heads, that no more of its surface was visible than if viewed through an artificial vista. On seeing her, we ran for some large rocks, where we could conceal ourselves, and kept ourselves in a stooping posture, to prevent those on board from seeing us until we had reached the rocks. While engaged in concerting our plans, the ship's boat suddenly came round the head, rowing close in shore in quest of a landing place, and soon I heard a clear voice say, 'There is a smoke,' for the speaker was looking at that which rose from our fire in the hut. My joy was great and we at once stood up and went down to the landing place and helped them in hauling up their boat. Their ship was the *Millwood*, Samuel G. Bailey, commander, from New York, bound to the Sandwich Islands and Canton. Imagine the contradictory and tumultuous state of my feelings, for Captain Bailey was an old and familiar acquaintance and now I should learn the situation of my kindred and friends.

"The men having filled the breakers, we entered the boat and rowed to the ship. When I reached the deck, Captain Bailey at first didn't recognize me, but soon he said, 'Barnard, whom did you marry?' And when I informed him he exclaimed in astonishment, 'We thought you were long since numbered with the dead,' and then hastily added, 'just before sailing I saw your wife and children, and I am happy to say they were enjoying good health.' Captain Bailey at once urged me to leave the island and proceed with him on his voyage round the world, an invitation which I gladly accepted for although it was the longest route, it probably was the surest, as some unforseen accident might happen to the *Eliza* which would prevent Captain Walker returning for me. Later in the day, the boat went ashore for more water. I went too and after gathering up my small possessions, I wrote with chalk on an old box, which I placed in a conspicuous situation, informing Captain Walker, if he should come, of the arrival of the American ship *Millwood,* of my embarking in her, of the peace, etc. Some years after I saw the then mate of the *Eliza* in New York and he told me they had stopped for me and read my information with much satisfaction.

"We bore away N., with an intention to sight the islands of Felix and Ambrose, and, on the 9th, saw them at daylight, bearing N. N. W., the distance being estimated at three leagues. These rocks stretch from the northwest to southeast about five leagues. The easternmost is a large, high, round rock, skirted with smaller ones: we ran between them, and found the passage good. There were fine winds and pleasant weather until the 27th, when we made the Gallipagoes Islands, bearing N. N. W. distant about seven leagues. Some of the crew exhibiting symptoms of the scurvy, Captain Bailey observed to me, that, as he now had a pilot on board, he would go in and get some terrapin, which would afford his crew a fresh diet, of a kind they all admired, and which he expected would be beneficial to those that had a scorbutic taint. At 5 P. M., came to, in Charles's Island harbor, with the small bower, in eight fathoms water, and moored ship.

"At 4 P. M. of the 28th of October, we accompanied Mr. Cole and ten men, in the pinnace, to the Black Beach, about three miles distant, to procure terrapin; we arrived there at daylight, and proceeded to the spring, about two miles from the landing. We found a great many terrapin there; they were generally too large for a man to carry, and it was only by culling them that one could be obtained to convey down to the shore. While the men were gone to the boat, Mr. Cole and myself searched among the surrounding rocks and brambles for more terrapin, and, by selecting the smallest, had procured one for each man, on his return from the beach.

"This spring of fresh water — the only one of living water on the island—is resorted to by the terrapin from the most distant parts of it, instinct only being their pilot. They remain round the spring several days, occasionally drinking, until they have filled their five internal reservoirs, when, having their twelve months' stock on board, they return to their burrows. While we were here, there was a continual stir among them; those that had obtained their stock were marching off, and others arriving to procure theirs. There was one remarkable for his size, as it was supposed he weighed six hundred pounds. Mr. Cole was desirous to get this mammoth on board, but to carry him to the pinnace was considered almost impracticable. I therefore instructed one of the boys how to manage and drive him, and calculated he would be able to reach the landing-place by sunset; but he was one quarter of a mile distant from it when we came up; for his rogue of a driver, when he thought he was not observed, would get on his back, but the terrapin, not being well broken, would not proceed far without stopping. We turned him over, and lashed him to a tree, to prevent his getting away, intending to terminate his land travels in the morning. On getting down to the beach, we found we had thirty-four fine terrapin there. On trial, we perceived the boat could not carry them all at once; and, accordingly, five of them were left, four men remaining at the spring. We started for the ship, but the boat was so deep, and rowed so heavily, that we made slow headway, and it was 10 o'clock before we got alongside. Captain Bailey had felt some uneasiness on our account; but we soon eased his anxiety, and his appetite for terrapin.

"On the 29th, we got out the long-boat before day-light, and, when it was light, Mr. Cole and six men left for the Black Beach, to procure as many terrapin as they could. Captain Bailey and myself each wrote a letter, to be deposited in the *post-office,* being the name assigned to a particular place, where voyagers deposit letters. Having enclosed them in a bottle, the first ship that arrives bound home takes them. We went on shore in the harbor, deposited them, caught six hair-seals, four terrapin, a green turtle, and a number of fine fish. At 6 P. M., the long-boat not appearing, I went in the pinnace, with a crew, to assist in getting her down, met and took her in tow, and got alongside about 8. Mr. Cole had forty-five terrapin in the boat, including the patriarch. Having now more than seventy on board,

Captain Bailey considered that number sufficient, hoisted in the long-boat, and got the ship ready to get under way in the morning.

"Strong breezes commencing from the southeast, on the 30th, at daylight, we began to unmoor the ship; at 9 A. M., got under way, and stood to the southwest to clear Albemarle Island, all sail set to advantage. Fine breezes prevailed the following day, with hazy weather: at 10 A. M., we passed the south cape of Albemarle, and shaped our course for the Sandwich Islands.

"On the 5th of December we passed the south part of the island of Owyhee, one of the Sandwich Islands, and two days later we stood into Carakooa Bay. A number of canoes filled with natives came off and circled about the ship, the occupants sporting and amusing themselves. Frequently a canoe would upset, but this, instead of lessening, rather increased the mirth. In one of the canoes was a native, seated on a platform, who appeared to be a personage of consequence. His two attendants at last rowed the canoe under the larboard quarter and the man suddenly spoke in plain English, asking, 'Don't you want a pilot?' Captain Bailey replied that he did, and much surprised to hear a native use English, inquired his name. 'My name,' said he, 'is Tom Knox.' 'Will you come on board, Mr. Knox, if you please,' said the Captain, and just as the carpenter placed the side ladder in position, Mr. Knox sprang into the mizzen chains and from there on the deck, coolly observing, 'I can get on board without a ladder.' He then piloted her safely to the anchorage in twelve fathoms of water.

"The deck was soon crowded with natives who continued on board the remainder of the day. Mr. Billy Pitt, the King's prime minister, accompanied by several chiefs, honored us with a visit. That evening a native by the name of Poar, a small chief, but a practiced thief, had the address to steal, and carry away undiscovered, my bedding, clothes, and a number of other articles. He entered by way of one of the cabin windows.

"At half past nine, the next morning, we got under weigh and stood out of the bay bound for Kirowah Roads, where we were to meet his majesty King Tamaammaah, who proved to be a venerable-looking Indian, who would enter into no agreement to supply us with sandal wood until he had consulted with old John Young, his adviser. On the 11th of December, he came on board accompanied by a great many natives of both sexes, who came to trade. John Young is the oldest white settler on the island and a bargain was soon concluded with him, as the King's representative, whereby we were to load sandal wood at the rate of $8.50 per picquel. The schooner *Columbia*, Captain Jennings, with Messrs. Bethuel and McDougal, partners in the Northwest Company, and Mr. Clanding, a clerk in the Company's service, was anchored near us and the next day the brig *Pedlar*, Captain Northrup, arrived from the Northwest coast, having on board a Doctor Shafford, a passenger, who was in the employ of the Russian government as a mineralogist and botanist.

"On the 15th we sailed for the island of Woahoo, having on board between fifty and sixty natives, who were going to collect the King's taxes. We also had on board, Mr. Marshall, late second officer of the *Lark*, of New York, which had been upset, some months previously, to the windward of these islands and drifted ashore on the island of Tourow. He was to serve as a linguist. On the second day after sailing we arrived at Woahoo and landed our unwelcome visitors who began collecting the exactions, consisting of rolls of tapa (a kind of cloth made of the fine inner bark of a tree) and bunches of dried fish handsomely covered with small mats. When all was collected, the ship was nearly full betwixt decks. On the 27th, the ship *Enterprize*, Captain Everett, direct from New York, arrived, bound on a trading voyage to the Northwest Coast.

"Having accomplished the business that brought us there we sailed for Owyhee and after landing our passengers and tribute we weighed and ran down on the 15th to Toai Bay, distant about thirty-five miles, where we were to load sandal wood. John Young was on board, to pilot the ship, and anchored her in an open road, one mile from shore, opposite a high rocky cliff. Here we remained for ten or twelve days, until we had taken on board all the sandal wood to be obtained, and then sailed for Woahoo where we took on board more wood but of a much inferior quality. While here, Young told me that twenty-five years before he had entered as a boatswain on board an American ship commanded by a Captain Medcalf, bound for a trading voyage to the Northwest Coast, and while at Caracooa Bay, his ship had sailed, leaving him on shore. After living among the natives for a time, King Tamaammaah had taken him into his service, since when he had prospered. He had married a native woman and one of his sons, a good seaman, had just returned from the

United States where he had fought on board an armed
vessel during the late war.

"On the 16th of February, 1816, we sailed for Canton,
and reached Whampoa on April 3d after an uneventful
voyage. Here we found the ship *Trumbull,* Captain
Aborn, from Rhode Island, and the schooner *Columbia,* Jennings, belonging to the Columbia River Company. Captain Bailey having been offered a freight
for his ship to Holland, the American Consul, Mr. Wilcox, suggested that I take passage on the *Trumbull,*
which was about to sail direct for the United States
and this I was soon able to arrange.

"The *Trumbull* having completed her cargo on
April 7th she proceeded down the river as far as the
first bar and came to for the night. I found on board
several officers and seamen who had been either
wrecked or captured and most of them had been in the
country for some time. This was the first opportunity
that offered to take passage for the United States.
Among them were Mr. Shute, midshipman, of the U.
S. Navy, and Messrs. Whitman and Lush of Boston.
In the course of the night, a boat filled with Chinese,
succeeded in getting under the stern without being perceived, and attempted to force open the dead lights
with an intent to enter the cabin and plunder. The
captain, officers and passengers, living on deck in the
coach-house, did not hear the noise, but the efforts of
the robbers at last alarmed the watch and they rowed
off leaving a large chisel stuck in the joint of a dead
light. The next morning the tide favoring, we proceeded down the river and at 4 P. M. left the Boca Tigris,
with a fine breeze from the eastward. At ten, the ship

General Scott, from New York for Canton was spoken.

"On the 18th of June, we descried the land on the coast of Natal, in Africa, bearing N. W., being distant about six leagues. This coast appears moderately high, with square, black heads. The 29th commenced with strong gales from N. N. E. At 3 P. M., the wind shifted suddenly into the N. E., with violent squalls, causing us to close-reef and take in the fore and mizzen topsails. As 6 A. M., we set them, and at 8 the wind was less furious; but suddenly the weather became hazy and dusky, and we could not discern any thing a mile from the ship. The atmosphere had a strange, threatening, and gloomy appearance, seeming as though we were enveloped in a thick cloud.

"About 9 the next morning, the weather was appalling. A sudden and tremendous squall, like an unexpected peal of thunder, from the southwest, struck our vessel, which, by powerful exertions, we kept before the wind; but, in spite of all our skill, the close-reefed maintopsail was rent in pieces, but the reefed foresail was saved. Our ship scudded four hours under bare poles, when she broached to, and fell on her beam ends. The violence of the gale was now dangerous and terrifying. Our ship was lying with her lower yards in the water, and we looked every moment for the hurricane to sweep us forever from the society of the living. The mizzenmast was cut away and the wreck cleared.

"Meridian. The tremendous gales and appalling seas yet menacing destruction to our storm-worn bark, all hands, except those whose fears had paralyzed their energies, were employed in using all possible means for the preservation of the ship, and the lives of those on board. At 4 P. M., we got the foreyard down, and jibboom in. About evening, as the ship was lying to, with the wind and sea a-beam, it was deemed conducible to our safety to get her before the wind, which we did, and scudded her under bare poles, the sea making a perfect breach over her decks, and in their fury dashing away the bulwarks. Some of the stanchions were driven in board on the starboard side, by the virulence of the sea when it struck her, and outward by the great pressure of water on her decks when she righted.

"The next morning, July the 30th, the violence of the wind began to abate, our ship having been violently strained and leaked badly. On examining our trunks in the coach-house, we found them filled with water, as was every thing else in this exposed place. On the 31st, swayed up the foreyard, and began to repair damages as well as our scanty means would admit. On examining my trunks more minutely, I had the vexation to find all my clothes, and the few articles that I had received as presents from my friends at Canton, ruined by the salt water. The following day, we cut away the rags of the maintopsail, and bent and set another. The carpenter we employed in calking the water-ways, and nailing battens over them. We lashed a spare topmast to the stump of the mizzen, for a jury-mast, rigged it, and set the spanker, and broke out the after hold for water. All which had been upon deck was lost in the gale; one of the seven casks had let out all the water, and, the state of the others being uncertain, we were constrained to go on allowance.

"On the 7th, the weather was squally with small rain and about the middle of the morning we saw a ship astern coming up rapidly. At 2 P. M., she was along-side and proved to be the *Herald*, of Salem, from Cal-cutta. She was 105 days out and had sustained some damage to her sails and rigging in the recent gale. The captain informed us that after the gale, they had ob-served wreckage — beds and pillows, floating on the sea. On the 10th of July, we saw another sail astern which at 1 P. M., came up with us and proved to be the brig *Pedlar*, Captain Hunt, one hundred and forty days out from Canton. He informed us of the loss of the ship *Fingal*, Captain Vibbets, in the Straits of Gas-par, and also that the ship *Bengal*, of Philadelphia, was thrown on her beam ends by a violent squall in the Straits of Sunda. She had put into the Isle of France badly damaged.

"Captain Hunt seeing that our ship had the appear-ance of being in distress, kindly offered to keep com-pany until we made St. Helena and in the event of our missing the Island to supply us with water to the ex-tent of his means. The breeze freshening we carried steering sails on both sides, but they were frequently down as the halyards and tacks being rotten and worn out, parted continually. The *Pedlar* kept astern un-der her topsails only. Our ship was then leaking at the rate of eighteen inches per hour.

At 1 P. M., on the 22d, Captain Aborn and I went on board the *Pedlar*, where I had the pleasure to find my old friends Captains Northrop, Hunt, and Mr. Halsey, well and hearty; we passed some time with them very agreeably. At 5 P. M., after leaving our let-ters and good wishes for their safe and speedy arrival at New York, we returned to the *Trumbull*, as there was no doubt of our seeing St. Helena next day. Three ships were in sight on the 23d, and at 2 P. M. our wishes were gratified by seeing the island of St. Helena from the deck, distant about ten leagues.

"At 4 P. M., we saw a vessel under the land; supposed her to be a lookout vessel; laid off, and after waiting for daylight, was boarded, at 7 A. M., by his Britannic majesty's brig *Julia,* one of the vessels stationed here to cruise round the island, and in its vicinity, to warn off all vessels, except those who were in actual distress. From our appearance, they did not hesitate to admit that our claim to be considered one of the excepted was well founded.

"The lieutenant inquired into the nature and extent of our wants, which were stated to him: they were all comprised in one article, viz., water, though strict veracity would not have been violated, had a number of others been included. The officer noted the quantity of water (six tons) required, and returned to the brig. In a short time, the boat came back with a sealed letter, accompanied by orders for us to stand in towards the anchorage, nearly but not quite abreast of the fort, and there to lay to until the admiral's boat should board us, when we were to deliver the letter to the boarding officer. We filled away, and stood in according to instructions, and then laid by for two or three hours, the fleet being in sight. At length we were boarded by a boat from the *Newcastle,* bearing the flag of Rear-Admiral Malcolm: the letter was delivered to the lieutenant. After reading it, he ordered flags to be brought from the boat on board of us, and signals to be made to the Newcastle, and repeated by her to the admiral,

ARRIVAL OF THE SHIP "MILLWOOD" AT MASAFUERO

From an engraving in Barnard's *Narrative of Sufferings and Adventures*, New York, 1829

VIEW OF THE ISLAND OF ST. HELENA
From a mezzotint by Edward Orme in the Macpherson Collection

who was at his residence on shore, the purport of which was to give notice of the arrival of an American ship in distress for water. This lieutenant also made a minute of the quantity required, and returned, leaving a midshipman on board to prevent any communication with the shore, and ordered us to remain where we were until further directions.

"As we were lying to in an unsheltered situation, and exposed to a heavy swell, after waiting a considerable time for further orders, we concluded to run past the fort, and get more under the lee of the land, to be protected from the wind and sea; as we had observed a country ship, from Bengal, under jury-masts, which had experienced the late tremendous gale off the Cape, being dismasted by the lightning, pass the fort, and anchor close in under the island; for we did not apprehend that such a procedure on our part could possibly excite the suspicion that our crippled, dull-sailing ship could, in the face of formidable batteries, and a strong fleet, liberate, or attempt the liberation of Napoleon. If we may be allowed to judge from the events that followed our movements towards the fort, such was the case; for, on our nearing it, a shot was fired ahead of us from the half-moon battery, which caused us to wear ship and stand on the other tack; after keeping off some time, fearing we should fall to leeward, we wore, and again stood towards the fort, which saluted us with another shot, that struck the water just ahead of us: on this, we again wore, and observed the admiral's boat coming to us. When alongside, the lieutenant told us to stand in; we then told him the reception the battery had already given us; he said that he would pull in and speak to them. When we saw that he was near the battery, we made sail, and soon met two men-of-war launches with water, who came alongside, and conveyed the water immediately into the ship's casks. We were then ordered to make sail, and proceed on our voyage without delay.

"Nothing remarkable occurred in crossing the Atlantic until the 23d October, when, at meridian, we sounded, and got ground in thirty-nine fathoms' water, mud, and dark sand. The clouds breaking away ahead, we were favored by the appearance of the haze off land, and, at 3 P. M., by the sight of Martha's Vineyard; at 4, we sounded, and got ground, of fine black, red, and white sand; at 5, Noman's Land bore N. W. by W., distant about three leagues. At 7, we saw the light on Gay Head, bearing N. W. by W., a bright revolving light, alternately dim; at 9, we tacked ship to the southward, being about one mile from No Man's Land; at 10, the wind came out from N. W. in a heavy squall, split fore-topsail and spanker; at daylight, the Vineyard appeared, bearing N. by E.; at 8 A. M., the ship wore, and stood N. N. E., with the wind blowing strong at N. W.; at meridian, found we had lost seven or eight miles during the night, and unbent foretopsail and spanker to repair. When within three miles of the Vineyard, a pilot-boat came off; but, as the pilot and captain could not agree respecting the pilotage, I took passage in the pilot-boat, and at about 7 arrived at the Vineyard, where I had once more the unspeakable happiness of finding myself on my native land.

"Who can describe the feelings of the weather-beaten sailor, and especially one who has endured as much as myself when he catches, upon the distant ocean, a view of the lighthouse and outstretched land, which are his heralds to the haven into which he is shortly entering? The thought of New York, with its lovely islands and indented bay; with its variegated stores, filled with plenty and laughing joy; with its sister rivers, pouring upon its sides the treasures and harvests of the country far and wide; with its numerous spires and towering edifices, overlooking thousands of freemen too happy to know their happiness, — was an astonishing contrast to my return to New Island when abandoned by all the crew. I scarcely had patience for the boat to reach the shore. Imagination must fill up the vacancy: suffice it to say, that I found my wife and children in good health, who mingled in the joy that transported my own heart. After an absence of four years and seven months, I had returned without a shilling in my pocket; but, notwithstanding my penury, my joy was far beyond the power of words.

"The next day after my arrival, I waited upon the owners of the *Nanina,* who expressed their happiness on my safe arrival, after so long and painful an absence. An interesting conversation followed, in the course of which they observed, that they had a fine brig unemployed, and tendered me the command; but, wishing to remain some time in the bosom of my family, I declined the offer.

"My father informed me that after I had left the vessel to go to the island to procure fresh provisions, as has been before stated, as soon as I was out of sight, the Englishmen rose, took possession of the brig, and commenced getting the topmasts up, and bending the sails, which they completed before night. The next morning they got under weigh. My father used the most earnest entreaties for them not to go away, and leave me and the boat's crew to perish on those barren islands, in the depth of a dreadfully-severe winter, without food, raiment, or shelter; but to all these supplications the cold-hearted British officers turned a deaf ear, and an impenetrable heart; and the British ministry afterwards sanctioned this unparalleled act of baseness, and rewarded the perpetrators by declaring the brig *Nanina,* after her arrival in London, to be a good prize."

THE ADVENTURES OF JOHN NICOL, MARINER, DURING THIRTY YEARS AT SEA.

HAVING reached the age of sixty-seven years, when I can no longer sail upon discovery, and weak and stiff, can only send my prayers with the tight ship and her merry hearts, at the earnest solicitation of friends I have here set down some account of my life at sea. Twice I circumnavigated the globe; three times I was in China; twice in Egypt; and more than once sailed along the whole land-board of America, from Nootka Sound to Cape Horn and twice I doubled it.

I was born in the small village of Currie, about six miles from Edinburgh, in the year 1755. The first wish I ever formed was to wander, and many a search I gave my parents in gratifying my youthful passion.

My father, a cooper, was a man of talent and information, and made it his study to give his children a good education; but my unsteady propensities did not allow me to make the most of the schooling I got. I had read Robinson Crusoe many times over, and longed to be at sea. Every moment I could spare was spent in the boats or about the shore.

When I was about fourteen years of age, my father was engaged to go to London. Even now, I recollect the transports my young mind felt, when he informed me that I was to accompany him. I counted the hours and minutes to the moment we sailed on board the Glasgow packet. It was in the month of December we sailed, and the weather was very bad; all the passen-

gers were seasick; I never was. This was in the year
1769, when the dreadful loss was sustained on the
coast of Yorkshire — above thirty sail of merchantmen
were wrecked. We were taken in the same gale, but
rode it out. Next morning, we could hardly proceed
for wreck; and the whole beach was covered. The
country people were collecting and driving away the
dead bodies in wagons.

My father embraced this opportunity to prejudice
me against being a sailor; he was a kind but strict par-
ent, and we dared not disobey him. The storm had
made no impression upon my mind sufficient to alter
my determination; my youthful mind could not sep-
arate the life of a sailor from dangers and storms, and
I looked upon them as an interesting part of the adventures I panted after. I enjoyed the voyage much,
was anxious to learn every thing, and was a great favorite with the captain and crew.

After my arrival in London, as I was going on an errand, in passing near the Tower, I saw a dead monkey
floating in the river. I had not seen above two or three
in my life; I thought it of great value; I stripped at
once, and swam in for it. An English boy, who
wished it likewise, but who either would or could not
swim, seized it when I landed, saying he would fight
me for it. We were much of a size; had he been larger
than myself, I was not of a temper to be easily wronged;
so I gave him battle. A crowd gathered, and formed
a ring; stranger as I was, I got fair play. After a severe contest, I came off victor. The English boy shook
hands, and said, "Scotchman, you have won it." I had
fought naked as I came out of the water; so I put on

my clothes, and carried off the prize in triumph; came home, and got a beating from my father for fighting, and staying my errand; but the monkey's skin repaid me for all vexations.

I remained in London scarcely twelve months, when my father sent me to Scotland to learn my trade. I chose the profession of a cooper, to please my father; but my heart was never with the business. While I was hooping barrels, my mind was at sea, and my imagination in foreign climes.

After my apprenticeship had expired, I entered the navy, and sailed for America in the *Proteus,* 20 gun ship, with ordnance stores, and one hundred men, to man the floating batteries upon Lake Champlain. After convoying the fleet to Quebec, and another from St. John's, Newfoundland, to the West Indies and back, I remained on shore in the Canadas for eighteen months, when I was ordered by Admiral Montague on board the *Surprise,* 28 gun frigate, commanded by Captain Reeves. Her cooper had been killed, a few days before, in a severe action with an American vessel. We kept cruising about, taking numbers of the American privateers. After a severe action, we took the *Jason,* of Boston, commanded by the famous Captain Manly, who had been commodore in the American service, had been taken prisoner, and broke his parole. When Captain Reeves hailed, and ordered him to strike, he returned for answer, "Fire away! I have as many guns as you." He had heavier metal, but fewer men, than the *Surprise.* He fought us for a long time. I was serving powder as busy as I could, the shot and splinters flying in all directions, when I heard the men call from one

of the guns, "Halloo, Bungs, where are you?" I looked
to their gun, and saw the two horns of my anvil across
its mouth; the next moment it was through the *Jason's*
side. The rogues thus disposed of my anvil, which I
had been using just before the action commenced, and
had placed in a secure place, as I thought, out of their
reach. "Bungs forever!" they shouted, when they saw
the dreadful hole it had made in the *Jason's* side.
Bungs was the name they always gave the cooper.
When Captain Manly came on board the *Surprise*, to
deliver his sword to Captain Reeves, the half of the
rim of his hat was shot off. Our captain returned his
sword to him again, saying, "You have had a narrow
escape, Manly." — "I wish to God it had been my
head," he replied.

When we boarded the *Jason*, we found thirty-one
cavalry, who had served under General Burgoyne, acting now as marines on board the *Jason*. During the
remainder of the American war, our duty was the same,
taking convoy and capturing American privateers. We
crossed the Atlantic several times. I became quite
weary of the monotonous convoy duty, and, having
seen all I could see, I often sighed for the verdant
banks of the Forth. At length, my wishes were gratified by the return of peace. We were paid off in March,
1783. When Captain Reeves came ashore, he completely loaded the long-boat with flags he had taken
from the enemy. When one of the officers inquired
what he would do with them, he said, laughing, "I will
hang one upon every tree in my father's garden."

I no sooner had the money that was due me in my
hat, than I set off for London direct, and, after a few

days of enjoyment, put my bedding and chest on board
a vessel bound for Leith: every halfpenny I had saved
was in it but nine guineas, which I kept upon my person to provide for squalls. The trader fell down the
river, but, there being no wind, and the tide failing, the
captain told us we might sleep in London, only to be
sure to be on board before eight o'clock in the morning.
I embraced the opportunity, and lost my passage.

As all my savings were in my chest, and a number
of passengers on board whom I did not like, I immedi-
cately took the diligence to Newcastle. There were no
mails running direct for Edinburgh every day, as now;
it was the month of March, yet there was a great deal
of snow on the ground; the weather was severe, but
not so cold as at St. John's. When the diligence set off,
there were four passengers — two ladies, another sailor,
and myself. Our lady companions, for the first few
stages, were proud and distant, scarcely taking any
notice of us. I was restrained by their manner; my
companion was quite at home, chatting to them, unmindful of their monosyllabic answers. He had a good
voice, and sung snatches of sea-songs, and was un-
ceasing in his endeavors to please. By degrees their
reserve wore off, and the conversation became general.
I now learned they were sisters, who had been on a
visit to a relation in London, and were now returning
to their father, who was a wealthy farmer. Before it
grew dark, we were all as intimate as if we had sailed
for years in the same ship. The oldest, who appeared
to be about twenty, attached herself to me, and listened
to my accounts of the different places I had been in,
with great interest. The youngest was as much inter-

ested by the conversation of my volatile companion.

I felt a something uncommon arise in my breast as we sat side by side; I could think of nothing but my pretty companion; my attentions were not disagreeable to her, and I began to think of settling, and how happy I might be with such a wife. After a number of efforts, I summoned resolution to take her hand in mine; I pressed it gently; she drew it faintly back. I sighed; she laid her hand upon my arm, and, in a whisper, inquired if I was unwell. I was upon the point of telling her what I felt, and my wishes, when the diligence stopped at the inn. I wished we had been sailing in the middle of the Atlantic; for a covered cart drove up, and a stout, hearty old man welcomed them by their names, bestowing a hearty kiss upon each. I felt quite disappointed. He was their father. My pretty Mary did not seem to be so rejoiced at her father's kind salutation as might have been expected.

My companion, who was an Englishman, told me he would proceed no farther, but endeavor to win the hand of his pretty partner. I told him my present situation, that my chest and all I had was on board the Leith trader, and no direction upon it; on this account, I was forced to proceed as fast as possible, or I would have remained and shared his fortunes with all my heart. I took leave of them with a heavy heart, resolving to return. I could perceive Mary turn pale, as I bade her farewell, while her sister looked joy itself when Williams told them he was to proceed no farther. Before the coach set off, I made him promise to write me an account of his success, and that I would return as soon as I had secured my chest and seen my father.

He promised to do this faithfully. I whispered Mary a promise to see her soon, and pressed her hand as we parted; she returned the pressure. I did not feel without hope. When the farmer drove off, Williams accompanying them, I only wished myself in his place.

When the coach reached Newcastle, I soon procured another conveyance to Edinburgh, and was at Leith before the vessel. When she arrived, I went on board, and found all safe. I then went to Borrowstownness, but found my father had been dead for some time. This was a great disappointment and grief to me. I wished I had been at home to have received his last blessing and advice; but there was no help. He died full of years; and that I may be as well prepared when I shall be called hence, is my earnest wish. After visiting his grave, and spending a few days with my friends, I became uneasy at not hearing from Williams. I waited for three weeks; then, losing all patience, I set off myself to see how the land lay. I took leave of home once more, with a good deal of money in my pocket, as I had been almost a miser at home, keeping all for the marriage, should I succeed.

The spring was now advancing apace, when I took my passage in a Newcastle trader, and arrived safe at the inn where I had last parted from Mary. It was night when I arrived, and, being weary, soon went to bed. I was up betimes in the morning; when I met Williams, he was looking very dull. I shook hands, and asked, "What cheer?" He shook his head, and said, "Why, Jack, we are on the wrong tack, and, I fear, will never make port. I had no good news to send, so it was of no use to write. I was at the farmer's last night;

he swears, if ever I come near his house again, he will
have me before the justice as an idle vagrant. My fair
jilt is not much concerned, and I can scarce get a sight
of her; she seems to shun me." I felt a chillness come
over me at this information, and asked him what he
meant to do. "Why, set sail this day; go to my mother,
give her what I can spare, and then to sea again. My
store is getting low here. But what do you intend to
do, Jack?" "Truth, Williams, I scarce know. I will
make one trip to the farm; and if Mary is not as kind
as I hope to find her, I will be off too."

Soon after breakfast, I set off for the farmer's, with
an anxious heart. On my arrival, I met Mary in the
yard. She seemed fluttered at sight of me; but, sum-
moning up courage as I approached, she made a distant bow, and coldly asked me how I did. I now saw
there was no hope, and had not recovered myself, when
her father came out, and, in a rough manner, demanded what I wanted, and who I was. This in a moment
brought me to myself; and, raising my head, which
had been bent towards the ground, I looked at him.
Mary shrunk from my gaze; but the old man came
close up to me, and again demanded what I wanted.
"It is of no consequence," I answered; then, looking at
Mary, "I believe I am an unwelcome visitor — it is
what I did not expect — so I will not obtrude myself
upon you any longer." I then walked off, as indifferent, to appearance, as I could make myself; but was
tempted to look over my shoulder more than once. I
saw Mary in tears, and her father in earnest conversation with her.

I made up my mind to remain at the inn the rest of

that day and all night, in hopes of receiving an appointment to meet Mary. I was loath to think I was indifferent to her; and, the feeling of being slighted is so bitter, I could have quarrelled with myself and all the world. I sat with Williams at the window all day; no message came; in the morning we bade adieu to the fair jilts, with heavy hearts — Williams for his mother's, and I for London.

After working a few weeks in London, at my own business, my wandering propensities came as strong upon me as ever, and I resolved to embrace the first opportunity to gratify it — no matter whither, only let me wander. I had been many times on the different wharves, looking for a vessel; but, the seamen were so plenty, there was great difficulty in getting a berth.

I met, by accident, Captain Bond, who hailed me, and inquired if I wished a berth. He had been captain of a transport in the American war. I had favored him at St. John's. I answered him, "It was what I was looking after." "Then, if you will come and be cooper of the *Leviathan*, Greenland ship, — I am captain, — you may go to 'Squire Mellish, and say I recommend you for cooper." I thanked him for his good-will, went, and was engaged, and on board at work next day.

We sailed in a short time for the coast of Greenland, and touched at Lerwick, where we took on board what men we wanted. In the first of the season, we were very unsuccessful, having very stormy weather. I at one time thought our doom was fixed; it blew a dreadful gale, and we were for ten days completely fast in the ice. As far as we could see, all was ice, and the ship was so pressed by it, every one thought we must either

be crushed to pieces, or forced out upon the top of the
ice, there ever to remain. At length, the wind changed,
and the weather moderated; and, where nothing could
be seen but ice, in a short time after, all, as far as the
eye could reach, was open sea. What were our feelings
at this change, it were vain to attempt a description of;
it was a reprieve from death. The horrors of our situation were far worse than any storm I ever was in. In a
storm, upon a lee shore, there, even in all its horrors,
there is exertion to keep the mind up, and a hope to
weather it. Locked up in ice, all exertion is useless;
the power you have to contend with is far too tremendous and unyielding; it, like a powerful magician,
binds you in its icy circle, and there you must behold,
in all its horrors, your approaching fate, without the
power of exertion, while the crashing of the ice, and
the less loud, but more alarming cracking of the vessel, serve all to increase the horrors of this dreadful
sea-mare.

When the weather moderated, we were very successful, and filled our ship with four fish. I did not like the
whale fishing; there is no sight for the eye of the inquisitive, after the first glance, and no variety to charm
the mind. Desolation reigns around — nothing but
snow, or bare rocks and ice. The cold is so intense, and
the weather often so thick, I felt so cheerless, that I resolved to bid adieu to the coast of Greenland forever,
and seek to gratify my curiosity in more genial climes.

We arrived safe in the river, and proceeded up to our
situation; but how strange are the freaks of fate! In
the very port of London, as we were hurrying to our
station, the tide was ebbing fast, when the ship missed

stays, and yawed round, came right upon the Isle of
Dogs, broke her back, and filled with water. There was
none of us hurt, and we lost nothing, as she was insured.
I was one of those placed upon her to estimate the loss
sustained amongst the casks, and was kept constantly
on board for a long time.

My next voyage was on board the *Cotton Planter*,
commanded by Captain Young, bound for the Island
of Granada, W. I. Under Captain Young, I was very
happy. We sailed in the month of October, and arrived
safe at St. George's, Granada.

I worked a great deal on shore, and had a number of
blacks under me. They are a thoughtless, merry race;
in vain their cruel situation and sufferings act upon
their buoyant minds. They have snatches of joy that
their pale and sickly oppressors never know. On the
evenings of Saturday and Sunday, the sound of the
benji and rattle, intermixed with song, alone is heard.
I have lain upon deck, of an evening, faint and exhausted from the heat of the day, to enjoy the cool
breeze of the evening; and their wild music and song,
the shout of mirth, and dancing, resounded along the
beach, and from the valleys. There the negroes bounded in all the spirit of health and happiness.

Captain Young did not keep his crew upon allowance; we had "cut and come again" always. I often
took a piece of lean beef and a few biscuits with me
when I went to the plantation, as a present to the
blacks. This the poor creatures would divide among
themselves, to a single fibre. There were two or three
slaves upon the estate, who, having once run away,
had iron collars round their necks, with long hooks,

that projected from them to catch the bushes, should they run away again; these they wore night and day. There was a black slave, a cooper, with a wooden leg, who had run away more than once; he was now chained to the block at which he wrought.

They are much given to talking and story-telling; the Scripture characters of the Old Testament are quite familiar to them; they talk with astonishment of Samson, Goliah, David, &c. I have seen them hold up their hands in astonishment at the strength of the white Buccaras. I have laughed at their personifications. Hurricane — they cannot conceive what it is. There are planters of the name of Kane on the island. "Hurricane," they will say, "he a strong white Buccara, he come from London."

There was a black upon the estate, who had been on the Island of St. Kitt's when Rodney defeated the French fleet. He had seen the action, and was never tired of speaking of it, nor his auditors of listening. He always concluded with this remark — "The French 'tand 'tiff, but the English 'tand far 'tiffer. De all de same as game cock; de die on de 'pot."

They are apt to steal, but are so very credulous, they are easily detected. Captain Young gave a black butcher, by the name of Coffee, a hog to kill. When the captain went to see it, Coffee said, —

"This very fine hog, massa, but I never see a hog like him in all my life; he have no liver, no light."

"That is strange, Coffee," said Captain Young, "let me see in the book." He took a memorandum-book out of his pocket, turned over a few leaves, and looked very earnest.

"I see, — Coffee go to hell bottom, — hog have liver and lights." Coffee shook like an aspen leaf, and said,—

"O massa, Coffee no go to hell bottom, — hog have liver and lights." He restored them and, trembling, awaited his punishment. Captain Young only laughed, and made him a present of them.

I one time went with Captain Young to a planter's, where he was to dine that I might accompany him back to the ship in the evening, as he was weakly. Upon our arrival, I was handed over to a black, who was butler and house-steward. He had been in England, and, as he said, seen London and King George. He was by this become a greater man than by his situation, among the other slaves; and was as vain in showing the little he knew, as if he had been bred at college; and was perpetually astonishing the other slaves, whom he looked down upon with the depth of his knowledge, and his accounts of London and King George. No professor could have delivered his opinions and observations with more pomp and dogmatism. One of the blacks inquired of me what kind of people the Welsh were. To enjoy the sport, as one of the crew, William Jones, a Welshman, was in company with me at the time, I referred him to the black oracle, who, after considering a moment or two, replied, with a smile of satisfaction upon his sooty features, "The English have ships, the Irish have ships, and the Scotch have ships, but Welshmen have no ships; they are like the negro man; they live in the bush." The Welshman started to his feet, and would have knocked him down, had I not prevented. He poured out a volley of oaths upon him; he heard him with indifference, and his assertion was not the least shaken, in the opinion of his hearers, by the Welsh-man's violence. It, like many others of equal truth, was quoted and received as gospel. It was long a by-word in the ship — "Welshman live in the bush like negro man."

We brought to England, as passenger from the is-land, a planter, who was very rich, and had a number of slaves. He had been a common seaman on board of a man-of-war, had deserted, and lived on shore con-cealed until his ship sailed. He afterwards married a free black woman, who kept a punch house, who died and left him above three thousand pounds. With this he had bought a plantation and slaves, and was mak-ing money fast. He brought as much fresh provisions and preserves on board as would have served ten men out and out, and was very kind to the men, in giving them liquor and fresh provisions.

Upon our arrival in London, I learned that my old officer, Lieutenant Portlock, now captain, was going out in the *King George,* as commander, in company with the *Queen Charlotte,* Captain Dixon, upon a voy-age of discovery and trade round the world. This was the very cruise I had long wished for; at once I made myself clean, and waited upon Captain Portlock. He was happy to see me, as I was an excellent brewer of spruce beer, and the very man he wished, but knew not where to have sent for me. I was at once engaged, on the most liberal terms, as cooper, and went away re-joicing in my good fortune. We had a charter from the South Sea Company, and one from the India House, as it was to be a trading voyage for furs, as well as dis-covery. This was in the year 1785.

With a joyful heart I entered on this voyage. The first land we made was Santa Cruz, in the Island of Teneriffe, where we staid ten days, getting fruit and provisions; then made the Island of St. Jago, — it belongs to the Portuguese, — where we watered, and took in fresh provisions. While here, we caught a number of fish called bass, very like salmon, which we ate fresh. The island is badly cultivated, but abounds in cattle. We exchanged old clothes for sheep, or any thing the men wanted. The Portuguese here are great rogues. I bought two fat sheep from one of them. The bargain was made, and I was going to lead away my purchase, when he gave a whistle, and my sheep scampered off to the fields. The fellow laughed at my surprise. I had a great mind to give him a beating for his trick, and take my clothes from him; but we had strict orders not to quarrel with the people upon any account. At length, he made a sign that I might have them again by giving a few more articles. I had no alternative but to lose what I had given, or submit to his roguery. I gave a sign I would; he gave another whistle, and the sheep returned to his side. I secured them before I gave the second price. With all their roguery, they are very careless of their money, more so than any people I ever saw. In walking through the town, I have seen kegs full of dollars, without heads, standing in the houses, and the door open, without a person in the house to look after them.

Having watered, we run for the Falkland Islands. When we arrived, we found two American vessels, the *Anchor* and *Hope,* busy whaling. We hoisted our colors and the Americans took us for Spaniards, and set off in all haste. When we landed, we found a great number of geese ready plucked, and a large fire burning; so we set to work, and roasted as many as served us all, and enjoyed them much.

Next morning, the Americans came near in their boats, and found out their mistake. Captain Portlock thanked them for their treat. We then had a busy time killing geese. There are two kinds, the water and upland. The water ones are very pretty, speckled, like a partridge. The penguins were so plenty, we were forced to knock them out of our way as we walked along the beach. The pelicans are plenty, and build their nests of clay; they are near each other, like a honey-comb. I was astonished how each bird knew its own nest. They appear to hatch in the same nest, until they are forced to change, by the accumulation of dung. They are so tame, I have stood close by when they arrived with their pouch distended with fish, and fed their young, without being in the least disturbed. We killed a number of hogs. Our doctor broke his double-barrelled gun in despatching one, and sold it afterwards, in China, for £42. What was of more value to us was, a great many iron hoops, and bees-wax, the remains of some wreck. We picked up some of the wax, but took every inch of the hoops; they were more valuable than gold to us, for trading with the natives.

When off Cape Horn, we perceived an object floating at a small distance from the ship. Not one of us could make out what it was. All our boats being fast, two men went down into the water, and swam to it, and made it fast in the slings. When it came on board, it was a cask, but so overgrown with weeds and barnacles,

the bung-hole could not be discovered. I was set to
work to cut into it. To our agreeable surprise, it was
full of excellent port wine. All the crew got a little of
it, and Captain Portlock gave us brandy in place of the
rest.

We next made Staten's Land; the weather was fine,
but very cold. We stood away for latitude 23°, where
we cruised about for some time in quest of islands laid
down in our charts. We could find none, but turtle in
great abundance. They were a welcome supply, but
we soon tired of them, cook them as we would, in every
variety. Not finding the islands, we bore away for
the Sandwich Islands. The first land we made was
Owhyee, the island where Captain Cook was killed.
The *King George* and *Queen Charlotte* were the first
ships which had touched there since that melancholy
event. The natives came on board in crowds, and were
happy to see us; they recognized Portlock and others,
who had been on the island before, along with Cook.
Our decks were soon crowded with hogs, bread-fruit,
yams, and potatoes. Our deck soon resembled sham-
bles; our butcher had fourteen assistants. I was as busy
and fatigued as I could be, cutting iron hoops into
lengths of eight and nine inches, which the carpenter
ground sharp. These were our most valuable commodity, in the eyes of the natives. I was stationed down in
the hold of the vessel, and the ladders were removed to
prevent the natives from coming down to the treasury.
The king of Owhyee looked to my occupation with a
wistful eye; he thought me the happieset man on
board, to be among such vast heaps of treasure. Captain Portlock called to me to place the ladder, and al-

low the king to come down, and give him a good long
piece. When the king descended, he held up his hands,
and looked astonishment personified. When I gave
him the piece of hoop of twenty inches long, he retired
a little from below the hatch into the shade, undid his
girdle, bent the iron to his body, and, adjusting his belt
in the greatest haste, concealed it. I suppose he thought
I had stolen it. I could not but laugh to see the king
concealing what he took to be stolen goods.

We were much in want of oil for our lamps. The
sharks abounding, we baited a hook with a piece of salt
pork, and caught the largest I ever saw in any sea; it was
a female, nineteen feet long; it took all hands to hoist
her on board; her weight made the vessel heel. When
she was cut up, we took forty-eight young ones out of
her belly, eighteen inches long; we saw them go into
her mouth after she was hooked. The hook was fixed
to a chain attached to our main-brace, or we never
could have kept her. It was evening when she snapped
the bait; we hauled the head just above the surface,
the swell washing over it. We let her remain thus all
night, and she was quite dead in the morning. There
were in her stomach four hogs, four full-grown turtle,
besides the young ones. Her liver, the only part we
wanted, filled a tierce.

Almost every man on board took a native woman for
a wife while the vessel remained, the men thinking it
an honor or for their gain, as they got many presents of
iron, beads, or buttons. The women came on board at
night, and went on shore in the morning. In the evening, they would call for their husbands by name.
They often brought their friends to see their husbands,

VIEW OF ST. GEORGE, GRENADA, W. I.

From a mezzotint by W. Daniel in the Macpherson Collection

View of Karakakooa Bay, Owyhee

From the engraving by W. Byrne, in Cook's *Voyages*, London, 1784

who were well pleased, as they were never allowed to go away empty. The fattest woman I ever saw in my life our gunner chose for a wife. We were forced to hoist her on board; her thighs were as thick as my waist; no hammock in the ship would hold her; many jokes were cracked upon the pair.

We had a merry, facetious fellow on board, called Dickson. He sung pretty well. He squinted, and the natives mimicked him. Abenoue, king of Atooi, could cock his eye like Dickson better than any of his subjects. Abenoue called him Billicany, from his often singing "Rule Britannia." Abenoue learned the air, and the words, as near as he could pronounce them. It was an amusing thing to hear the king and Dickson sing. Abenoue loved him better than any man in the ship, and always embraced him every time they met on shore, or in the ship, and began to sing, "Tule Billicany, Billicany tule," &c.

We had the chief on board who killed Captain Cook, for more than three weeks. He was in bad health, and had a smelling-bottle, with a few drops in it, which he used to smell at; we filled it for him. There were a good many bayonets in possession of the natives, which they had obtained at the murder of Cook.

We left Owhyee, and stood down to Atooi, where we watered, and had a feast from Abenoue, the king. We took our allowance of brandy on shore, and spent a most delightful afternoon, the natives doing all in their power to amuse us; the girls danced, the men made a sham fight, throwing their spears; the women, standing behind, handed the spears to the men, the same as in battle, thus keeping up a continued shower of spears.

No words can convey an adequate idea of their dexterity and agility. They thought we were bad with the rheumatism, our movements were so slow compared with their own. The women would sometimes lay us down, and chafe and rub us, making moan, and saying, "O rume! O rume!" They wrestled, but the stoutest man in our ship could not stand a single throw with the least chance of success.

As the summer now advanced apace, we stood over to Cook's River, on the Northwest Coast of America, where we arrived in 1786, eleven months after we left England.

At the entrance of Cook's River is an immense volcanic mountain, which was in action at the time, and continued burning all the time we lay there, pouring down its side a torrent of lava as broad as the Thames. At night, the sight was grand, but fearful. The natives here had their spears headed with copper; but, having no one on board who could speak their language, we had no means of learning where they obtained the copper. While we lay here, it was the heat of summer; yet the ice never melted, and the snow was lying very deep on the heights. What a contrast from the delightful islands we had so lately left!

Our long boat, decked and schooner-rigged, proceeded up the river, in hopes of finding an outlet, or inland sea. After proceeding with great difficulty and perseverance, until all hopes of success vanished, they returned. We then bore to the southward, to Prince William's Sound, to pursue our trade with the Indians. They are quite different from the Sandwich Islanders in appearance and habits; they are not cruel, but great thieves.

I was employed on shore brewing spruce all day, and slept on board at night. One night, the Indians, after starting the beer, carried off all the casks; they were iron-hooped. All our search was vain; no traces of them were to be discovered. To quarrel with the Indians would have defeated the object of our voyage. At length, they were discovered by accident, in the most unlikely place, in the following manner: One of our boats had been, on a trading excursion, detained so long, we became alarmed for its safety. Captain Portlock sent some of our men, armed, to the top of a high hill, to look out for the boat. To the surprise of the men, they found the staves and ends of the barrels, and some large stones they had used in breaking them to pieces. How great must their labor have been in rolling up the barrels, and then in dashing them to pieces! yet I have no doubt they thought themselves richly rewarded in obtaining the iron hoops. The men brought back a stave or two with the ship's name branded on them, to evidence the truth of their discovery. We then moved the brewing-place to the other side of the island, within sight of the ship. I was much annoyed by the natives for some time, while working; they would handle the hoops, and every now and then a piece would vanish. There was only a quarter-master and boy with me. While the natives swarmed around, I felt rather uncomfortable. They became more and more bold. The captain, seeing, from the deck, my disagreeable situation, hailed me to set Neptune, our great Newfoundland dog, upon them, saying they would fear him

more than fifty men. I obeyed with alacrity, and
hounded Neptune, who enjoyed the sport as much as
I, to see the great fellows run, screaming like girls, in
all directions. I was soon left to pursue my labor un-
molested; and, whenever they grew troublesome, Neptune, without orders, put them to running and screaming. When one approached, if Neptune was near, he
would stretch out his arms, and cry, "Lally, Neptune;"
that is, *friend,* in their language.

One Sabbath day, all the ship's company, except the
captain, two boys, and the cook, were on shore, amusing themselves. During our absence, an immense number of the natives came alongside, and took complete
possession of the vessel, and helped themselves to whatever took their fancy. The captain, boys, and cook,
barricadoed themselves in the cabin, and loaded all the
muskets and pistols within their reach. Their situation
was one of great danger. The surgeon and myself were
the first that arrived upon the beach; the captain hailed
us from the cabin window, and let us know his disagreeable situation, telling us to force the Indians to
put us on board. We having our muskets, they complied at once. Thus, by adding strength to the captain,
we gained new assurance; and the others, doing as we
did, were all put on board as they came to the beach.
The Indians offered no violence to the ship; and, when
the crew were nearly all on board, they began to leave
the vessel, shipping off their booty. Captain Portlock
ordered us to take no notice of the transaction in way
of hurting the Indians, but to purchase back the articles they had taken away that were of use to us; but
they had only taken what pieces of iron they found

loose about the ship. After having hid the things they had stolen, they began to trade, as if nothing had happened; and we bought back what few bolts they had taken. They had plundered the smith's tent in the same manner, although they looked upon him as a greater man than the captain. He was a smart young fellow, and kept the Indians in great awe and wonder. They thought the coals were made into powder. I have seen them steal small pieces, and bruise them, then come back. When he saw this, he would spit upon the anvil while working the hot iron, and give a blow upon it; they would run away in fear and astonishment when they heard the crack.

One or other of our boats, often both, were absent for some time upon trading voyages. In one of these trips, our boat was nearly cut off, and would, in all probability, had it not been for the presence of mind of an American, one of the crew, Joseph Laurence. I never was more alarmed for my safety, in the whole voyage. We were rowing through a lagoon, to get a near cut to the ship; the tide was ebbing fast; the boat took the ground, and, before we could do any thing to get her off, the whole bay was dry. The natives surrounded the boat in great numbers, and looked very mischievous. We knew not what to do. In this dilemma, Laurence, who knew their ways, took a small keg of molasses, and went to the beach; at the same time, he sat down by it, and began to sing and lick, inviting them to follow his example. They licked, and listened to him for a good while, and even joined him in singing; but the molasses wore down, and they were weary of his songs. We looked about in great anxiety, and discovered a small height that commanded the boat. To this we ran, but dared not to fire, even while they were plundering the boat; they could have killed us all with spears and stones, had we even shot one hundred of them, and wasted all our ammunition. We stood like bears at the stake, expecting them every moment to commence the attack, resolved to sell our lives as dear as we could. At length, the wished return of tide came, and we got to the boat, and she floated soon after. Then we cared not one penny for them. We began to trade, and bought back the articles they had stolen. Even our compass we were forced to buy back. We set sail for the *King George,* resolved to be more circumspect in future, and happy we had escaped so well.

The party who had taken possession of the vessel on the Sabbath day, the next time they came back, had their faces blacked, and their heads powdered with the down of birds. They had done this as a disguise, which showed they had a consciousness of right and wrong. Thinking we knew them not, as we took no notice of them, they were as merry and funny as any of the rest.

While the boats were absent on a trading voyage, the canoe was sent to haul the seine for salmon. There were fourteen men and boys in it. About half-way between the vessel and the shore, she filled with water; those who could swim made for the beach; the boys, and those who could not, clung to the canoe. Captain Portlock saw from the deck the danger they were in, and requested the boatswain, who was an excellent swimmer, to go to their assistance; he refused. The sail-maker and myself leaped into the water. I had a line fixed round my waist, as I swam first, which he supported at a short distance behind, to ease its weight. When I came up to the canoe, they were nearly spent. I fixed the line to the canoe, and we made a signal to the ship, when those on board drew her to the vessel, John Butler and I attending to assist and encourage them. There was a son of Sir John Dick's, and a son of Captain Gore's, among the boys. Captain Portlock never could bear the boatswain afterwards. Before this, he was a great favorite.

While in Prince William's Sound, the boat went on an excursion to Snug Corner Cove, at the top of the sound. She discovered the *Nootka*, Captain Meares, in a most distressing situation from the scurvy. There were only the captain and two men free from disease. Two-and-twenty Lascars had died through the course of the winter; they had caused their own distress, by their inordinate use of spirits on Christmas eve. They could not bury their own dead; they were only dragged a short distance from the ship, and left upon the ice. They had muskets fixed upon the capstan, and man-ropes that went down to the cabin, that, when any of the natives attempted to come on board, they might fire them off to scare them. They had a large Newfoundland dog, whose name was Towser, who alone kept the ship clear of the Indians. He lay day and night upon the ice before the cabin-window, and would not allow the Indians to go into the ship. When the natives came to barter, they would cry, "Lally, Towser," and make him a present of a skin, before they began to trade with Captain Meares, who lowered from the window his barter, and in the same way received their furs. The *Beaver*, the *Nootka's* consort, had been cut off in the beginning of the winter, and none of her people were ever heard of. We gave him every assistance in our power, in spruce and molasses, and two of our crew to assist in working the vessel, Dickson and George Willis, who stopped at Canton until we arrived; then, wishing him well, took our leave of him. Captain Portlock could have made a fair prize of him, as he had no charter, and was trading in our limits; but he was satisfied with his bond not to trade on our coast; but the bond was forfeit as soon as we sailed, and he was in China before us.

We now stood for Nootka Sound, but encountered a dreadful gale, and were blown off the coast, and suffered much in our sails and rigging, which caused us to stand for the Sandwich Islands to refit, which gave us great joy. The American coast is a hostile region, compared with the Sandwich Islands. The American Indians are very jealous; and if any of our men were found with their women, using the least freedom, they would take his life, if it was in their power; but their women are far from being objects of desire, they are so much disfigured by slitting their lips, and placing large pieces of wood in them, shaped like a saucer. I have seen them place berries upon it, and shake them into their mouth, as a horse would corn out of a mouth-bag, or lick them in with their tongue. The men have a bone, eight inches long, polished, and stuck through the gristle of their nose; we called it their spritsail-yard. We had suffered a good deal of hardship on this coast, and bade it adieu with joy.

Soon as we arrived at Owhyee, our old acquaintance flocked on board to welcome us, each with a present.

Then such a touching of noses and shaking of hands took place! "Honi, honi," — that is, touch nose, — and "How are you?" were the only words to be heard. Our deck was one continued scene of joy.

Having refitted, and taken in provisions, we again set sail for Cook's River, Prince William's and Nootka Sound, to obtain more fur-skins. We were pretty successful. While on shore in Prince William's Sound, brewing spruce beer, I and the quarter master made an excursion up the river, and discovered a large space covered with snakeroot, which is of great value in China. My comrade, who had been in China, informed me of its value. It is the sweetest smelling plant I ever was near, when it is growing. We set to work, and dug up as much as we chose, and dried it, letting no one know, for lessening the value of what we got. It was got safe on board the day before we sailed, and we sold it well at Wampoa.

We parted company from the *Queen Charlotte.* She had been absent for a long time, when a party of Indians came to the *King George,* having in their possession a pair of buckles that belonged to one of the people on board our consort; we became alarmed for her, thinking she had been cut off. We immediately set sail for Nootka Sound, leaving a large quantity of salmon, half dried. After waiting in Nootka Sound, our place of rendezvous, for some time, and she not appearing, we immediately set sail for Owhyee, but got no word of our consort until we came to Atooi, when we perceived Abenoue in his single canoe, making her scud through the water, crying, "Tattoo for Potipoti," as he jumped upon deck with a letter from Captain Dixon, which removed our fears, and informed us he had discovered an island, and got a very great number of skins, and had sailed for China. We watered, and laid in our provisions as quick as we could, to follow her.

After taking on board as much provisions as we could stow, we sailed for China. At the Ladrones, or Mariana Islands, a number of pilots came on board. The captain agreed with one. The bargain was made in the following manner: He showed the captain the number of dollars he wished by the number of cass — a small brass coin — the captain taking from the number what he thought too much, the pilot adding when he thought it too little. He was to pilot the *King George* to the Island of Macao. From thence we sailed up the Bocca Tigris to Wampoa, where we sold our cargo of skins. We were engaged to take home a cargo of tea for the East India Company.

I was as happy as any person ever was to see any thing. I scarcely believed I was so fortunate as really to be in China. As we sailed up the river, I would cast my eyes from side to side: the thoughts and ideas I had pictured to my mind of it were not lessened in brilliancy, rather increased: the immense number of buildings, that extended as far as the eye could reach; their fantastic shapes and gaudy colors; their trees and flowers, so like their paintings, and the myriads of floating vessels; and, above all, the fanciful dresses and gaudy colors of their clothes, — all serve to fix the mind of a stranger, upon his first arrival.

Soon as we cast anchor, the vessel was surrounded with sampans; every one had some request to make. Tartar girls requested our clothes to wash, barbers to

A MAN OF PRINCE WILLIAM'S SOUND
From the engraving by J. Basire, in Cook's *Voyages*, London, 1784

Whampoa, China

From an engraving by E. Duncan, in the Macpherson Collection, after a painting by W. J. Huggins, showing the view from Dane's Island looking towards Canton

shave the crews, others with fowls to sell — indeed, every necessary we could want. The first we made bargain with was a barber, Tommy Linn. He agreed to shave the crew, for the six months we were to be there, for half a dollar from each man, and he would shave every morning, if we chose, on board the ship, coming off in his sampan. The Tartar girls washed our clothes for the broken meat, or what rice we left at mess. They came every day in their sampans, and took away the men's shirts, bringing them back the next, and never mixed the clothes. They all spoke less or more English, and would jaw with the crew as fast as any women of their rank in England.

I was on shore for a good while at Wampoa, making candles, for our voyage home. I had a number of Chinese under me. My greatest difficulty was to prevent them from stealing the wax. They are greater and more dexterous thieves than the Indians; a bambooing for theft, I really believe, confers no disgrace upon them. They will allow no stranger to enter the city of Canton. I was different times at the gate, but all my ingenuity could not enable me to cross the bar, although I was eight days in the suburbs.

The Chinese, I really believe, eat any thing there is life in. Neptune was constantly on shore with me at the tent; every night he caught less or more rats. He never ate them, but laid them down, when dead, at the tent door. In the morning, the Chinese gave vegetables for them, and were as well pleased as I was at the exchange.

After the candles were made, I removed to Banks Hall, to repair the cooper work, and screen sand and dry it, to pack the tea-boxes for our voyage home. One day, a boy was meddling rather freely with the articles belonging to me. Neptune bit him. I was extremely sorry for it, and, after beating him, dressed the boy's hurt, which was not severe. I gave the boy a few cass who went away quite pleased. In a short time after, I saw him coming back, and his father leading him. I looked for squalls; but the father only asked a few hairs out from under Neptune's fore leg, close to the body; he would take them from no other part, and stuck them all over the wound. He went away content. I had often heard, when a person had been tipsy the evening before, people tell him to take a hair of the dog that bit him, but never saw it in the literal sense before.

A short time before we sailed, all the crew got two months' pay advance, for private trade, and purchased what articles they chose. The dollars are all stamped by the captain, as the Chinese are such cheats, they will dexterously return you a bad dollar, and assert, if not marked, it was the one you gave.

With all their roguery, they are not ungrateful. One day, two Chinese boys were playing in our boat; one of them fell overboard. The current was strong, and the boy was carried down with rapidity. I leaped into the river, and saved him with great difficulty, as the current bore us both along until my strength was almost spent. By an effort I got into the smooth water, and soon had the pleasure of delivering him to his father, who stood upon the beach wringing his hands. I wished to go on board, but the Chinese would have me to his house, where I was most kindly received, and got my dinner in great style. I like their manner of setting out the table at dinner. All that is to be eaten is placed upon the table at once, and all the liquors at the same time. You have all before you, and you may make your choice. I dined in different houses, and the same fashion was used in them all. The Chinese never thought he could show me kindness enough.

Having completed our cargo, we set sail for St. Helena, where we made a present to the governor of a number of empty bottles; he, in return, gave us a present of potatoes, — a valuable gift to us. While here, I and a number of the crew were nearly poisoned by eating albicores and bonettos. We split and hung them in the rigging to dry; the moon's rays have the effect of making them poisonous. My face turned red and swelled; but the others were far worse; their heads were swelled twice their ordinary size; but we all recovered. In a few days, we set sail for England, where I arrived without any remarkable occurrence, after an absence of three years, having, in that time, circumnavigated the globe. We came into the River Thames in the month of September, 1788.

I now returned to Scotland with a sensation of joy only to be felt by those who have been absent for some time. Every remembrance was rendered more dear, every scene was increased in beauty. A piece of oaten cake tasted far sweeter in my mouth than the luxuries of Eastern climes. I was for a time reconciled to remain; the love of country overcame my wandering habits. I had some thought of settling for life, as I had saved a good deal of my pay. In the middle of these musings, and before I had made up my mind, a letter

I received from Captain Portlock upset all my future plans, and rekindled my wandering propensities with as great vigor as ever.

The letter requested me to come to London without delay, as there were two ships lying in the river, bound for New South Wales, the *Guardian* and *Lady Julian,* in either of which I might have a berth. The *Guardian* was loaded with stores and necessaries for the settlement. There was a vine-dresser, and a person to superintend the cultivation of hemp, on board. She sailed long before us. The *Lady Julian* was to take out female convicts.

I would have chosen the *Guardian,* only she was a man-of-war; and, as I meant to settle in Scotland upon our return, I could not have left her when I chose. My only object was to see the country, not to remain at sea; I therefore chose the *Lady Julian,* as she was a transport, although I did not, by any means, like her cargo; yet, to see the country, I was resolved to submit to a great deal.

We lay six months in the river, before we sailed, during which time, all the jails in England were emptied to complete the cargo of the *Lady Julian.* When we sailed, there were on board 245 female convicts. There were not a great many very bad characters; the greater number were for petty crimes, and a great proportion for only being disorderly, that is, street-walkers; the colony, at the time, being in great want of women.

One, a Scottish girl, broke her heart, and died, in the river; she was buried at Dartford. Four were pardoned on account of his majesty's recovery. The poor young Scottish girl I have never yet got out of my mind; she was young and beautiful, even in the convict dress, but pale as death, and her eyes red with weeping. She never spoke to any of the other women, or came on deck. She was constantly seen sitting in the same corner from morning to night; even the time of meals roused her not. My heart bled for her; she was a countrywoman in misfortune. I offered her consolation, but her hopes and heart had sunk. When I spoke, she heeded me not, or only answered with sighs and tears; if I spoke of Scotland, she would wring her hands, and sob, until I thought her heart would burst. I endeavored to get her sad story from her lips, but she was silent as the grave to which she hastened. I lent her my Bible to comfort her, but she read it not; she laid it on her lap, after kissing it, and only bedewed it with her tears. At length, she sunk into the grave, of no disease but a broken heart.

I went every day to the town to buy fresh provisions and other necessaries for them. As their friends were allowed to come on board to see them, they brought money, and numbers had it of their own; particularly a Mrs. Barnsley, a noted sharper and shoplifter. She herself told me her family, for one hundred years back, had been swindlers and highwaymen. She had a brother, a highwayman, who often came to see her, as well dressed and genteel in his appearance as any gentleman. She petitioned the government agent and captain to be allowed to wear her own clothes in the river, and not the convict dress. This could on no account be allowed; but they told her she might wear what she chose when once they were at sea. The agent, Lieutenant Edgar, had been with Captain Cook, was a kind, humane man, and very good to them. He had it in his power to throw all their clothes overboard when he gave them the convict dress; but he gave them to me to stow in the after-hold, saying they would be of use to the poor creatures when they arrived at Port Jackson.

Those from the country came all on board in irons; and I was paid half a crown a head by the country jailers, in many cases, for striking them off upon my anvil, as they were not locked, but riveted. One day, I had the painful task to inform the father and mother of one of the convicts, that their daughter, Sarah Dorset, was on board; they were decent-looking people, and had come to London to inquire after her. When I met them, they were at Newgate; the jailer referred them to me. With tears in her eyes, the mother implored me to tell her if such a one was on board. I told them there was one of that name; the father's heart seemed too full to allow him to speak, but the mother, with streaming eyes, blessed God that they had found their poor, lost child, undone as she was. I called a coach, drove to the river, and had them put on board. The father, with a trembling step, mounted the ship's side; but we were forced to lift the mother on board. I took them down to my berth, and went for Sarah Dorset; when I brought her, the father said, in a choking voice, "My lost child!" and turned his back, covering his face with his hands; the mother, sobbing, threw her hands around her. Poor Sarah fainted, and fell at their feet. I knew not what to do. At length, she recovered, and, in the most heart-rending accents, implored their pardon. She was young and pretty, and had not been two years from her father's house at this present time; so short had been her course of folly and sin. She had not been protected by the villain that ruined her above six weeks; then she was forced by want upon the streets, and taken up as a disorderly girl; then sent on board to be transported. This was her short but eventful history. One of our men, William Power, went out to the colony when her time was expired, brought her home, and married her.

Mrs. Nelly Kerwin, a female of daring habits, banished for life for forging seamen's powers of attorney, and personating their relations, when on our passage down the river, wrote to London for cash, to some of her friends. She got a letter, informing her it was waiting for her at Dartmouth. We were in Colson Bay when she got this letter. With great address she persuaded the agent that there was an express for him and money belonging to her lying at Dartmouth. A man was sent, who brought on board Nell's money, but no express for the agent. When she got it, she laughed in his face, and told him he was in her debt for a lesson. He was very angry, as the captain often told him Kerwin was too many for him.

We had on board a girl, pretty well behaved, who was called, by her acquaintance, a daughter of Pitt's. She herself never contradicted it. She bore a most striking likeness to him in every feature, and could scarce be known from him as to looks. We left her at Port Jackson.

When we were fairly out at sea, every man on board took a wife from among the convicts, they nothing loath. The girl with whom I lived — for I was as bad

in this point as the others — was named Sarah Whitelam. She was a native of Lincoln, a girl of a modest,
reserved turn, as kind and true a creature as ever lived.
I courted her for a week and upwards, and would have
married her upon the spot, had there been a clergyman
on board. She had been banished for a mantle she
had borrowed from an acquaintance. Her friend pros-
ecuted her for stealing it, and she was transported for
seven years. I had fixed my fancy upon her from the
moment I knocked the rivet out of her irons upon my
anvil, and as firmly resolved to bring her back to England, when her time was out, my lawful wife, as ever I
did intend any thing in my life. She bore me a son in
our voyage out. What is become of her, whether she is
dead or alive, I know not. That I do not is no fault of
mine, as my narrative will show. But to proceed. We
soon found that we had a troublesome cargo, yet not
dangerous or very mischievous, — as I may say, more
noise than danger.

When any of them — such as Nance Ferrel, who was
ever making disturbance — became very troublesome,
we confined them down in the hold, and put on the
hatch. This, we were soon convinced, had no effect, as
they became, in turns, outrageous, on purpose to be
confined. Our agent and the captain wondered at the
change in their behavior. I, as steward, found it out
by accident. As I was overhauling the stores in the
hold, I came upon a hogshead of bottled porter, with a
hole in the side of it, and, in place of full, there was
nothing but empty, bottles in it. Another was begun,
and more than a box of candles had been carried off.
I immediately told the captain, who now found out

the cause of the late insubordination and desire of con-
finement. We were forced to change the manner of
punishing them. I was desired by the agent, Lieutenant Edgar, who was an old lieutenant of Cook's, to
take a flour barrel, and cut a hole in the top for their
head, and one on each side for their arms. This we
called a wooden jacket. Next morning, Nance Farrel,
as usual, came to the door of the cabin, and began to
abuse the agent and captain. They desired her to go
away between decks, and be quiet. She became worse
in her abuse, wishing to be confined, and sent to the
hold; but, to her mortification, the jacket was produced, and two men brought her upon deck, and put it
on. She laughed, and capered about for a while, and
made light of it. One of her comrades lighted a pipe
and gave it to her. She walked about, strutting and
smoking the tobacco, and making the others laugh at
the droll figure she made; she walked a minuet, her
head moving from side to side, like a turtle. The agent
was resolved she should be heartily tired, and feel, in
all its force, the disagreeableness of her present situation. She could only walk or stand; to sit, or lie down,
was out of her power. She began to get weary, and
begged to be released. The agent would not, until she
asked his pardon, and promised amendment in future.
This she did, in humble terms, before evening, but, in
a few days, was as bad as ever; there was no taming
her by gentle means. We were forced to tie her up,
like a man, and give her one dozen, with the cat-o'-
nine-tails, and assure her of a clawing every offence;
this alone reduced her to any kind of order.

The first place we stopped at was Santa Cruz, in the

Island of Teneriffe, for water. As we used a great quantity, the agent, at the captain's request, had laid in tea and sugar in place of beef or pork allowed by government. We boiled a large kettle of water, that served the whole convicts and crew, every night and morning. We allowed them water for washing their clothes, any quantity they chose, while in port. Many times they would use four and five boat-loads in one day.

We then stood for Rio Janeiro, where we lay eight weeks, taking in coffee and sugar, our old stock being now reduced very low.

In crossing the line, we had the best sport I ever witnessed upon the same occasion. We had caught a porpoise the day before the ceremony, which we skinned to make a dress for Neptune, with the tail stuffed. When he came on deck, he looked the best representation of a merman I ever saw painted, with a large swab upon his head for a wig. Not a man in the ship could have known him. One of the convicts fainted, she was so much alarmed at his appearance, and had a miscarriage after. From Rio Janeiro we sailed for the Cape of Good Hope, where we took on board seventy-three ewes and a ram, for the settlement.

At length, we sailed for Port Jackson. We made one of the convicts shepherdess, who was so fortunate in her charge of the flock as not to lose one. While we lay at the Cape, we had a narrow escape from destruction by fire. The carpenter allowed the pitch pot to boil over upon the deck, and the flames rose in an alarming manner. The shrieks of the women were dreadful, and the confusion they made running about drove every one stupid. I ran to my berth, seized a pair of blankets to keep it down until the others drowned it with water. Captain Aitken made me a handsome present for my exertions.

At length, almost to our sorrow, we made the land upon the 3d of June, 1790, just one year, all but one day, from our leaving the river. We landed all our convicts safe. My charge, as steward, did not expire for six weeks after our arrival, as the captain, by agreement, was bound to victual them during that time.

The days flew on eagles' wings; for we dreaded the hour of separation, which at length arrived. It was not without the aid of the military we were brought on board.

They have an herb in the colony they call sweet tea. It is infused and drank like the China tea. I liked it much; it requires no sugar, and is both a bitter and a sweet. There was an old female convict, her hair quite gray with age, her face shriveled, who was suckling a child she had borne in the colony. Every one went to see her, and I among the rest. It was a strange sight; her hair was quite white. Her fecundity was ascribed to the sweet tea. I brought away with me two bags of it, as presents to my friends; but two of our men became very ill of the scurvy, and I allowed them the use of it, which soon cured them, but reduced my store. When we came to China, I showed it to my Chinese friends, and they bought it with avidity, and importuned me for it, and a quantity of the seed I had likewise preserved. I let them have the seed, and only brought a small quantity of the herb to England.

Upon our arrival at Wampoa, I renewed my ac-

quaintance with my Chinese friends, and was as happy as I could be, with the thoughts of Sarah's situation
upon my mind; but this was the dullest voyage I ever
made. We touched at St. Helena on our way to England. When we arrived, I was paid off, and immediately made every inquiry for a ship for New Holland;
but there was none, nor any likely to be soon.

There was a vessel called the *Amelia,* Captain
Shiels, fitting out as a South Sea whaler. She belonged
to 'Squire Enderborough, Paul's Wharf, London. I
got myself engaged as cooper of her. The whole crew
were on shares. I, as cooper, had a larger share than
a seaman; but this was not my present aim, neither
did I think of gain. I had all my money secured about
my person, sewed into my clothes, ready for a start,
and with it to pay the passage of Sarah and my son to
England.

In two months after my leaving the *Lady Julian,* I
was again at sea, in hopes of reaching Port Jackson by
some means or other. In our first offset, we were
stranded upon the Red Sand, near the Nore. While we
lay in distress, the Deal men came out, and wished to
make a wreck of us, by cutting away our masts. I, with
alacrity, aided the captain, and stood guard, with a
brace of pistols, and threatened to blow out the brains
of the first man of them that offered to set his foot upon
our deck. The weather, fortunately, was moderate.
We, having no long boat, carried out our anchor between two boats, into deep water; and, as the tide
flowed, we got her off. To my great disappointment,
we were forced to put back into dock to have her examined, by removing the copper sheathing. All the

crew left her, except myself, as the engagement was broken by our return to dock, and the men would not continue in her, as they thought no good would come of the voyage; her stranding was an omen of her bad luck.

There was no ship in the river for New South Wales; and the Indiamen would not sail until about the month of March; the *Amelia* would still be the first vessel. I had no inducement, therefore, to leave her. We were soon again ready for sea, and set sail with an entire new crew. The first land we made was the Island of Bona Vista, which belongs to the Portuguese, where we took in live stock, and salt to salt down our seal-skins, then stood for St. Jago and took in more live stock; from thence to the Falkland Islands for geese and swine. We next made Staten Land, and passed the Straits of Magellan and Straits le Mair, but did not go through either of them. We doubled the Cape, then stood down to our fishing-ground, which was between latitude 18° and the line. We had nothing to do but commence, as we had been busy all the voyage, preparing and fitting our tackle.

Our boilers were fitted up before we left England, as, in the South Seas, the spermaceti is all boiled upon the deck. The boiler is built up with fire brick, and a space left between the lower tier and the deck, about nine inches high, quite water-tight. When once the fire is kindled, — which is never after allowed to go out until the ship is fully fished, — the space between the bricks and the deck is kept full of water. There are two plug-holes, one on each side; so that, when the water heats, and would melt the pitch, upon whatever tack the ship may be, the plug is drawn from the under side, and the space immediately filled with cold water from the higher side. Great attention is required to watch the boilers. We do not require to carry out fuel to boil our oil, as the refuse of the oil is used ever after the first fire is kindled. The ashes of the fire is better than any soap. Let our clothes be ever so black and greasy, as they must be from our employment, one shovel full of ashes in a tub of water, will make them as clean as when we bought them.

I pursued my labors with all the ardor of a seaman. After taking a sufficient quantity of spermaceti, we stood as far down as latitude 3°, to the Island of Lopes, where we killed thirty thousand seals. We had a busy time chasing and killing them. When we had a sufficient number, we began to kill sea-lions, to get their skins for the ship's use. One of their skins was a sufficient load for two men. We used to stand in a gap of the rocks in the morning, and knock them down with our clubs as they approached the sea, then stab them with our long knives.

George Parker, our mate, made a blow at one, and missed him; he made a snap at George, and sent his tusk right through his arm, a little above the wrist, and walked away at his leisure with him into the sea, Parker roaring like a bull, from the pain and terror. Robert Wyld, perceiving his danger, rushed into the water to rescue him, and was up to the arm-pits before he succeeded in despatching the unwieldly monster. He then dragged them both on shore, where, with difficulty, the tusk was drawn from between the bones, it was so firmly jammed.

After visiting Payta and Lima, on the western coast of South America, we returned into the Atlantic, and put into Rio Janeiro for refreshments.

The governor's linguist came on board the *Amelia*, and requested, as a personal favor, that Captain Shiels would allow four of his men to go on board the commodore, to assist in the voyage home, as it would be a winter's passage. I immediately volunteered. I hoped by this means to reach England sooner, and obtain more money for Sarah, as I would receive a full share of the *Amelia* in England, the same as if I had continued in her. Had I known the delays, the fatigue and vexations, I was to endure from these execrably superstitious Portuguese sailors, I never would have left the *Amelia* for any reward the commodore could have given me; and he was very kind to us. He knew our value, and his whole reliance was upon us. We were to work the ship, and fight the ship, should an enemy lay us alongside. He had been forty years trading between Lisbon and Rio Janeiro, and, in all that time, never had made a winter's voyage. The Portuguese are the worst sailors in the world, in rough or cold weather, and we had plenty of both; but, worse than all, we had a black fellow of a priest on board, to whom the crew paid more attention than to the captain. He was forever ringing his bell for mass, and sprinkling holy water upon the men. Whenever it blew harder than ordinary, they were sure to run to the quarter-deck, to the black priest. We were almost foundered, at one time, by this unseamanlike conduct. The whole crew ran to the quarter-deck, kneeling down, resigned to their fate, the priest sprinkling holy water most profusely upon them, while we four Englishmen were left to steer the vessel and hand the sails. It required two of the four to steer, so that there were only two to hand the sails. The consequence was, she broached to. William Mercer and I ran and cut the fore-gears, and allowed the yard to swing; at the same time, the captain, mate, and boatswain, hauled in the fore-brace, and she righted in a moment. Had her commons not been very high, she must have filled while she lay upon her beam ends. The sea was all over her deck, round the hatch; but so soon as she righted, and we were going to make sail, the Portuguese left their priest, and lent us a hand.

We were wrought almost to death, and never could have made out the voyage had we not been well fed, and the captain given us plenty of liquor. The black priest rung his bell at his stated time, whatever we were doing; and the Portuguese would run to their berths for their crosses. Often, the main tack was left half hauled aboard, at the sound of his bell, and the vessel left to drift to leeward until prayers were over. As two men could do nothing to the sail, when the wind was fresh, after prayers they would return, and begin bawling and hauling, calling upon their saints, as if they would come to assist. We were thus almost driven to distraction by them, and could scarce keep off our hands from boxing their ears. Many a hearty curse they and their saints got. Then they would run to the captain or priest, and make complaint that the Englishmen had cursed St. Antonio, or some other of their saints. I often wondered the captain did not confine the priest to his cabin in foul weather, as he was sure to be busiest then. When they complained, the captain

The Entrance of Port Jackson and Part of the Town of Sydney, New South Wales

From an engraving in the Macpherson Collection, after a drawing by Major Taylor, 48th Regiment, made in 1822

VIEW OF LISBON FROM THE TAGUS

From an engraving in the Macpherson Collection, after a drawing made in 1792 by Noel

took our part, and overawed the Portuguese, or I really believe they would have thrown us overboard.

At length, after a tedious voyage of three months, I got out of this vile crew. When we reached the Tagus, the Portuguese began to quarrel, and knock us about. We stood our ground the best way we could, until the captain got five of them sent on shore under a guard of soldiers. We remained at the captain's house until we got our wages. The owners gave us a doubloon a-piece, over and above our agreement, for saving the ship, as the captain did us every justice to the owners at the time, saying, "If the English were as careful of their souls as they are of their bodies, they would be the best people in the world."

We assisted at a religious ceremony before we came away, at the special request of our kind friend, the captain. The foresail, that was set when she broached to, was given, as an offering, to the church, as the black priest told them it was through it they were s a v e d . Although the worst sailor in the ship knew it was the sail that would have sunk us, they dared not contradict the priest. The whole ship's crew carried it through the streets of Lisbon upon handkerchiefs to the church, where it was placed upon the altar with much mummery. We came away and left them; but the owners of the vessel bought back the sail again, after the priests had blessed it to their minds, as the church had more use for money than foresails.

With a joyful heart, I set sail for London, to look out for an Indiaman, that I might get to Bombay, and inquire for S a r a h ; for she was still the idol of all my affections. At this time, I was all anxiety to reach England. I often hoped she had reached her father's house, and was there pining at my absence. I used, for days, to flatter myself with these dreams.

When we arrived at Gravesend, a man-of-war's boat came on board to press any Englishman there might be on board. William and I did not choose to trust to our protections, now that we were in the river. So we stowed ourselves away among some bags of cotton, where we were almost smothered, but could hear every word that was said. The captain told the lieutenant he had no more hands than he saw, and they were all Portuguese. The lieutenant was not very particular, and left the brig without making much search. When the boat left the vessel, we crept from our hiding-hole; and, not long after, a custom-house officer came on board. When we cast anchor, as I had a suit of long clothes in my chest, that I had provided, should I have been so fortunate as to have found Sarah at Port Jackson, to dash away with her a bit on shore, I put them on immediately, and gave the custom-house officer half a guinea for the loan of his cocked hat and powdered wig; the long gilt-headed cane was included in the bargain. I got a waterman to put me on shore. I am confident my own father, had he been alive, could not have known me, with my cane in my hand, cocked hat, and bushy wig. I inquired of the waterman the way to the inn where the coach set out from, for London; I, at the same time, knew as well as he. I passed for a passenger. At the inn, I called for a pint of wine, pens and ink, and was busy writing any nonsense that came in my head, until the coach set off. All these precautions were necessary. Had the waterman suspected me to be a sailor, he would have informed the press gang in one minute. The waiters at the inn would have done the same. By these precautions, I arrived safe in London, but did not go down to Wapping until next day, where I took up my old lodgings, still in my disguise. My landlord went on board, and brought on shore my bedding and chest. I left them under his charge while I went to Lincoln, to Sarah's parents, where I made every inquiry; but they knew not so much of her as I did myself. The last information they had obtained was from the letter I had put in the post-office for them, before I sailed in the *Amelia*. I immediately returned to London, where, to my disappointment, I found there was not a berth to be got in any of the Indiamen who were for Bombay direct. They were all full. I then, as my next best, went to be engaged as cooper on board the *Nottingham*, for China direct, depending on Providence, if we were ever to meet again. To find some way to effect my purpose, my landlord took me to be impressed. He got the six guineas allowed the bringer, which he returned to me. He was from Inverness, — as honest a man as ever lived. I had always boarded in his house when in London. A curious scene happened at my entry. There were a few more impressed on the same day, one an old tar. When asked by C a p t a i n Rogers, in his examination, how they hauled the main tack aboard, he replied, "I can't tell, your honor, but I can show." He clapped his foot into Captain Roger's pocket, at the same instant leaped on his shoulders, tore his coat to the skirts, saying, "Thus we haul it aboard." Captain Barefoot, of the *Nottingham,* and the other captains, laughed heartily, as well as Rogers, who said, rather peevishly, "You might have shown without tearing my coat." "How could I, your honor?" was the reply.

I thus again set off as cooper of the *Nottingham,* in 1793. Nothing worthy of notice happened. I did not get any intelligence from Sarah, nor did I ever hear from her again. As I have gone over the same voyage before, I will not detain the reader; but one circumstance, that I witnessed off the Cape of Good Hope, I cannot avoid mentioning, as a dreadful example of what man will dare, and the perils he will encounter, to free himself from a situation he dislikes. A man-of-war had been washing her gratings, when the India fleet hove in sight. They are washed by being lowered overboard, and allowed to float astern. Four or five men had slipped down upon them, cut them adrift, and were thus voluntarily committed to the vast Atlantic, without a bit of biscuit, or a drop of water, or any means of guiding the gratings they were floating upon, in the hope of being picked up by some vessel. They held out their arms to us, and supplicated, in the wildest manner, to be taken on board. The captain would not. The *Nottingham* was a fast-sailing ship, and the first in the fleet. He said, "I will not; some of the stern ships will pick them up." While he spoke, these unfortunate and desponding fellow-creatures lessened to our view, while their cries rung in our ears. I hope some of the stern ships picked them up. Few things I have seen are more strongly impressed upon my memory, than the despairing looks and frantic gestures of these victims in quest of liberty. Next morning, the frigate they had left came alongside of us, and inquired if we had seen them. The captain gave an indirect answer to their inquiries, as well he might.

On my return home from China, nothing uncommon happened, until we reached the Downs. I had allowed my beard to grow long, and myself to be very dirty, to be as unlikely as possible, when the man-of-war boats came on board to press the crew. As we expected, they came. I was in the hold, sorting among the water-casks, and escaped. They took every hand that would answer. I rejoiced in my escape, but my joy was of short duration. One of the men they had taken had a sore leg; the boat brought him back, and I had the bad luck to be taken, and he was left. Thus were all my schemes blown into the air. I found myself in a situation I could not leave, a bondage that had been imposed upon me against my will, and no hopes of relief until the end of the war — not that I disliked it, but I had now become weary of wandering, for a time, and longed to see Scotland again. My heart always pointed to my native land. Remonstrance and complaint were equally vain.

I therefore made up my mind to it, and was as happy as a man in blasted prospects can be. I was taken on board the *Venerable,* Admiral Duncan. She was the flag-ship, and commanded by Captain Hope, now Admiral Hope. The *Venerable's* boats had made a clean ship of the *Nottingham.* She was forced to be brought up the river by ticket-porters and old Greenwich men. Next morning, sixty of us, who had belonged to the *Nottingham,* were turned over to the *Edgar,* 74, Captain Sir Charles Henry Knowles. This was on the 11th June, 1794. I was stationed in the gunner's crew.

We shortly after sailed on a cruise in the North Seas, and encountered a dreadful gale on the 17th October. I never was in such danger in all my life. The *Edgar* was only newly put in commission, and her rigging was new, and not properly seasoned. We in a few hours carried away our bowsprit and foremast in this dreadful night; then our mizzen and maintopmast. With great difficulty we cut them clear. Soon after, our mainmast loosened in the step, and we every moment expected it to go through the bottom. Then no exertion could have saved us from destruction. The carpenter, by good fortune, got it secured. We lost all our anchors and cables in our attempts to bring her to, save one. At length, it moderated a little, when we rigged jury masts, and made for the Humber, where we brought to with our only remaining anchor, when the *Inflexible,* Captain Savage, hove in sight, and took us in tow. When in this situation, the coasters, as they passed, called to the *Inflexible,* "What prize have you got in tow?" A fresh gale sprung up, and the *Inflexible* was forced to cast us off. The weather moderated again, and we proceeded up the Swain the best way we could, into Blackstakes, Chatham. My berth, during the storm, as one of the gunner's crew, was in charge of the powder on deck we used in firing our guns of distress. The ship rolled so much, we were often upon our beamends, and rolled a number of our guns overboard. We were forced to start all our beer and water, to lighten the ship; but we rode it out, contrary to our expectation, and were shortly after turned over, captain and all, to the *Goliah,* 74 guns, and sailed to join Sir John Jervis in the blockade of Toulon. We boarded a Spanish ship, and found on board thirty Austrian prisoners. They every man entered with us as marines.

We next sailed for St. Forensa Bay, in the Island of Corsica, to water, but found the French in possession of the watering-place, and could get none. I belonged to the launch, and had charge of the powder and match. I was constantly on shore, when any service was to be done in destroying stores, spiking guns, blowing up batteries, and enjoyed it much. We carried off all the brass guns, and those metal ones that were near the edge of the rocks we threw into the sea. This was excellent sport to us; but we were forced to leave it, and sail to Gibraltar for water and provisions, but could obtain no supplies, and sailed for Lisbon, where we got plenty, having been on short allowance for some time before.

While we lay at Lisbon, we got private intelligence, overland, that the Spanish fleet was at sea. We, with all despatch, set sail in pursuit of them. We were so fortunate as to come in sight of them by break of day, on the 14th of February, off Cape St. Vincent. They consisted of twenty-five sail, mostly three-deckers. We were only eighteen; but we were English, and we gave them their Valentines in style. Soon as we came in sight, a bustle commenced not to be conceived or described. To do it justice, while every man was as busy as he could be, the greatest order prevailed. A serious cast was to be perceived on every face, but not a shade of doubt or fear. We rejoiced in a general action; not that we loved fighting, but we all wished to be free to return to our homes, and follow our own pursuits. We knew there was no other way of obtaining this than by defeating the enemy. "The hotter war, the sooner peace," was a saying with us. When every thing was cleared, the ports open, the matches lighted, and guns run out, then we gave them three such cheers as are only to be heard in a British man-of-war. This intimidates the enemy more than a broadside, as they have often declared to me. It shows them all is right, and the men, in the true spirit, baying to be at them. During the action, my situation was not one of danger, but most wounding to my feelings, and trying to my patience. I was stationed in the after-magazine, serving powder from the screen, and could see nothing; but I could feel every shot that struck the *Goliah;* and the cries and groans of the wounded were most distressing, as there was only the thickness of the blankets of the screen between me and them. Busy as I was, the time hung upon me with a dreary weight. Not a soul spoke to me but the master-at-arms, as he went his rounds to inquire if all was safe. No sick person ever longed more for his physician than I for the voice of the master-at-arms. The surgeon's mate, at the commencement of the action, spoke a little; but his hands were soon too full of his own affairs. Those who were carrying, ran like wild creatures, and scarce opened their lips. I would far rather have been on the decks, amid the bustle, for there the time flew on eagle's wings. The *Goliah* was sore beset; for some time, she had two three-deckers upon her. The men stood to their guns as cool as if they had been exercising. The admiral ordered the *Britannia* to our assistance. Iron-sides, with her forty-twos, soon made them sheer off. Towards the close of the action, the men were very weary.

One lad put his head out of the porthole, saying, "Damn them, are they not going to strike yet?" For us to strike was out of the question.

At length, the roar of the guns ceased, and I came on deck to see the effects of a great sea engagement; but such a scene of blood and desolation I want words to express. I had been in a great number of actions with single ships, in the *Proteus* and *Surprise*, during the seven years I was in them. This was my first action in a fleet; and I had only a small share in it. We had destroyed a great number, and secured four three-deckers. One they had the impiety to call the Holy Ghost, we wished much to get; but they towed her off. The fleet was in such a shattered situation, we lay twenty-four hours in sight of them, repairing our rigging. It is after the action the disagreeable part commences; the crews are wrought to the utmost of their strength; for days they have no remission of their toil, repairing the rigging, and other parts injured in the action; their spirits are broke by fatigue; they have no leisure to talk of the battle; and when the usual round of duty returns, we do not choose to revert to a disagreeable subject. Who can speak of what he did, where all did their utmost? One of my messmates had the heel of his shoe shot off; the skin was not broken, yet his leg swelled, and became black. He was lame for a long time. On our return to Lisbon, we lost one of the fleet, the *Bombay Castle*. She was stranded, and completely lost. All her crew were saved. We were in great danger in the *Goliah;* Captain Sir C. H. Knowles was tried for not lending assistance, when he needed it himself. The court-martial honorably acquitted him.

Collis, our first lieutenant, told us not to cheer when he came on board; but we loved our captain too well to be restrained. We had agreed upon a signal with the coxswain, if he was, as he ought to be, honorably acquitted. The signal was given, and in vain Collis forbade. We manned the yards, and gave three hearty cheers. Not a man on board but would have bled for Sir C. H. Knowles. To our regret, we lost him to our ship at this very time. He was as good a captain as I ever sailed with. He was made admiral, and went home in the *Britannia*.

Captain Foley took command of the *Goliah*, and we joined the blockade of Cadiz, where we remained, sending our boat to assist at the bombardments, and covering them until Admiral Nelson came out again, and picked out thirteen seventy-fours from the fleet; the *Goliah* was one. She was the fastest sailing ship in the fleet. We did not stay to water, but got a supply from the ships that were to remain, and away we set, under a press of sail, not knowing where. We came to an anchor in the Straits of Messina. There was an American man-of-war at anchor; Captain Foley ordered him to unmoor, that the *Goliah* might get her station, as it was a good one, near the shore; but Jonathan would not budge, but made answer, "I will let you know I belong to the United States of America, and will not give way to any nation under the sun, but in a good cause." So we came to an anchor where we could. We remained here but a short time, when we got intelligence that the French fleet were up the Straits. We then made sail for Egypt, but missed them, and came back to Syracuse, and watered in twenty-four hours. I was up all night filling water. The day after we left Syracuse, we fell in with a French brig, who had just left the fleet. Admiral Nelson took her in tow, and she conducted us to where they lay at anchor in Aboukir Bay.

We had our anchors out at our stern port with a spring upon them, and the cable carried along the ship's side, so that the anchors were at our bows, as if there was no change in the arrangement. This was to prevent the ships from swinging round, as every ship was to be brought to by her stern. We ran in between the French fleet and the shore, to prevent any communication between the enemy and the shore. Soon as they were in sight, a signal was made from the admiral's ship for every vessel, as she came up, to make the best of her way, firing upon the French ships as she passed, and "every man to take his bird," as we, joking, called it. The *Goliah* led the van. There was a French frigate right in our way. Captain Foley cried, "Sink that brute; what does he there?" In a moment, she went to the bottom, and her crew were seen running into her rigging. The sun was just setting as we went into the bay, and a red and fiery sun it was. I would, had I had my choice, been on the deck; there I should have seen what was passing, and the time would not have hung so heavy; but every man does his duty with spirit, whether his station be in the slaughter-house or the magazine.

I saw as little of this action as I did of the one on the 14th February, off Cape St. Vincent. My station was in the powder magazine, with the gunner. As we entered the bay, we stripped to our trousers, opened our ports, cleared, and, every ship we passed, gave them a

broadside and three cheers. Any information we got
was from the boys and women who carried the powder.
The women behaved as well as the men, and got a present for their bravery from the Grand Seignior. When
the French admiral's ship blew up, the *Goliah* got such
a shake, we thought the after-part of her had blown up,
until the boys told us what it was. They brought us,
every now and then, the cheering news of another
French ship having struck, and we answered the cheers
on deck with heartfelt joy. In the heat of the action, a
shot come right into the magazine, but did no harm, as
the carpenters plugged it up, and stopped the water
that was rushing in. I was much indebted to the gunner's wife, who gave her husband and me a drink of
wine every now and then, which lessened our fatigue
much. There were some of the women wounded; and
one woman, belonging to Leith, died of her wounds,
and was buried on a small island in the bay. One woman bore a son in the heat of the action; she belonged to
Edinburgh. When we ceased firing, I went on deck to
view the state of the fleets, and an awful sight it was.
The whole bay was covered with dead bodies, mangled,
wounded, and scorched, not a bit of clothes on them except their trousers. There were a number of French,
belonging to the French admiral's ship, the *L'Orient*,
who had swam to the *Goliah,* and were cowering under
her forecastle. Poor fellows! they were brought on
board, and Captain Foley ordered them down to the
steward's room, to get provisions and clothing. One
thing I observed in these Frenchmen, quite different
from any thing I had ever before observed. In the
American war, when we took a French ship, — the

Duke de Chartres, — the prisoners were as merry as if they had taken us, only saying, "Fortune de guerre, — you take me to-day, I take you to-morrow." Those we now had on board were thankful for our kindness, but were sullen, and as downcast as if each had lost a ship of his own. The only incidents I heard of are two. One lad, who was stationed by a salt-box, on which he sat to give out cartridges and keep the lid close, — it is a trying berth, — when asked for a cartridge, he gave none, yet he sat upright; his eyes were open. One of the men gave him a push; he fell all his length on the deck. There was not a blemish on his body, yet he was quite dead, and was thrown overboard. The other, a lad who had the match in his hand to fire his gun. In the act of applying it, a shot took off his arm; it hung by a small piece of skin. The match fell to the deck. He looked to his arm, and, seeing what had happened, seized the match in his left hand, and fired off the gun, before he went to the cockpit to have it dressed. They were in our mess, or I might never have heard of it. Two of the mess were killed, and I knew not of it until the day after. Thus terminated the glorious first of August, the busiest night in my life.

Soon after the action, the whole fleet set sail with the prizes, and left the *Goliah* as guard-ship. We remained here until we were relieved by the *Tigre,* 74, when we sailed for Naples, to refit. After refitting, we sailed for Malta, to join in the blockade, where we remained eight months, without any occurrence worthy of notice. At length, the *Goliah* became so leaky, we were forced to leave our station and sail for Gibraltar, where after watering, we sailed for England. We got some marines

from the Rock, to reënforce the *Goliah's* complement,
— one of them a tall, stout Englishman, who had been
cock of the Rock. He was very overbearing. There are
often quarrels at the ship's fires, when the men are
boiling their kettles. We had a stout little fellow of an
Irishman, who had been long in the *Goliah;* the marine pushed his kettle aside. Paddy demanded why he
did so. "Because I choose to do it." "I won't allow
you while the life is in me," was the reply. "Do you
wish to fight?" said the Englishman. "Yes, and I do,"
said Paddy; "I will take the Gibraltar rust out of you,
or you shall beat the life out of my body before we are
done." A fight was made up in a minute; and they
went well forward on the deck, to be out of sight of the
officers. To it they went, and fought it out, we forming
a ring, and screening them from observation. Paddy
was as good as his word; for he took the rust off the marine so well, he was forced to give in; and we were all
happy to see the lobster-back's pride taken out of him.
On our arrival, she was put out of commission, and the
crew turned over to the *Royal William,* the guard-ship,
and had two or three days' liberty on shore, by the admiral's order.

I was next draughted on board the *Ramillies,* and
sailed for Belleisle, but remained only a short time in
her, when I was turned over to the *Ajax,* Captain Alexander F. Cochrane, upon preferment. We sailed for
Ferrol, and attempted to cut out some vessels, but did
not succeed; then stood for Algiers to water, having a
fleet of transports with troops on board under convoy.
The troops were commanded by Sir Ralph Abercrombie. Having watered, we sailed with the army to Ma-

marice Bay, and the troops were encamped upon a fine piece of ground, with a rivulet running through the centre. The French had just left the place, having first done all the mischief in their power. While we lay here, an engineer, named William Balcarras, went, in a frigate to reconnoitre the French works. He landed, and, having attained his object, was coming off in his boat, when he was followed by another from the shore, and shot dead before he reached the frigate. We left Mamarice Bay, and sailed to Rhodes, where we took in forage for the cavalry. We then sailed for Alexandria, and landed the troops.

I belonged to one of the boats. Captain A. F. Cochrane was beach master, and had the ordering of the troops in the landing. We began to leave the ships about twelve o'clock, and reached the shore about sunrise in the morning. We rowed very slow, with our oars muffled. It was a pleasant night; the water was very still; and all was silent as death. No one spoke; but each cast an anxious look to the shore, then at each other, impatient to land. Each boat carried about one hundred men, and did not draw nine inches of water. The French cavalry were ready to receive us; but we soon forced them back, and landed eight thousand men the first morning. We had good sport at landing the troops, as the Frenchmen made a stout resistance. We brought back the wounded men to the ships.

For some time, we supplied the troops on shore with provisions and water. After the advance of the troops into the country, I was with the seamen on shore, assisting at the siege of Alexandria, and working like a laborer in cutting off the branch of the Nile that sup-

plied the city with water. One of the *Ajax's* boats, at
Sir Ralph Abercrombie's request, carried him, after
receiving his wound, on board the hospital ship.

Of all the countries I was ever in, in all my wanderings, I could not remain in Egypt, the air is so dry, and
I felt so disagreeable. It is, on the whole, sandy and
barren; yet what I saw of it that was cultivated is very
agreeable. For some days before the town surrendered,
I had been so bad with the flux, I was forced to go on
board. After the town surrendered, and the operations of the army ceased, we sailed for Malta. At this
time, I was blind with the ophthalmia, and continued
thus for six weeks. My sufferings were most acute. I
could not lie down for a moment, for the scalding water, that continually flowed from my eyes, filled them,
and put me to exquisite torture. I sat constantly on
my chest, with a vessel of cold water, bathing them. If
I slept, I awoke in an agony of pain. All the time, the
flux was most severe upon me, and the surgeon would
not dry it up, as it, he said, relieved my eyes. When we
came to Malta, a French surgeon cured me by touching the balls of my eyes with tincture of opium; but the
pain of the application was very severe. Thank God,
however, I soon after recovered my health and spirits.
From Malta, we sailed to Gibraltar, where we watered,
then sailed for England, where, to my joy, I found that
peace was concluded. We were all paid off shortly after
our arrival. I was ship's corporal when I was discharged.

I was once more my own master, and felt so happy, I
was like one bewildered. Did those on shore only experience half the sensations of a sailor at perfect lib-

VIEW OF VALETTE, MALTA

From an engraving made in 1818 and now in the Macpherson Collection

erty, after being seven years on board ship without a
will of his own, they would not blame his eccentricities,
but wonder he was not more foolish. After a few days,
my cooler reason began to resume its power, and I began to think what should be my after pursuits. It was
now seven years since I had been pressed from the
Nottingham. In that time, the thoughts of Sarah had
faded into a distant, pleasing dream. The violent desire I at one time felt to repossess her was now softened
into a curiosity to know what had become of her.

I could not settle to work, but wandered up and
down. At length I fell in with a cousin of my own. We
had been playfellows, and a friendly intimacy had continued until I went to sea. I fixed my affections on her,
and we were married. I gave her my solemn promise
never again to go to sea, during her life. I then thought
sincerely of settling, and following my trade. I bought
a house in the Castle Hill, and furnished it well; then
laid in a stock of wood and tools. I had as much work
as I could do for a soapwork at the Queen's Ferry. For
one year, my prospects were as good as I could have
wished, and I was as happy as ever I had been in my
life. But, in a few months after, the war broke out
again, and the press-gang came in quest of me. I could
no longer remain in Edinburgh and avoid them. My
wife was like a distracted woman, and gave me no rest
until I sold off my stock in trade and the greater part
of my furniture, and retired to the country. Even, until I got this accomplished, I dared not to sleep in my
own house, as I had more than one call from the gang.

For eleven years I lived at Cousland. Year followed
year, but still no views of peace. I grew old apace, and

the work became too heavy for me. I was now fifty-eight years of age, and they would not have taken me, had I wished to enter the service. I therefore removed to Edinburgh, and again began to work for myself. My first employers had failed in business long before. The times were completely changed; I could not get constant employment for myself. I therefore wrought for any of the other masters who were t h r o n g ; but the cooper business is so very poor, I have been oftener out of employment than at work. Few of them keep journeymen. They, like myself, did all their work with their own hands.

I never had any children by my cousin during the seventeen years we lived together. Margaret, during all that time, never gave me a bad word, or made any strife by her temper; but all have their faults. I will not complain; but more money going out than I by my industry could bring in, has now reduced me to want in my old age.

At her death, which happened four years ago, I was forced to sell all my property, e x c e p t a small room, in which I live, and a cellar where I do any little work I am so fortunate as to obtain. This I did to pay the expenses of her funeral, and a number of debts that had been contracted unknown to me. As my poverty will not allow me to pay for a seat in a church, I go in the evenings to the Little Church; but my house is in the Tolbooth parish.

I eke out my subsistence in the best manner I can. Coffee, made from the raspings of bread, (which I obtain from the bakers,) twice a day, is my chief diet. A few potatoes, or any thing I can obtain with a few pence, constitute my dinner. My only luxury is to-bacco, which I have used these forty-five years. To beg I never will submit. Could I have obtained a small pension for my past services, I should then have reached my utmost earthly wish, and the approach of utter helplessness would not haunt me, as it at present does, in my solitary home. Should I be forced to sell it, all I could obtain could not keep me and pay for lodgings for one year; then I must go to the poor's house, which God, in his mercy, forbid. I can look to my death-bed with resignation; but to the poor's house I cannot look with composure.

I have been a wanderer, and the child of chance, all my days; and now only look for the time when I shall enter my last ship, and be anchored with a green turf upon my breast; and I care not how soon the command is given.

A JOURNAL OF A VOYAGE IN THE BRIG *SPY*, OF SALEM (1832-1834), JOHN B. KNIGHTS, MASTER.

O N THE 8th of August, 1832, I sailed from Salem in the brig *Spy*,* myself master, bound on a trading voyage among the islands in the Pacific Ocean. We experienced very fine weather until passing the Cape Verde Islands when the trade wind, which is usually baffling at this season of the year, left us with S. W. and S. S. W. winds and heavy squalls of thunder, lightning and rain.

On the 8th of September, in the act of reducing sail, to receive a squall which had made its appearance in the N. W., the brig took some rolls which carried away both fore and maintopmasts, started the bowsprit and rendered us a complete wreck. To add to the horror of the scene, the armorer, Israel W. Roundy of Beverly, fell overboard from the top and not being a swimmer sunk immediately. The scene in the meantime baffles description; the vessel rolling gunwale and gunwale; the vivid flashes of lightning in contrast with the succeeding darkness rendering it doubly terrible (it being 8.30 P. M.) ; and the broken spars, thrashing across and athwait the deck, rendering it impossible for us, for a time, to pass forward of the main mast. In a short time, as the wind came on and I was enabled to keep the vessel before it, we succeeded in cutting away the

---

*The brig *Spy*, 98 tons, was built at Medford, Mass., in 1823, and at first was schooner-rigged. At the time of this voyage she was owned by Stephen C. Phillips.

THE SCHOONER "SPY," OF SALEM, MASS.

From a copy of a watercolor in the possession of Stephen W. Phillips

rigging and getting the spars and sails down. At midnight the decks were cleared and the two following days were employed in getting up jury masts for I determined to steer for St. Salvadore. The vessel did not leak and after a most disagreeable and miserable chance we arrived safe at St. Salvadore on the 28th of October. Here I remained, suffering great inconvenience from the slowness of the carpenters and want of the necessary supplies, until the 29th of November when I again set sail for the Pacific.

My crew, which came from Salem, was composed chiefly of landsmen, the greater part of whom, with two seamen who had probably got tired of the vessel, deserted me at St. Salvadore and obliged me to ship another set, principally Portuguese, and two Englishmen who had deserted from the Brazilian service. In fact, I had no choice but was obliged to put up with such as came along. The vessel behaved but little better; her masts, however, being reduced and better stayed, there was little danger of their again going although she labored and strained tremendously. I had a speedy and pleasant passage to the longitude of the Cape of Good Hope; but then experienced several tremendous gales attended with a mountain sea and found I had a vessel but ill suited to contend with either; twice, all my bulwarks were carried away by the sea.

On the 23d of January, 1833, in the evening, I made the Island of St. Paul; it being pleasant and moderate and ran close to it and lay by with the intention of going into the basin, on the morrow, for the purpose of fishing, as great quantities of the finest fish are said to be caught there in a short time. When morning, however, arrived, the wind had shifted and increased to a gale, which obliged me to give up the intention and proceed on my course. I had a boisterous and gloomy passage to Van Diemans Land and arrived at the Bay of Islands, New Zealand, on the 25th of March, 1833, and found several English whaling ships, in the harbor.

The anchor was scarce down, before my decks were filled with natives of both sexes. I had been told by a whaling captain, whom I spoke coming in, that I must allow the natives on board at first or they would be offended and bring me no supplies. The place I anchored at was the second village from the entrance of the Bay, on the larboard hand, called Couradica. Seeing the shipping I hauled in and came to anchor among them. The natives brought on board abundance of fish, squashes and potatoes, all of which I readily obtained for a little tobacco, of which they are excessively fond. At dark I was obliged to drive the females out of the vessel.

The next day I set about making enquiries respecting the place and how I had best proceed. I had much to do about my vessel, beside watering, &c. and there being so many vessels here, the watering place was continually in requisition. The noisy conduct of these whaling crews also was setting a wretched example to mine, who thus far had behaved pretty well; at least, they were in a proper state of subordination. Added to this, — *rum* that *curse* to the *sailors,* — was plenty on the beach, in the hands of some white men who got along then by supplying sailors when on shore. Taking all this into consideration, I was not a little pleased to hear there was another settlement, about

five miles up the river, where I might lie more quiet
and be less annoyed by the natives and be also equally

Having obtained the necessary knowledge of the
handy for watering.

ground, at noon we got under way with a fair wind and
ran up and let go the anchor about two miles below the
village, called the Par. Immediately after I was much
gratified to see a ship standing up, for me, under the
flag of my *country* and went to meet her in my boat.
She proved to be the *Loan,* Capt. Jason Luce, of Edgar-
town. He had discovered that I was an American and
steered to join me. During the afternoon the chiefs of
the place, Chiva Chiva and Poo Murry, came on board
of us and seemed very glad to find us in their territories.
Both spoke English and they conducted themselves
with the utmost propriety. We got abundance of fine
peaches, potatoes, pumpkins and cabbages, for which
we exchanged tobacco. Pigs were scarce, owing to the
number of vessels which had lately been there and were
now in the place.

On the next morning I manned my boat and proceeded, unarmed, to pay a visit to the chiefs at the village. On landing I was shown to the cabin of Chiva
Chiva, by a white sailor who was residing among them.
The chief appeared much gratified on seeing me; invited me in; said his wife was sick and he wished me to
give her some medicine to cure her. The place they
lived in was a shed covered with moss, some fifteen feet
square, of only one room with no floor, but with planks
to walk on when the ground was wet. On each side
were tiers of berths for sleeping, similar to those we
had on board ship. The room contained a chest, sev-

eral muskets in fine order and large parcels of potatoes, peaches, &c. in baskets, thrown about in the utmost confusion. In one of the berths lay the sick wife, a young and interesting female apparently about twenty-three years old, with the complexion of a Spanish brunette. She told me in English, her head was sick and I promised if her husband would go on board with me, to give him something that might make her better. He agreed to come off soon and after looking round the village a short time, I returned on board much gratified with my excursion. The chief soon followed and I gave him a few *See's Pills* and instructed him how they were to be administered. He said he would take one *himself*, to try them, which he did and soon after left me and went on board Captain Luce.

The following day, the wife being better, they came to visit me together, bringing as a present, two large hogs and a quantity of vegetables and peaches. The chief said, "Your name is now my name and my name yours," and we must be great friends; and during my stay of three weeks, I had not the least cause to complain of his breach of profession. I never visited them armed; neither did this chief or his brother show the least timidity of visiting me alone; on the contrary, several times, when either of them had been a distance, from home and night overtook them, they came alongside and begged to be allowed to stop till morning. Though naturally brave, these people are very superstitious and very timid in the *night*.

My friend Captain Luce, had some difficulties, owing to his being obliged to allow half his men to be at liberty in port at all times. They, at times, got into trouble with the tribes in the lower part of the bay, the principal causes being insults offered to the women in their drunken, brutal scrapes. This, of course, would bring on a fight and the sailors generally came off with the worst of it. After one of these encounters, on a Sunday, I happened to be dining on board the *Loan*, when two of the seamen were brought on board badly wounded. The natives followed and were clamorous in demanding payment for their outrages, but on giving them a hearing they went away perfectly satisfied when they *were assured* that the fellows were sufficiently punished. The natives would have been perfectly justified, in *my opinion*, had they killed the pair of *scoundrels*. One, I was told, was saved by the interference of a girl he had previously formed an intimacy with.

These natives, it is said, do not like to kill a white, from a superstitious dread, instilled into them by the missionaries, from a circumstance which took place some years since and which was related to me by one of that class.

An English vessel had come from New Holland to this island, to procure flax and the captain took on board a chief's son, at one of the neighbouring settlements, to go round the islands with him. The captain flogged the boy repeatedly. After some time, finding he could not succeed in obtaining a cargo of flax, he concluded to take on board spars. At this time he was apparently on good terms with the native and consulted with him as to the best place to go for the purpose of obtaining a supply. He strongly recommended the settlement where his *father* was chief, assuring the cap-

tain there was plenty of fine timber to be easily procured there and also that he would interest his father
to assist him. The captain, suspecting no evil intention, went in and on arrival found abundance of trees,
as was stated, and immediately agreed with the chief
for sufficient to load his vessel, proceeding forthwith to
cut it down and raft it off. In this labourious part of
the undertaking, he was necessarily obliged to employ
large numbers of the natives, and at times to have a
large part of his crew on shore. At one of these periods,
the captain with the carpenter and part of the crew,
being at work on shore, the natives (instigated by the
chief's son) attacked the party and massacred the
whole. They then dressed themselves in the clothes of
those they had killed and pulled for the ship, this being
the signal and the officer of the deck having no suspicion that all was not right, those who were on board
rose and overpowered and killed the rest and on the
arrival of the boat they slipped the cables and ran the
vessel on to the beach.

It now remained to share the spoil among the tribe
who had assembled in great multitudes, on the beach,
for that purpose. They at length got to the powder,
which they were dealing by *handfuls*, with *lighted pipes*
in their mouths, when a spark was dropped, which blew
the ship into the air and sent seven-eighths of the tribe
into *eternity*. The missionaries, of course, took care,
as this singular account spread among the natives, to
represent it as a judgement, immediately from God,
for their wickedness and a *signal instance* of his awful
power.

So far, well, — if such delusion can *serve* to render

them more *humane;* and far, very far, be it from me to question the power of the *Almighty.* Still I think no one can read this tale without perceiving immediately that the *loss* of the *ship* and *lives* was entirely owing to the cruelty and folly of the captain. There are far too many, even in these enlightened days, who "think the name of *savage* and *pagan"* is a sufficient excuse for every injury and insult they can offer. In my honest opinion, if the English missionaries at the Bay of Islands, would set more of an example of *humility* and *self-denial,* both in their manner of living and in their intercourse with the natives, it would tend much more toward civilizing the inhabitants, than their *pompous* prayers, their formal lessons, and fanciful stories about the horrors and torments of a future state.

The weather, being fine, I got along fast with my work until the last week of our stay. My people had behaved well and I indulged a hope that I should have no trouble with them. I had seen plenty on board the whaling ships and felt a great degree of pride that among so large a crew as mine, with the worst example possible before them, all things should continue so uniform. But as is the common lot of humanity I was here doomed to meet with disappointment. A Frenchman, I had as armourer, ran away from me and I shipped an English blacksmith in his stead who proved a great villain. This fellow instilled into my men's heads that they were not allowed the same privileges as the English sailors in port and in fact put them up to the asking of favours which they themselves were well aware would not be granted. The blacksmith then refused to go the voyage, I not having as yet let him enter himself on my articles. I put him out of the vessel immediately and was sorry to find, the next day, that the two English sailors had deserted and joined him, as previously they had been obedient and peaceable. I therefore left on the 20th of April, 1833, for the Fegee Islands, with two men short.

A description of the manners, customs and appearance of the New Zealanders, may be deemed superfluous from me as much has been before written by other voyagers; still, perhaps, something amusing, possibly instructing, may have been observed by me which might have been passed unheeded by others. At any rate, "my friends," for whose gratification *alone* I have sketched these remarks, will, I doubt not, consider them of more value than those of a far more finished but unknown writer. Should they accidentally fall into other hands, criticism will be wasted on remarks taken from a record of daily occurrences; penned amid perplexity and care; in places when life and property were only protected by untiring watchfulness and constant preparation; and by one whose least ambition is that of being *an author*.

The men of New Zealand are of a light olive complexion with uniform and regular features, tall and straight in figure and manly in their movements. They disfigure their faces wretchedly by tattooing them, those of the chiefs being so marked as to leave less than a third of the skin natural. The women are much lighter in color, some of them being as clear as many dark complexioned English women, and the blush of modesty is far less a stranger on their faces, than on those of many of the Europeans who reside among them. The

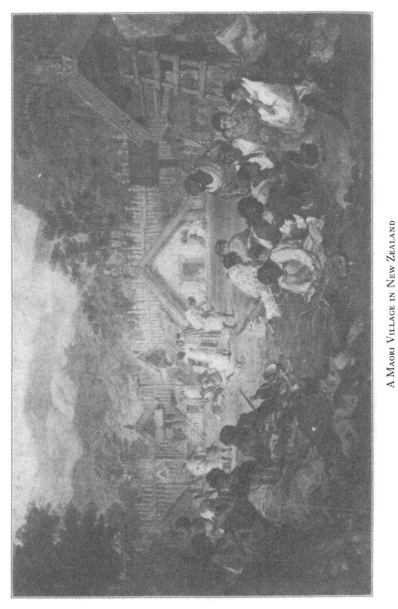

A MAORI VILLAGE IN NEW ZEALAND

From a photograph in the Peabody Museum of Archæology and Ethnology, Cambridge, Mass.

A New Zealand Girl
From a photograph in the Peabody Museum, Salem, Mass.

women are not tattooed except a single line round the lips, perhaps merely to remind them where to find the mouth. Some of them are quite handsome when dressed neatly in the European style, which many of them do. In fact, I have seen children of European fathers and native mothers, who were certainly as interesting and beautiful children as I have ever beheld. The affection which the mother's entertain for these children is worthy of remark. It is absolutely impossible to get them to consent to part with them either by entreaties, rewards or promises to return them. They would sooner die. I happened to be present when an English captain was using every persuasion to obtain a boy to carry home and educate,—promising the most sacredly if he lived he should return. All, however, was unavailing and so fearful was the poor creature that her child would be taken from her, that she put him immediately into the charge of her chief for protection.

They have a singular custom when they lose a friend by death, of cutting and scratching their bodies with shells until the body is buried, which is done with much solemnity. After the body has laid in the grave six moons, they dig it up again and have another great lamentation over it. This last is called the raising of the bones, at which all the tribe assemble. After the mourning is over there is a grand feast and as night comes on they take care to sleep in company for fear the dead should come back among them. The burial grounds are tabooed; that is, they are not to be entered by any one except at a burial or disinterment. These taboos are sacredly inviolable and I very much doubt if they are ever known to be broken by a native. For instance; a chief dies and the survivor thinks proper to cause the river to be tabooed. No native will then think of catching a fish or digging a clam in it. So, also, a married woman or a betrothed maid are tabooed and these contracts are as sacred as in any country on earth and according to my impressions more so. In fact, these people are as happy as it is possible for human beings to be.

Their government seems like those of old, under the Patriachs, the chief being considered as the father of the tribe, seemingly beloved and valued by all. Punishments are very rare, the greatest is depriving the delinquent of his or her property. I never discovered an instance of any of a tribe quarrelling with each other and what is more remarkable, I do not believe *slander* is ever practised among them. Their generosity is proverbial. If a stranger happens among them at meal time, they will not eat themselves till he has sufficiently eaten, or at least, until they are satisfied he has the food by him.

In war with other tribes, when they take prisoners, they make cookies or slaves of them, but they are treated as well in all respects as they treat each other. I saw no difference except in name. They were as happy and contented as the rest of the tribe. If any of the enemy are killed in battle, they are probably eaten. Wars are, however, very seldom carried on now in the vicinity of the Bay of Islands, and the chiefs are ashamed to confess they have eaten human flesh. If they have ever done so, it is far from home and I have particularly observed that it is very disagreeable to them to have any allusion made to the practice when they are in company with their wives and women who shrink with horror at the bare mention of the outrageous custom. At the South island, the most desolating wars are continually waging and such is the horrid ferocity of the combatants, that I was told they would pluck out their enemies' eyes while living and *eat them.*

Muskets are now used altogether as war instruments by the natives on the North island and they are now as good judges, and keep them in as good order, as the Europeans. They are good marksmen and some of the chiefs more than ordinarily so.

The country, particularly the North island, is extremely fertile; the climate mild and healthy and the scenery about the Bay and up the rivers, indescribably beautiful. I know of no spot on earth that presents such beautiful, romantic and at times magnificent scenery, as a sail up this Bay and the Kidde Kidde river, excepting only our own lordly Hudson. The forests abound with wild fowl, such as pigeons, robins and partridges, and the seaside, with wild ducks, geese and beach birds. In the villages are abundance of hogs, some fowls and geese, the latter have been given them, and they are taken great care of. The river and bay furnish any quantity of the finest fish and the flats abound in oysters and round clams. Of the latter, the natives seem to almost subsist and they are indeed fine. Such is the astonishing quantity of these clams, or, as the natives call them, pipies, that a long boat might be filled with them on any part of the beach in a half hour. In truth, Nature here scatters her blessings with an unsparing hand. The natives raise large quantities of Indian corn, potatoes, squashes, &c. much of which they exchange, as well as hogs, to the shipping and the missionaries for tobacco, blankets and muskets, calicoes and prints. They are now getting fond of clothing for their wives and children. They manufacture very beautiful mats and this is the only article of note, I know of their making.

It is now necessary that I should give some account of the whites who reside there and I presume it useless to say that they are all English, as Port Jackson is so near. They should be divided into two distinct classes. Among the first, may be placed the missionaries and the adventurers from New Holland, called settlers. The latter have traded with the natives for a piece of land, part of which they cultivate and they also keep shops for supplying the shipping and trading with the natives for pork, flax, &c. They likewise have sheds for blacksmiths and carpenters to work in, when they can fall in with those trademen, who are often found among the renegadoes who escape from Port Jackson and get over here. These settlers it is impossible to place in too low a light. I have had occasion to see all those who reside there and they are decidedly the greatest sharpers and descend to the meanest and lowest subterfuges of any men I have ever before fallen in with. There is not a spark of honourable or manly principal to be found among them and consequently they cannot be trusted for a moment. In general they are punctual in their attendance at Church and may be considered appendages to the Mission as some of them go about on Sundays catechising the native children. The missionaries, having a bank at Sydney, frequently furnish them the means of making very considerable purchases from vessels, that are sometimes obliged to sell their oil to pay for repairing and putting in order. And woe betide the captain, who allows his respect to the *outward forms* of religion, to lull him into a belief that all are morally honest who pay the strictest attention to them. If closely observed there is one part of their conversation which leads, even a stranger to suspect them. On inquiring of them the reputation of another, who is not at the time present, you will hear very nearly his true character. I have observed repeatedly, that the principle topic of their conversation consists in declaiming about the dishonesty of those who are *absent*. Instead of living in harmony and friendship and uniting together for common protection, they set an opposite example and the natives wonder that white men are so unkind to each other.

The other class are far less to be feared because they act in character and seem, what they in reality are, "bare-faced villains." These consist of run-away sailors and convicts who have escaped from Botany Bay and who reside under the protection of some chief and sell *rum* to the crews when they come on shore; and to give this beverage more stimulus, they infuse into it a goodly portion of tobacco and when their victims get well crazed, they persuade them to desert from their vessel and assist them to get their effects privately on shore. Having thus far succeeded, they keep them until they have eaten and drank what they consider the value of their clothes and then they get them shipped, if possible, on board some other vessel in want of men, probably, still more in their debt, which the new captain is frequently obliged to pay before they

can come on board. The English whaling ships that
frequent this port, make the state of things much worse
than they would other ways be, for their men are on
shares and discipline is loose in comparison with our
merchant vessels. Their captains have frequently told
me that the length, hardship and dangers of the voyage,
oblige them to grant many indulgences to be able to
get along at all.

The Mission here is Episcopalian and Methodist.
The latter is located some distance up the river and the
former makes quite a village, of white, handsome
houses located between Couradica and the Par. They
have no connection with the shipping, alleging that it
is the *only obstacle* in the way of their doing good.
That the conduct on board of some and even the greater part of the shipping is far, very far, from moral, I
certainly know; but at the same time, I also know, that
some captains, try as hard to have good order on board
their vessels, as do the missionaries to place them in
their worst possible light. That these spiritual guides
are aiming, at temporal power over the natives, there is
no doubt; as, also, that it is their interest to place their
exertions and its *fruit,* in its best light to the world
which is furnishing them, from the *hard earnings of
industry,* the means of lolling in princely luxury and
comparative idleness.

On the 20th April, 1833, being ready, I set sail for
the Fegee Islands and experienced continual head
winds until the 4th of May, when the wind came round
to N. E. and continued principally from that quarter
the greater part of the passage although I was all the
time in the space where the S. E. trade wind is ex-

pected to blow, constant and fresh. On the 6th of May, I made Sunday island and ran near, seeing no reef off it, and lowering the boat pulled in for the shore, but on getting near found the surf too furious to risk landing and so was obliged to go on board again. I saw no appearance of any inhabitants, and did not make soundings until within three boats-length, of the shore. The shore was as steep as a church.

On the 14th, was called by the officer of the watch at day break and told that land was in sight. It proved to be two small, beautiful islands, placed on no chart or book. We sailed as near them as prudence allowed, as they were encircled by coral reefs. There was no smoke or appearance of inhabitants.

On the 18th May, saw the island of Mythogue, one of the Fegee group, and soon after, Toa Toa, Marla, and others, of the group. On the next day several canoes came off from Marla, from which I obtained a little shell and abundance of bananas, yams, a goat, &c. for all which I paid a few beads and scissors. They made me understand that the island was Marla and were very anxious to get me to go on shore with them. For that kind of trap I was, however, too old. These people have in one or two instances, enticed captains on shore and then obliged the mates to redeem them by large presents. As this is not an island for trading, I merely lay by till morning and then proceeded to Goora, the largest of the islands, about sixty-five miles from Marla.

I continued among these islands until the 26th June, during which time I was employed in trading for and going in quest of shell. I had much anxiety and trou-

ble from various causes. In the first place, the early
misfortunes of my voyage would alone have prevented
my meeting with the bark *Peru,* Capt. Eagleston, with
whom my voyage was calculated to connect. That vessel had long since left the islands in a leaky condition
from having been on shore and narrowly escaping shipwreck. From her, my calculations were to obtain not
only much information, but extra hands and an interpreter. Now, I was deficient in both; nor had I a single person on board who had the slightest knowledge
of a chart. I also found the journal of a previous voyage and the accompanying chart of this group, fatally
erroneous and so was obliged to depend entirely on
running with a look-out aloft, without a person who
knew the land, as I made it, although the man I had
as mate had been cast away the voyage previous and
resided here ten or twelve months. My feelings, amid
all these disappointments can be better judged by a
seaman than described by me. On any doubt or perplexity I had none who could answer to a remark
other than by a shrug or a grin.

At anchor, under the lee of an island called Over-
low, near to Bow, the residence of the King, I was
boarded, by a parcel of white men who resided on the
island and who had deserted from the different vessels which had been there. They were partly Americans and one was a Salem fellow, by the name of
Magoun. From these men I received information of
the *Peru,* as above stated. They told me there was a
revolution going on among the islands; that the natives had driven the King from Bow and placed another in his stead; that part of the islands had de-

clared in favour of one, the other part for the other; that owing to this cause it would be impossible to procure a cargo of fish, as the natives at the places where it was to be procured, were under such continual apprehension that they would not be persuaded to fish for me; they said that part of them would go and assist a larger vessel, if there was a chance of succeeding, but my vessel was too small for them to risk themselves in. All this I did not believe, notwithstanding my mate was sanguine in his encomium on the integrity of a greater part of these fellows.

During the time I lay near Bow, picking up what shell I could find, I fell in with a Frenchman, at an island called Beaver, who had been left some time since by a French brig, to trade there. He had a lot of beach de mer cured which he wished to dispose of in exchange for trade, as he said he could not store it safely. This I obtained. It was brought on board in double canoes and invariably the fellows took care to come alongside in the night. Whatever were their intentions they always found me prepared. I took it in over the stern; had the two forward gunades pointed aft with three hundred bullets in each, matches lighted and everything ready in case an assault should be made. Having it all on board on the 21st of June, and satisfied I could get no more shell as I have taken a chief as hostage, I sent one of my officers, *twice*, to Bow, with presents to the headmen and they returned without being able even to see any, I got under way and went to the white men's town to get wood and water. My second officer, after behaving in a most outrageous manner, left me and joined these white

men and I firmly believe the unprincipled young man
thought, as my anxieties and cares were so great, that
I should be compelled to bear with any insults and
that now was the time to push them. In this supposition he found he was mistaken.

At this place my vessel came within a hair's breadth
of being cut off, by my own inattention, I am compelled to admit. I had heard much talk and, as I considered, *nonsense* from some of the whites respecting
conversations they pretended to have overheard
among the natives about attacking my vessel. This I
considered was done to try my feelings and render me
as uncomfortable as possible. One David Whippey,
from Nantucket, who appeared to be the principal
man among them, was the only one I had the least
confidence in. He it was, at this time, who saved the
vessel and ourselves from destruction.

The plot was laid in the following manner: — I had
agreed with the chief of the place to pay a keg of powder, he to fill my water casks, bring them alongside
and furnish me with a sufficient quantity of wood.
Part of the water and all the wood was on board and the
remaining casks were on shore filling, when one night,
a large double canoe full of men came from the neigh-
bourhood. The fellows went to the chief and proposed their taking part of the water in their canoe,
while the chief's canoe was alongside and helping
hoist in, when, on a *signal,* their chief, who was to
have some shell on board to sell, was to seize me and
the rest, who were forward, were then to rush upon
the mate and people and close the business with clubs
hid in their tappey or belt of cloth, wound round their

bodies. The substance of this story, the chief told David Whippey in the morning and as the large canoe was hauling up to the stern while the other was discharging, David, came over the side from a small canoe he had himself paddled off. He seemed much agitated, caught up two cold balls from their places and called to me to have all hands armed which was immediately done. At sight of these preparations part of the natives jumped overboard and all went into their canoes. We then secured the water casks, which were towing alongside, and drove the canoes away. The only reasons I can give for the men nor myself not being armed, was partly the assurances that Whippey had given me of the peaceable disposition of his chiefs and tribe and partly the men's being at hard work and in great haste to get the water on board. I felt mortified that I should have departed for a moment from my usual preparation of defence.

The next day was calm and I was ready for sea. The following day the wind was ahead and at 1 P.M. David came on board again and told me the natives were mortified that they had been so easily frustrated in their purpose and had determined to attack me that coming night and had got lines in readiness to draw the brig on shore. All things being ready and not wishing to run farther risk with only twelve on board, I hove up the anchor and stood through the weather passage of the reef and at 5 P.M found myself among a parcel of *sunken rocks*. While going eight knots through the water we rubbed broadside lightly upon one not two feet under water. I was in this perilous situation about ten minutes but got clear and into deep water. The two following days we had hard gales from the eastward and were obliged to carry a heavy press of sail to keep off the reefs. On the third night having cleared the Group and pitching bows under at every sea, drowning my hogs and half drowning ourselves, I brought the vessel under easy sail and concluded to run back to New Zealand, restow and put my fish in order, which had been taken on board, but not properly, to remain a length of time. Besides, I feared the weather might have damped it. Thus ended my excursion among these Islands.

The natives of the Fegee islands are probably the most uncivilized of any of the inhabitants of the islands in the Pacific which have been visited by Europeans. They are complete cannibals and cruel in the last extreme to one another. In personal appearance they are far from being equal to the New Zealander for they are much darker; in size very tall, few being below five feet ten inches, and their general appearance, at first sight, gives one a disgust which is not easily got over. The hair, on the heads of the chiefs, is wadded or frilled, eight or ten inches above the top of the head and is, of course, full of vermin as no comb can go through it. They have two long wooden needles, stuck over each ear, with which they dig into the hair when its inhabitants get too outrageous. In this case, too, they frequently dip their heads into hot ashes and water, the remains of which they allow to remain on their faces as an ornament. At first sight I took these marks for tattooing, like the New Zealanders. They *do not* mark their bodies otherways, than by cutting off a finger or toe when a relation dies.

Few, even of the children, have all these members perfect and when the King dies, one of his wives is killed to go to wait upon him in the other world. Both sexes go naked with the exception of a piece of tapper, or cloth, round their middle which scarcely answers the purpose decency requires.

Their canoes, some of which are very large, are dug out of long trees. Double canoes, as they are called, are two of these lashed together, with a staging built up in the middle, of eight or ten feet high, on which the chiefs sit. These stagings sometimes are so high as to look over the rail of the largest vessels. I have had a canoe near me, which was two-thirds as long as my brig. When there is no wind for their sails these canoes are skulled by means of paddles placed between the two. They very much resemble a horse ferry boat.

The ceremony of courtship among them is singular. When a young man takes a fancy to a girl, he kills all the pigs he can muster, for a feast to which he invites the relatives of the girl. When it is over, he sends the remains of the banquet to them and if this is accepted it amounts to an engagement. The girl's friends then give a similar entertainment and the marriage is thus completed, no other ceremony being necessary. The girl goes home with her husband but the next day she is obliged to go back to her parents and deliver up the mat she has hitherto worn and receive another which distinguishes her as a woman to whose society she is now admitted. Before that she was considered a child and treated as such.

The females at this group, are in no condition better than slaves and, in fact, not so well used by their

husbands as are the slaves by their masters, for they
are obliged to perform all the labourious and menial
offices, while the brutish husband lounges in utter
idleness from day to day.

Many of their customs are connected with others of
too disgusting a nature to be mentioned. The men
are cruel and base in the extreme, but not by any
means sagacious, as they will, not unfrequently, inform others of mischiefs they are at the time meditating. They are treacherous as the Devil himself, but
at the same time great cowards. Their bodily strength
is immense; still they fear to trust it in combat with
the White Man. They appear to have no idea of a
Supreme Being, as I understand from a white man
who has resided long among them.

With respect to there being a doubt of their cannibalism, as I have heard such expressed, I can answer
for the fact that they eat even the bodies of their own
tribe, who offend them, and two men corroborated a
story of being eye-witnesses to a chief's killing one of
his wives, who had contradicted him, and ordering her
to be *cooked*. They will all tell you, by signs, how
much they prefer it to the flesh of turtle or hogs.

In fine, I saw many things to disgust, without a
single one to admire, in the character of a Fegee man,
and to a friend who had a fancy which led him to wish
to go on a Fegee voyage, and asked my advice, I would
say to him — "That if he had a desire to view human
nature in its most *disgusting colours,* pass a considerable portion of his own life in intense anxiety, subsist entirely on *oily pork* and *yams,* without a shadow

of *pleasure* to cheer his dull hours; Go, my friend, go a *Fegee voyage*."

On the night of the 15th of July, I again arrived at the Bay of Islands, New Zealand, and cast anchor some distance outside of Couradica, it being very dark. I found the weather very cold and having been in sight of the Capes two days, the wind blowing directly out, just as evening came on I had a fair wind and feeling well enough acquainted, I ran in without being able to see at all. I feared being caught out in the equinoxial gale and judging by the distance run by the watch, that I was within a short distance of Tarpecker point which makes out from Couradica, I let go the anchor in three fathoms. In the morning I found myself exactly where I calculated and got under way and ran for my former anchorage. Two days after, experienced a tremendous gale from the eastward and parted my bower cable with three anchors ahead. The gale lasted forty hours. To judge of its fury,— I had every yard and *mast down* on deck, notwithstanding which she drifted, the spray flew over her like rain and when the gale abated, I could toss a biscuit on the rocks to leeward. The missionary cutter drove high and dry ashore and the tide was so driven in as to carry away the settler's fences. Hove up the two anchors and towed out into a safer berth. I tried repeatedly but could not recover my lost anchor as it had settled in the mud.

It was now cold and wet and this weather detained me putting my rigging in order and restowing the fish until the 18th of August. During this time I saw much less of the natives than on my former visit, but was treated by them with the same respect and kindness, although I was, the best part of the time, the only vessel in the Bay. The weather being so cold the natives kept much in their huts and the place, wore a gloomy appearance when compared to my former visit. Now, when they had hogs to sell, they would take no other article than blankets in exchange, consequently I could do nothing in that line. I parted with the only one I had for two hogs, in fact, I suffered from cold and want of some necessaries. My stock of sugar, coffee, tea and flour, were all expended, the fish we found so plenty before, would not bite now and the natives said it was too cold to set their nets, tho' I promised them tobacco to bring me some. All the fish food we got were clams, but for the want of butter to cook them, they tasted insipid and they would get cold in the shell e'er we could eat them. I exhausted my description of this place when here last and now I was too cold and hungry to enlarge upon it. I will only add, that I saw no reasons to alter opinions before expressed, relative to the missionaries, the British settlers or the natives.

From information here received, I again set sail for the Caroline Group. I had a favourable chance and in seven days made the westermost island of the Fegee Group, called *Beta Lib* or Big Land. Three days after, being August the 28th, I made the island of Rotumah and concluded to stop for yams and other refreshments so at 12 the next day, came to anchor in sixteen fathoms in the roads. Here I found an Englishman who had been a second mate of a whaler and left here sick and producing recommendations from

Captain Eagleston and others, as interpreter. I employed him as such.

Rotumah, consists of three small, high islands, instead of one, as laid on the chart, and can be seen sixty or seventy miles distance. It is laid down forty miles too far east, on the charts and books. Immediately on my arrival I had abundance of canoes alongside with various kinds of fruits, vegetables and shells; all of which I obtained easily for beads, scissors and coarse cottons, — the latter of which they are extremely fond of. They are a *harmless, good natured* people and one need not have the least anxiety when among them.

But there are at least *twenty convicts* among them who are *dangerous fellows.* I was aware of this, as I knew Captain Eagleston had landed an English sailor here the voyage previous, by his request, and paid him and these rascals murdered him the first night for his money which was tied round him, in gold. Besides, I had been frequently cautioned by several English captains, if I stopped here, to admit none of them on board. I had *never* allowed any sailor from shore to come on board at New Zealand and here I gave my mate strict orders to the same effect. Several were alongside the first day but were ordered off. The next day twelve or fourteen were alongside in the different canoes with the natives and in spite of the mate, two came on board. I soon drove them over the bow with a few cuts with a ropes-end, as they knew my previous orders and *were insolent.*

The next day I was under the necessity of going on shore to purchase a lot of yams, and on landing on the beach I was met and surrounded by *nine* of these *vaga-*

bonds, part of them entirely naked. They saluted me with "You threatened to flay *me* if *I* came on board, your ship." I answered that I did and would either or *any of them* who did so contrary to *my orders.* They told me then, with much insolence, "*We* were on *equal terms* and to do it *then.*" Being armed with loaded pistols and a dirk, which they had not seen, I drew a *pistol,* cocked it and then *assured them solemnly,* if a *hand* was raised or an *impediment* put in my way of proceeding, I would silence *at least* a pair of them and then proceeded through the gang without seeming to take farther notice and finished my business. When I got back to the boat with the yams, these fellows were still about but not game enough to run the risque of attacking me. I must confess I did not feel very easy, while on shore, and I well knew that the least signs of dread or moving from the purposes of my visit would, in all probability, be the *finishing of me.* Consequently I was *not a little* happy on getting once more safe on board.

I was very much pleased with the manners and conduct of these natives. They shew no disposition to take the least trifle from the decks. On the following Sunday, I went on shore at one of the islands called Ware, about three miles from my anchorage and two from the large island, — Rotumah, — with Mr. Emery (who resided there), to try to obtain some goats, and my jaunt there deserves particular mention. I went in Emery's canoe, having two natives with us. Emery had told me the landing was bad which was the reason of my not taking my own boat. When we got there it *was* bad indeed and required all the nerve I had to get through.

The rocks were perpendicular and the sea rose and fell fifteen to eighteen feet. A native stood on the summit with a rope, which he hove for me to take and by its help, when the canoe was on the top of the sea, I made a spring and landed safe. On looking back, the canoe with Emery in it, was fifteen feet and upwards below me. He came the next time in the same manner.

I found the island difficult of access, after being safe on shore, the rocks being rugged and steep. I here saw the greatest natural curiosity it has ever before been my fortune to witness. It was, a fountain situated in a solid rock about one hundred feet long and from five to ten feet wide and four to twelve feet deep, kept constantly filled with pure, crystal water by a brook running from the summit above. About eight feet from one side of this fountain was the edge of the precipice; perpendicular, with the dark of the ocean below. Over this tremendous fall, which I have no doubt was over two thousand feet, ran the overplus water. It really made one dizzy to look over. In fact, I recoiled back with a feeling not unmixed with *horror*. I know nothing which has so great a tendency to bring one's mind so thoroughly to a sense of *his own* comparative nothingness, as the view of some stupendous work of nature.

Into this lovely bathing tub we went and swam upwards of an hour and I never recollect of having enjoyed a greater refreshment. After walking farther we arrived at the house of Emery where we got dinner consisting of roast fowls, fried bananas and bread fruit. The house was very good; in fact, good enough for the climate. It was built by putting up four posts and cross-pieces; then poles fastened to these instead of joists; then the whole was covered with palm leaf, perfectly impervious to water. The sides were opened, when necessary, to let the wind pass through. He had it quite well and neatly furnished and it reminded me of the cabin of Robinson Crusoe, in his best estate; but superior, to poor Crusoe, as he had friendly natives, a wife and a pretty good quantity of books. I afterward learned from an English captain, whom I spoke off Ascension, that Emery, whom he knew well, was a worthy and respectable man and the reason of his living at this island, was his having a *wicked and abandoned woman* for a wife in England, from whom, on his last return there, he had tried to get divorced but did not succeed. After dinner, the goats had ranged away and could not be got, so we spent a greater part of the afternoon ranging about this beautiful place where Nature seems to have spread her table in the choicest abundance for the supply of those simple children of hers and left them only the trouble to devour it.

I particularly noticed, what to me indicated a refined and somewhat of a poetic feeling even in a simple native and this was the care, evidently bestowed upon their burial ground, — a space of perhaps half an acre, which was walled in with large rocks about five feet above the ground. This space was then filled with fine sand brought from the sea shore of one of the other islands, which must have been a great labour. In this space the bodies are deposited and a head and foot stone, even, placed at each grave, to designate where each body was buried to prevent them from digging again in the same place.

These people, to my mind, approach by nature nearer to civilization than the New Zealander: Planting and cultivating their grounds as carefully and regularly as our farmers at home and as a whole they present an appearance of industry which is very pleasing. Their hospitality is worthy of much remark. I also have found that the uncultivated savage, generally, possesses little or even none of that principle we term meanness. This certainly (granting the statement to be true) corroborates the notion that mankind, are not naturally selfish beings, but made so by the cravings which are caused by the artificial wants of cultivated life.

During our walks about the island, when we happened to fall in with a house, which were in some places far apart, I always observed some one would come out and offer us refreshments. At one of these times I was alone and saw an aged female making a mat in front of her cottage. She came up to me, as soon as she saw me, and offered the water of a green cocoa nut. As I was very thirsty at the time and the weather very warm, I received it gratefully and sat by her to rest myself and see her work. On going away I gave her some tobacco for which she appeared quite overjoyed. Some hour or two afterward, while at dinner at Emery's, an old man brought a large bunch of bananas to the door, as much as he could well carry and told Emery that it was for the White Chief who had passed his house some time since and given his wife some tobacco. I, of course, gave the poor old fellow a present.

We ascended, during the afternoon, the highest mountain, to enjoy the freshness of the trade wind. The ascent was not so very difficult, as I could lay hold of roots and bushes to draw myself along. The descent, however, was to me both difficult and dangerous. We had met, on the summit, two natives who were amusing themselves by throwing stones into the ocean below and these kind-hearted fellows, seeing me descend slowly and with difficulty, in comparison to my companion, came to me and one wished to take me on his back. I accepted his assistance so far as to place an arm on his shoulder; the other, went directly in front to pick out the best tract and prevent my falling. To prove all this was not done for the sake of reward, let me say that they were off before I knew of it after we were down and Emery found some difficulty in finding them to reward them as they deserved.

When evening came, the wind, which had been blown fresh all day, had raised such a surf on the landing place as to render it dangerous to launch the canoe and consequently I was obliged to content myself on shore in the best manner circumstances would admit. After tea, I joined the natives on the green where they had collected, male and female, in a ring, singing the songs of their country and keeping the most perfect time by the clapping of hands. Their music was wild, but to me far from unpleasant. About ten o'clock the party broke up and I retired to bed in Emery's cottage.

Early in the morning we got two natives and went to the landing. The surf was breaking much higher than when we landed but I had determined, if Emery would risk it, to go on board if possible. We took our seats in the canoe and the natives pushed it to the edge of the precipice and when the sea was at the highest, pushed off and sprung in and I have no hesitation in stating that in five seconds we were twenty feet below and safe, with only a trifle of water in the bottom. At seven o'clock I was once more on board the *Spy*.

I continued peaceably to trade with this interesting people until the 4th of September when I made sail and continued our route toward the Caroline Islands.

On the 27th of September, in lat. 1.05 S., long. 169.35 East, I saw a small island which was not on any chart. Bowditch, however, lays Gardner's Isle near here, which this must be. From this time until the 9th of November, I was drifting about with W. N. W. and N. W. winds and squalls from the same quarter and never less than a two mile hour current setting me dead to the eastward. In truth, there were times when it appeared that there was small prospect of ever getting to the N. W. I was set 6″ dead off and found myself among the Ralick chain of islands which, by the way, are placed wretchedly out of the way in both books and charts, being seventy miles further to the northward than placed.

On the 27th of November, I made a large high island, which I presumed to be Ascension, though sixty-five miles to the westward of its situation on the chart. I had sailed over that and saw no other appearance of land than some birds and floating cocoanut trees. The current setting strong to the eastward I steered west and at length saw land. I continued standing off and on for several days without being able to find any opening in the reefs (with which the island was surrounded) to obtain an anchorage for the vessel. The natives came off, when the weather admitted (I had frequent and very heavy squalls) and some of them brought considerable quantities of shell.

On the 20th day, a canoe came off with an Irishman in her, who said he could show me a fine harbour. After assuring him that his life should be the immediate forfeit if he led me into any trap, I followed his directions and found an opening in the reef of ¼ to ½ mile wide, and ran in and anchored in three fathoms in as secure a place as possibly could be. I should think that 150 canoes came to meet me as I rounded the point but I suffered none to come on board. As they were so numerous I fired four guns and being the first vessel, so far, in I named the port *New Salem*. Got up my boarding nettings and stationed a sentry on each side the deck and another in the foretop and then commenced trading with the natives who had a great abundance of vegetables, fowls, &c. with a considerable quantity of shell.

The white man told me that a Botany Bay ship left the coast only ten days before, after obtaining upwards of seven hundred pounds of shell and in consequence I should find it much scarcer than usual. Very soon, however, a lot of whites came off with a quantity of shell which I purchased. These fellows had been put into the canoes of the natives, by the Botany Bay whalers as they passed the island and undoubtedly were convicts who had hid away on board before the ships sailed, which is often the case. As I thought it probable the interest of my voyage would be forwarded by keeping on the right side of these fellows, who could probably get more shell, I determined to do so if possible and agreed with them to cut my wood and fill the water casks, which they did and enabled me to keep all my men on board. I found by experience that these natives were great thieves as they were soon trying to draw the iron out of the sides of the vessel. The *whites* assured me that they would steal anything they could lay their hands on. These people were smaller than any I had seen and were about the colour of the Rotumah people. I was so continually surrounded with them as not to be able to leave my vessel at all. Their customs, on shore, I consequently know nothing about. The goodness of their nature and the politeness of their manners may be judged by this account of their treatment of me.

I told the white man who piloted me in and served me also as interpreter, to assure the natives I came among them as a friend; that my intention was to trade with them on *fair terms* and pay them for every thing they brought me which I wanted; and that I expected to receive in return the same treatment; and by all means, for them to be careful never to approach my vessel in the night, as I should in that case certainly fire upon and kill them, which I should be very sorry to be obliged to do. On the third day, I found to my astonishment, they had ripped up and stolen two guard irons from the channels. I again told the interpreter to tell them I should resent this kind of conduct. On the same afternoon, while upwards of a hundred canoes were alongside, and during a heavy fall of rain, the chief mate caught a fellow in the act of stealing another guard iron. He fired a bread fruit at him. On the same instant we were attacked by a shower of stones from their slings. I, being below, seized my pistols and ran to the deck where the stones and spears were flying about like hail.

The 2d officer was at this instant struck down by a stone which hit him on the head and laid him senseless. I lost no time in opening a fire of musketry upon them which soon had the effect desired and caused them to drop off. As they saw some of their number fall they took good care to keep out of reach of the big guns by arranging themselves ahead and astern. When the man on board fell, they set up a shout which lasted till one or two of their number paid for it. By the time they had retreated too far for their stones to reach us our muskets would not go off; in fact, if they had possessed the courage to have pushed on and boarded, it is very doubtful how the fortune of the day would have turned for there were not less than seven hundred natives alongside. When the conflict was over there were a parcel of canoes under the bows, — the natives in them afraid to move. They begged for quarter and protested, they were not concerned. I ordered all away. I found my 2d officer much injured but not seriously so.

On the following day many canoes came alongside. The natives in them did not appear at all intimidated. I could not tell but that part of them were the same fellows who had attacked us the previous day. In the afternoon the King came in a large painted canoe and pulled round and round the vessel and appeared to be afraid to come on board. I ordered him to be called and assured of his safety. He then came on board. He was a miserable looking old fellow and had no particular marks of respect shown him by the other natives. I told him of the manner his subjects had treated me and he answered "they were bad men and I must kill them if they wanted to take the vessel, &c." He made me a present of a mat and a live turtle and some shell. I, also, gave him some trifles. He wanted some rum, of which I had none to give, and he soon left me.

During the following night I was awakened from sleep by a noise similar to that of a rat. I had a lamp *always* burning in my cabin and on drawing aside the curtain, I saw a pole with a hook on it drawing away my clothes, which I had placed on my chest on going to bed. I jumped out not doubting my appearance would startle the fellow. It was bright moonshine and I could see him plainly but instead of drawing away, he seized his spear and was preparing his aim at me through the slatting of my cabin window, when I gave him a shot from one of my pistols. The other fellow with him, backed the canoe astern and was now fired at by the watch on deck. This watch must have been careless not to have seen them before. The cook and a black sailor, who were both sick, wished to be discharged here and as they were useless fellows I paid them off and took a fellow from shore who had been cook before and also two others who begged hard to be allowed to work their passages to Manilla.

During this forenoon, while overhauling the muskets, found some one of the whites from shore had stolen one and so I forbid their coming any more on board. At the same time those who were going on the voyage were not to go any more on shore. Little or no trade off that day. Bought a handsome canoe for which I paid a hatchet. Prepared for sea and during this

forenoon the natives stole the canoe, which was fastened to the stern by a line. I fired at them but they
kept on. I then armed the boat to go after them. No
sooner was the boat gone than a large number of war
canoes came round the point, sounding their war
shouts and steering toward the vessel. I gave them the
bow gun, elevated over them to cause them to return,
but they, finding it did not hurt them, redoubled their
shouts and brandishing their spears at us, the boat put
back. On the firing of the gun, the jib was hoisted to
pay the brig round so that the gun would bear. I gave
them a charge of langrage and bullets which made
things wear a different aspect among them and they
stopped short and turned off in a returning direction
and after this I saw no more of them for that day.

During this forenoon I saw with much pleasure a
bark pass close outside of the reef and in the afternoon
her boat pulled in. She proved to be the English bark
Nimrod, late McColliff, of Sydney. Her master had
been killed, with two of his crew, three days previous
at McAskill island and the present captain informed
me he had overheard one of the whites who had come
on board his vessel while drunk, tell his people that
they, — the white men, — were about joining with the
natives to take my vessel. That she was small, had few
men, and the *damned Yankee* should not reign king
there much longer. This was the reason, he said, he
had pulled in. I questioned their power. The captain
said that he had left nine here himself, who came off
from McAskill's island and assisted him against the
natives and as they were afraid to go back, he agreed to
land them here. That all of them had muskets and

would without doubt join the others. I knew the rascals were desperate enough for any thing. He advised my endeavouring to get out during the night, but that would have been madness as I could not get through the first reach without a fair wind, and the entrance was not more than a quarter to a half mile wide with the wind blowing dead in. I engaged, however, to get under way and try at daylight and he agreed to lay near in and assist us in case the brig struck.

The night was rainy with heavy squalls from the eastward. At daybreak I hove short and as soon as I could well see got under way, got safe through the first reach but at 8 A. M. struck on a ledge of sunken rocks in the centre of the passage which could not be seen by the lookout aloft. As the sun was low in the horizon and very bright, I hove all aback and prepared to defend the vessel from the natives, who were collected in large numbers on the beach and raising their war shouts in triumph. The vessel rubbed *hard* upon the rocks (which were coral) about five minutes and then she swung round and I once more had charge of her. Until this time I had not seen the bark but in about half an hour she made her appearance, standing in, at 11 A. M. the captain came on board. We continued beating, in this narrow place, until 1 P. M. without gaining a fathom ahead when providentially a thunder squall came over the island and by keeping all sail on, she went staggering through and once more we were in *deep water,* all hands of us pretty well beat out. We had tacked every ten minutes and had not had time to eat until 3 P. M. I then went on board the other ship and gave the captain a keg of powder for his kindness and returned and then shaped a course for Manila.

On Dec. 7th, 1834, made the island of Guam, — an island the Spaniards have used as a place on which to put convicts. Ran within a mile of the west side but saw no boats. This island is laid down twenty miles too far eastward. On the 19th of December, hauled into the entrance of St. Bernardino Strait, between the islands of Luconia and Samar.

On the next night, when off the island of Monduque, I was insulted by one of the fellows whom I had taken to work his passage from Ascension. I had been told, the day before, by one of my Portuguese sailors, that he had proposed taking the vessel but could get none of the crew to join him. I therefore had my eye on him and was well armed as well as my mates. At this time I had heard a loud noise forward and on enquiry found it proceeded from this fellow. I called him to desist or I would iron him or shove him ashore. He then *defied me* to do either. I ordered the boat lowered and four men and the second mate to put him on shore. Another fellow who had shipped as cook, swore he would go to, so he went along, but after being gone three hours, they returned in the evening and to my mortification brought them *back*. The *officer* said "they had said they would *lose their lives* sooner than be left on a desolate island" and this miserable fellow, with four men, let them come again on board. One of the sailors told me if the order had been given by the officer, he himself would have undertaken to put them out of the boat. As I was within a short distance of Manilla and a fair wind had sprung up, I concluded to take them in and on the 22d December, arrived safe at Manilla and delivered the mutineers to the officer. I left them in prison, to be sent away the first chance to some other place. The government would not try them and they will probably, hereafter, get *imposed* as honest men, on some one else, being British subjects, as there was no British consul to take charge of them.

The *Spy* being totally unfit for the business for which she was intended, was here sold to the Spaniards and on the 28th of January, 1834, I took passage for New York on board the ship *Moscow,* Capt. Rishworth Mason.

THE REMARKABLE TRANSACTIONS WHICH
TOOK PLACE AT THE TONGA ISLANDS, IN
THE SOUTH PACIFIC OCEAN, DURING THE
CAPTIVITY OF WILLIAM MARINER, ONE
OF THE SURVIVORS OF THE "PORT AU
PRINCE," PRIVATEER, WHICH WAS DE-
STROYED BY THE NATIVES.

ON Tuesday, February 12, 1805, at eleven
o'clock A. M. the privateer *Port au Prince,*
Captain Duck, weighed anchor at Gravesend,
made sail, and worked down the river. She was a ship
of five hundred tons burthen, carrying ninety-six men
and mounting twenty-four long nine and twelve
pounders, besides eight twelve pound carronades on the
quarter-deck. After passing through the Downs, with
a fair wind, she sailed down the Channel, and proceeded on her voyage. No circumstances worth mentioning
occurred during several weeks. The wind continued
fair, but variable. On the 20th March, in the afternoon, the mizzenmast gave way, by the jerk of a swell,
and was found much decayed under the copper, in the
way of the mizzen gaff; this damage, however, by the
next day, was completely repaired. On her arrival in
latitude 21° 55′ S., longitude 38° 38′ W., a very heavy
gale came on. The foretopsail yard, being now discovered to be rotten in the slings, was sent down and re-
placed by a new one. The gale continued to increase
and, from 3 to 5 in the morning, continual flashes of
lightning came on from different quarters with loud

and repeated claps of thunder, succeeded by very heavy rains. After cruising in the vicinity of the River of Plate, she proceeded for the Pacific Ocean and on the 17th of June, Cape Horn bore W. by S. four leagues. The weather was very snowy and the ship leaked badly.

On the 3d of July, having doubled the Cape, she fell in with the *Earl St. Vincent*, a south whaler, homeward bound, by whom she despatched letters for England. She received at the same time, from on board this vessel, Thomas Turner, harpooner, concerning whom it may be interesting to state a few particulars. He went out, at first, on board a south whaler; she made a very successful voyage and on her return home, fell in with the *Earl St. Vincent*, outward bound. Turner, being encouraged by his late good success, got permission to go on board the *Earl St. Vincent* and went accordingly with the view of doubling his good fortune. This vessel was also very successful. On his return home a second time, he fell in with the *Port au Prince* and went on board of her, as just related, with the same views of enjoying a continuation of the good success hitherto attending him. But the favors of Fortune were now at an end; by grasping at more he soon lost all; meeting with a most severe fate, as will be hereafter related.

The *Port au Prince* having received information from the *Earl St. Vincent*, that two south whalers had been captured by the Spaniards and were lying at Conception, it was resolved that she should proceed, as it lay in her voyage, to endeavor to cut them out. On the 20th of July, she arrived off Quiriquina, an island near the Bay of Conception. Here, four boats, well armed and manned, were sent on shore to procure stock. The boats represented to the inhabitants that the *Port au Prince* was an American, whilst they received information, in return, that there were two English whalers in the bay, exactly as was stated by the *Earl St. Vincent.* The boats waited till dusk and then proceeded from the island to Conception, being well assured by Thomas Turner that there were no guns mounted there nor any batteries; and of this he was fully convinced, he said, having formerly been on shore there.

The weather, unfortunately, was now calm, which circumstance prevented the *Port au Prince* from getting into the bay to assist the boats. They, however, very well succeeded, the night being dark, in boarding one of the whalers (the *Albion*) and having secured the Spaniards and cut the cables, towed her about a quarter of a mile, the calm rendering her sails useless; and no doubt they would have succeeded in towing her quite clear of the forts, — for such there were, notwithstanding Turner's account, — had it not been for an accident occasioned by this unfortunate man. He was employed steering one of the boats, when, happening to look to the priming of his pistols, one of them unluckily went off. This alarming the sentinels on shore, two batteries were immediately opened upon them; keeping up a smart fire with well-directed shot, which hulled the ship several times. It was here that Turner met his fate. To avoid the fire, he stooped his body bringing his chin near his knees, where a shot took away his lower jaw, his left arm as far as the elbow, and his right hand, grazing, at the same time, his left side and carrying off the upper, fleshy part of his right thigh.

It did not, however, immediately kill him. The boat was much shattered and one lad was slightly wounded by a splinter. The calm still continuing and the enemy keeping up a constant fire, they were obliged to relinquish the prize and pull on board as fast as they were able, leaving the shattered boat behind them. About six hours afterwards Turner died of his wounds.

After taking several prizes of no great value and making several unsuccessful attempts to plunder the small towns on the coast of South America, the ship entered the Bay of Pisagua with her prizes; and having summoned the village of Guiana to surrender, upon a refusal, the boats were sent with forty-five men on board of a prize brig, which anchored before the town, and men were landed at the same time. Whilst landing, the enemy opened a smart fire of musketry which mortally wounded one man and slightly wounded two others. The men, being all landed, took refuge behind a rock, whence, seeing a fit opportunity, they rushed forth, drove the Spaniards out of the town and took possession of it. In one house they witnessed a scene sufficiently ludicrous, viz., the commandant and a fat friar so drunk that they could not stand; these they secured without much trouble in hopes of receiving a ransom for them.

As the enemy were expected to come shortly in great numbers from the country, to defend themselves better they took possession of the church and mounted a swivel on the steeple. In the mean while the men plundered and pillaged the place of every thing valuable; nor was it possible to restrain them. Silver candlesticks, chalices, incense pans, crucifixes, and images, also of silver, constituted a rich booty; those of wax and wood, of course, were not appropriated, but, notwithstanding, sadly abused. The next morning the enemy not having yet made his appearance, the officers and men secured all the plate that could be found as well as the two prisoners, who had by this time become sober. They then set fire to the town and returned on board.

Having sunk her prizes she sailed out of the bay on the 14th of September. At 10 A. M., a boat was seen pulling towards the ship, which, in the course of an hour, came alongside with six men and proved to belong to the *Minerva,* south whaler, Capt. Obit Cottle, of London. The boat's crew stated that the remainder of the ship's company, nineteen in number, had mutinied, shot the captain and allowed them to have the two boats; but, after having been ten days at sea, the four, being much fatigued, went on shore in the jollyboat; since which the remaining six had been fourteen days in the whaling boat before they fell in with the *Port au Prince.* When they left the *Minerva,* the mutineers hoisted the black flag and declared themselves at war with all nations.

On the 22d, the *Port au Prince* fell in with the *Lucy,* privateer, from London, and in whose company on the following day she came to an anchor off Chinca. The boats were then sent on shore with forty armed men from each ship. In the afternoon they returned, having succeeded in plundering the town, without, however, finding any thing of much value.

On the 4th of October, a sail being seen standing in for Paita, the two ships gave chase; the *Lucy,* being ahead, took her and found her to be a king's tender, bound to Paita, laden with pork, bread, and olive oil for the Spanish frigate *Astraea,* lying at anchor in Paita roads. The circumstance of this frigate being there prevented a meditated attack upon the town. The frigate soon got under weigh and gave chase to the two ships, which immediately stood out of the bay; but, at 2 P. M., being three leagues from the shore, they tacked ship and stood towards the *Astraea* and in half an hour commenced a close action with her, when she bore up for the lee shore and engaged before the wind. At half past 4, the *Port au Prince* was close on the lee shore, in four or five fathoms water, where she lost her mizzentopmast which was shot away and fell athwart the main yard, preventing it, consequently, from bracing about. This was not her only damage for her mizzen was shot down, maintopsail and topgallantsail shot away, foretopsail yard shot down, jib and foretopmast staysail halliards carried away and most of her braces and bowlines likewise. In this situation, on a lee shore, she was obliged to discontinue the engagement. The *Lucy,* who had not received so much damage in her rigging, had hauled off some time before and made sail. The enemy, seeing this, hauled off on the same tack. The *Port au Prince* immediately bent a new maintopsail, when the *Astraea,* finding she did not gain ground, wore ship and stood in for Paita. The *Port au Prince* was not able to follow her and renew the action, on account of her fore cap being shot away, besides the other damage in her rigging and hull. She had only one lad killed, by a grape shot; three others were slightly wounded.

On the afternoon of the 8th, being to windward of

Paita, the two ships bore up for the roads, where the *Astraea* was seen hauled close up in the head of the bay. They immediately stood in and recommenced action with the frigate, which was continued for more than an hour, during which the *Port au Prince* received considerable damage. As the *Astraea* was hauled in shore, firm as a battery, with springs on her cables, her shot were sure to tell; and, as the two ships were obliged to engage her under way, they found it impossible to take her.

The two ships now stood out of the bay in company, proceeded on their voyage and made for the Gallipagos Islands for refreshments, where they separated. On Sunday, the 3d of November, having parted company with the *Lucy*, the *Port au Prince* gave chase to one of three ships which appeared in sight and coming up, found her to be the American ship *Neutrality*, Captain Folger; the other two were the *Britannia* and *British Tar*, of London.

The ship had now arrived on her whaling ground and therefore kept a good lookout for whalers, according to her instructions, but owing to the scarcity of whales, had very little success. On the 4th of February, she captured the *San Pedro*, bound to Point St. Helena for salt, and on Thursday following, still keeping a lookout for whales, she fell in with a strange sail, boarded her, and found her to be the Spanish brig *Santa Rosa del Calmo*, laden with salt, flour and tallow. She was brought alongside, discharged of her cargo, and the next day, putting twenty prisoners on board, she was given up as a cartel.

About the 1st of March, 1806, the *Port au Prince*

came to anchor in Tola roads and in response to a letter the Governor politely sent out a boat containing six pigs, a number of fowls, etc. During the time the ship remained at this place, the officers were very well received and entertained at the Governor's house. He was a very gentlemanly old man and had an only daughter, a very agreeable girl of about sixteen, who had just come from a nunnery where she had received her education. She had heard of the depredations committed by the *Port au Prince,* when the church at Hilo was plundered, and with considerable agitation she expressed her sentiments in tolerably good English, to young Mariner,* then about fourteen years of age, telling him she was certain his ship would never again reach England and predicting that he would never again see his father and mother. The lad told her that if she were in England she would stand a chance of being punished as a witch which produced a laugh accompanied by a pretty smart box on the ears.

After wooding and watering and laying in a good supply of fresh provisions, the *Port au Prince* weighed anchor and made sail; before she had been out long, however, it was found that she was leaking and a course was set towards the island of Cocos, to careen. When she came to anchor in Chatham Bay, the water casks were sent on shore to fill and they began to careen the ship. On running the guns over to starboard

---

*William Mariner was born September 10, 1791, at Highbury Place, Islington, England. He was the son of Magnus Mariner, formerly commander of a hired armed vessel, who had served under Lord Cornwallis in the American Revolution. His son William, became very anxious to go to sea and eagerly grasped the opportunity offered by Captain Duck, to sail with him on the *Port au Prince,* owned by Robert Bent of London. Captain Duck took young Mariner under his immediate protection and during the voyage he served in the capacity of captain's clerk.

and heeling the ship four strakes, the leak was found to proceed from a graving-piece not properly secured under the forechains. The copper under the larboard bow was found to be in bad shape and it was accordingly stripped off and three-quarter inch board was used for sheathing. The principal leaks having been stopped and the ship righted, she weighed anchor and made sail towards the whaling ground, where she cruised for several weeks without success so that the men began to be discontented. On the 12th of May, four whales were caught making a total of fifteen taken during the voyage.

Early in June, a Spanish corbetta was cut out of the harbor of St. Blas, and was found to be laden with pitch, tar and cedar boards. A Spaniard on board informed Captain Duck that two vessels laden with cocoa were expected daily at Acapulco and this news occasioned a dispute between the captain and the whaling-master, Mr. Brown, who contended that the whaling cruise should alone occupy their attention. It was finally determined that the *Port au Prince* should proceed to the island of Ceros and there make up for her ill-success in her whaling cruise, by laying in a cargo of elephant oil and seal skins, this being part of her instructions. Here it may with propriety be remarked, that had the ship been fitted out solely as a privateer, she might have made a good voyage; but having two objects in view and all operations being fettered by the rigidness of the instructions, her success was far less than what it otherwise would have been.

The island of Ceros, one of the San Benito islands, appeared in sight on July 30th and a boat sent on shore brought back information that the place was well stocked with sea-elephants and seals. The next day Captain Duck, finding himself very ill, went ashore and on the 11th of August he died. He was buried two days afterward, the captain and crew of the ship *O'Caen,* of Boston, U. S. A. just arrived, attending the ceremony. A cedar board was erected at the head of the grave, in place of a tombstone, on which the name, age, and profession of the deceased were carved out: he was indeed a very worthy man, bore a most excellent character, and was much lamented by the crew, many of whom shed tears of unfeigned sorrow on the occasion.

On the 19th of September, the ship stood out to sea bound for the Island of Owhyee. The leak was now found to have increased so as to be at the rate of seventeen feet in twenty-four hours. On the 27th, it was found to be considerably decreased; although it had been blowing fresh for three days. On reaching Owhyee, the chief of the island, hearing that they had a sick man on board, refused them permission to enter the close harbor for repairs, being afraid of introducing disease into the country.

The vessel, being plentifully supplied with refreshments proceeded towards Otaheite on the 26th of October, having received eight of the natives on board, who offered their services, as she was in want of hands on account of the leak. This last-mentioned island was the nearest where assistance was to be expected. As she proceeded on her course, the leak was alarmingly increased to the rate of nine inches and a half per hour. In order to ease the ship, it became necessary to remove the carronades from off the quarter-deck, down below; the try-works were also taken down, and the bricks thrown overboard. On the 18th of November, as well as several days preceding, the pumps were obliged to be worked every half hour out of two. By this time, finding she had missed Otaheite, by reason of an adverse current, she steered to the westward for the Tonga Islands, and, on the 27th, saw that part of them called the Hapai Islands, bearing W. twelve miles. The leak had now increased to eighteen inches per hour.

On the 29th of November, 1806, at 4 P. M., the *Port au Prince,* brought to, for the last time, in seven fathoms water, at the northwest point of one of the Hapai Islands, called Lefooga, in the same place where Captain Cook had formerly anchored. In the evening, a number of chiefs came on board with a large barbacued hog, and a quantity of ready-dressed yams as a present to the ship's company. With them came a native of Owhyee, who spoke a little English, which he had formerly learned on board an American ship that had taken him from the Sandwich Islands to Manilla and thence had brought him to the Tonga Islands. This man, whose name was Tooi Tooi, endeavored by all the means of expression that lay in his power, to convince the ship's company that the natives were disposed towards them in the most friendly manner. Another Sandwich Islander, whom the *Port au Prince* had brought along with her, declared his opinion that the Indians had hostile intentions and he advised Mr. Brown, the new captain, to keep a watchful eye over them and even to send all out of the ship, excepting a few chiefs, by treating whom in a friendly way, the produce of the islands might be procured. Captain Brown, however, disregarded this sage admonition and ordered the man to quit the quarter-deck and even threatened to flog him — a treatment which the poor fellow little deserved, for his opinion of the natives was but too well founded, although his less honest country- man Tooi Tooi had spoken so well of them; and, had not the captain unfortunately been above receiving good advice, the *Port au Prince* might again have reached England in safety and thus he might have preserved his own life and the lives of many others.

On Sunday morning, the 30th of November, the men were ordered to be busily engaged in careening the ves- sel, at which they all demurred and some absolutely re- fused, being desirous of going on shore as they had been accustomed to do on Sundays, at whatever place they had touched during the voyage; and to this they were further encouraged by the pernicious invitations of the natives. It is, indeed, sometimes extremely difficult under such circumstances to preserve good order and prompt obedience among the men; and yet the state of the ship at this time, perhaps, fully required the greatest exertions and the most watchful care. Mr. Brown, irritated by these symptoms of discontent, — the fault of which was in no small degree to be laid to his own account, — seemed to have less use of his own judgment at a time when he required it most. The men came aft to request permission to go on shore; this he preemptorily refused, telling them they might go to hell, if they pleased, but that they should not go on shore till the work was done on board and ordered them immediately to quit the quarter-deck. They instantly complied. A short time after, James Kelly jumped up on the gangway with a Spanish stiletto in his hand and swore by God he would run the first man through who attempted to stop him. He then hailed a canoe. His example was instantly followed by three others, George Wood (the carpenter's mate, who swore he would never rig the pumps again), William Baker and James Hoay, taking with them all their clothes. Not much time elapsed before fifteen others took the same step.

In the afternoon, the remainder of the crew came aft with a complaint that a considerable number of the natives had assembled between decks, armed with clubs and spears, and whose behavior gave ample grounds to suspect that they intended to take the vessel. This was, indeed, their object, having already digested their plan, which Mariner afterwards learned from a young chief named Vaca-ta-Bola. It will be well to relate it here in its proper place, although they did not at this time succeed. During the present interval, Vaca-ta-Bola and another chief were sitting in the cabin with Mr. Brown, Mr. Dixon and young Mariner. While they were there, a canoe was to come under the stern and Vaca-ta-Bola was to rise up suddenly and call out, with seeming great earnestness, to the people in the canoe; on which it may be supposed that Mr. Brown and Mr. Dixon would naturally turn their heads, out of curiosity, to see what was going forward in the canoe; at which moment, the two chiefs were to knock them down with short iron-wood clubs which they had concealed under their dress. Before the canoe arrived, however, Mariner happening to go into the steerage, was met by the men who were coming to inform Mr. Brown of the threatening appearance of the natives. Mr. Brown seemed at first not much inclined to pay attention even to this new warning of danger, but when Mariner assured him that what the men stated was correct and that, at all events, it would be but common prudence to inquire into it and satisfy their apprehensions, he went upon deck leading Vaca-ta-Bola by the hand, Mr. Dixon and the other chief followed. During this time, Mariner could not help observing that the two chiefs turned pale and were evidently much agitated; which he attributed to fear, occasioned by the bustle which appeared, without their understanding the cause; though the truth was, they imagined their plot discovered and their fate inevitable.

When they arrived upon deck and were given to understand that Mr. Brown did not like to have so many men on board armed with clubs and spears, they pretended to interest themselves very much in throwing their arms overboard and in ordering the natives out of the ship. Mariner noticed that they took great care not to throw away the best and most handy clubs, but contrived to get them safe into the canoes by passing them from one to another. This he also attributed to a wrong motive, imagining that they wished to save them merely on account of their goodness, while the bad ones they threw away without reluctance. Mr. Brown, with a view of wearing also a pacific appearance, ordered the tomahawks, boarding-pikes and other arms, to be removed below.

In the evening, after the natives had gone on shore, the carpenter and sailmaker spoke to Mr. Brown on the propriety of having the muskets up and placing

sentinels on deck to keep the natives off, as their number prevented them from working; but, unfortunately,
too self-willed and obstinate in error, he treated every
wholesome admonition with indifference and accordingly no such measures were taken.

The following fatal day, Monday, the 1st December, 1806, at eight o'clock in the morning, the natives
began to assemble on board and soon increased to three
hundred, in different parts of the ship. About nine
o'clock, Tooi Tooi, the Sandwich Islander, who had
endeavored to inspire the ship's company with a good
opinion of the friendly disposition of the natives, came
on board and invited Mr. Brown to go on shore and
view the country; he immediately complied and went
unarmed. About half an hour after he had left the ship,
young Mariner, who was in the steerage, went to the
hatch for the sake of the light, as he was about to mend
a pen, and looking up saw Mr. Dixon standing on a
gun, endeavoring by signs to prevent more of the natives from coming on board. At this moment, he heard
a loud shout from the Indians and saw one of them
knock Mr. Dixon down with a club. Seeing now too
clearly what was the matter, he turned about to run
towards the gun-room, when an Indian caught hold of
him by the hand; he luckily escaped from his grasp,
ran down the scuttle and reached the gun-room, where
he found the cooper. Considering the magazine the
safest place, they ran immediately there and having
consulted what was best to be done, they came to the
resolution of blowing up the vessel and, like Samson of
old, to sacrifice themselves and their enemies together.
Mariner went to the gun-room to procure flint and

steel but was not able to get at the muskets without making too much noise, for the arm-chest lay beneath the boarding-pikes, which had carelessly been thrown down the scuttle the preceding evening. The noise occasioned by clearing them away, as the uproar above began to cease, would undoubtedly have attracted the notice of the Indians and he therefore returned to the magazine, where he found the cooper in great distress of mind over his impending fate.

Mariner next proposed that they should go at once upon deck and be killed quickly while their enemies were still hot with slaughter, rather than by greater delay subject themselves to the cruelties of cooler barbarity. After some hesitation, the cooper consented to follow if Mariner would lead the way. The latter thereupon went up into the gun-room and lifting up the hatch a little, saw Tooi Tooi and Vaca-ta-Bola examining Captain Duck's sword and other arms that were in his bed-place. Their backs being turned, he lifted off the hatch entirely and jumped up into the cabin. Tooi Tooi instantly turning round, Mariner presented his hands open, to signify that he was unarmed and at their mercy. He then uttered, "Aroghah!" (a word of friendly salutation among the Sandwich Islanders), and asked, partly in English and partly in his own language, if he meant to kill him as he was ready to meet his fate. Tooi Tooi replied in broken English, that he should not be hurt as the chiefs were already in possession of the ship, but that he wished to be informed how many persons there were below; to which Mariner answered that there was only one, and then called up the cooper who had not followed him the whole way. Tooi

Tooi led them upon deck towards one of the chiefs who had the direction of the conspiracy.

The first object that struck Mariner's sight, on coming upon deck, was enough to thrill the stoutest heart. There sat upon the companion a short, squab, naked figure, of about fifty years of age, with a seaman's jacket, soaked with blood, thrown over one shoulder; on the other rested his iron-wood club, spattered with blood and brains; and what increased the frightfulness of his appearance, was a constant blinking with one of his eyes and a horrible convulsive motion on one side of his mouth. On another part of the deck, there lay twenty-two bodies, perfectly naked, and arranged side by side in even order. They were so dreadfully bruised and battered about the head, that only two or three of them could be recognized. At this time, a man had just counted them and was reporting the number to the chief, who sat in the hammock-nettings; immediately after which they began to throw them overboard. Mariner and the cooper were now brought into the presence of the chief, who looked at them a while and smiled, probably on account of their dirty appearance. Mariner was then given in charge to a petty chief, to be taken on shore, but the cooper was detained on board.

In a little while he was landed and led to the most northern part of the island, to a place called Co-oolo, where he saw without being much affected at the sight, the cause of all that day's disasters, — Mr. Brown, the whaling-master, lying dead upon the beach. The body was naked and much bruised about the head and chest. They asked Mariner, by words and signs, if they had done right in killing him and as he returned no answer, one of them lifted up his club to knock out his brains, but was prevented by a superior chief who ordered them to take their prisoner on board a large sailing canoe. While here, he saw, upon the beach, an old man, whose countenance did not speak much in his favor, parading up and down with a large club in his hand. At this time, a boy, who had just come into the canoe, pointed to a fire at a little distance and speaking to Mariner, pronounced the word *máte* (meaning to *kill*) and made such signs that could give him to understand nothing less than that he was to be killed and roasted. This idea roused him from his state of mental torpor and gave him some alarm which was not lessened by the sight of the old man who appeared to be an executioner, waiting for his victim. About half an hour afterwards, a number of people came to the canoe, landed him and led him towards the fire, near which he saw, lying dead, James Kelly, William Baker and James Hoay, three of those who had first mutinied. Some hogs were now brought to be cooked and Mariner was soon undeceived respecting what he had understood from the gestures of the boy in the canoe, who had merely meant to imply that some of the crew lay dead where he pointed and that they were going to roast or bake some hogs there.

From this place he was led towards the Island of Foa. On the way they stopped at a hut where they stripped him of his trousers, notwithstanding his earnest solicitations to retain them for he already felt the effect of the sun on his back and he dreaded a total exposure to its heat. He was now led about barefooted and without any thing to cover him, the heat blistering his skin in a most shocking manner. Every now and then some of the natives came up from motives of curiosity and felt his skin, to compare it with their own, or likened it, rather (as he afterwards understood) to the skin of a scraped hog from its whiteness. From malice, or rather wantonness, they spit upon him, pushed him about and threw sticks and cocoa-nut shells at him so that his head was cut in several places. After having thus tantalized and led him about for a considerable length of time, as fast as the soreness of his feet would permit him to walk, a woman, happening to pass near at hand, from motives of compassion gave him an apron made of the leaves of the chee-tree, with which he was permitted to cover himself. Coming, at length, to a hut, they entered and sat down to drink cava, putting him in a corner and desiring him by signs, to sit down, it being considered very disrespectful to stand up before a superior. While his persecutors were regaling themselves, a man entered the hut in great haste and having said something to the company, took Mariner away with him. As they were going along, they met one of the Sandwich Islanders whom the *Port au Prince* had brought from Anahooroo Bay, who gave Mariner to understand, that Finow, the king of the islands, had sent for him.

When he arrived in the king's presence, the king beckoned to him and made signs that he should sit near him. As he entered the place, the king's women, who sat at the other end of the room, at the sight of his deplorable condition, uttered a cry of pity, beating their breasts and exclaiming, "*O yaoo! chiodofa!*" (Alas! poor young man!) Fortunately for Mariner, Finow

WILLIAM MARINER IN TONGA ISLAND COSTUME
From the engraving by Abel Bowen, published in 1820

A FIATOOKA OR MORAI, TONGA ISLANDS

From an engraving by W. Ellis, in Cook's *Voyages*, London, 1784

had taken an extraordinary liking to him from the first moment he had seen him on board. He thought he was the captain's son or at least a young chief of some consequence in his own country and he, accordingly, had given orders that if they found it necessary to kill the white men, they should at any rate preserve young Mariner's life. The king put his nose to his forehead (a mark of friendly salutation) and, soon after, observing that he was very dirty and much wounded, he directed one of the women attendants to take him to a pond within the fencing of the house, where he might wash himself. Here, he made himself as clean as mere water could make him; but finding the dirt did not come readily off his feet, she brought some sand and began to scrub them with it and when he complained that this hurt him, she said something which, at that time, he did not clearly understand, implying that such was the Tonga mode of washing. After being pretty well washed, he again came into presence of the king and was sent to the other end of the house where he was oiled all over with sandal-wood oil, which felt very agreeable, alleviating the smart of his wounds and greatly refreshing him. He now received a mat to lie down on, where, overcome by fatigue, he soon fell fast asleep. During the night he was awakened by one of the women who brought him some baked pork and some yam; but being prejudiced against the pork, lest it should be human flesh, he did not taste it, but ate heartily of the yam, not having tasted anything since breakfast the preceding day.

In the course of the morning, Finow took him on board the ship, where he was much gratified to find several of the crew who had been ordered on board to bring the ship close in shore. The king's orders being understood, they cut the cables and worked her in shore, through a very narrow passage, so full of rocks and shoals that, untried, it would have been considered unnavigable. Through the medium of Tooi Tooi, the king had been previously informed that unless his men (which were about four hundred in number) were to sit down and remain perfectly quiet, it would be impossible to work the ship; the Englishmen being only about fourteen in number. The moment Finow had given orders to his men, he was most implicitly obeyed. They sat down and not a word was spoken nor the least perceptible noise made by them during the whole time. The ship was brought within half a cable's length of the shore, through the narrow passage and then run aground, according to Finow's orders.

After the ship was aground, the next two or three days were employed in striking the masts and conveying on shore two of the carronades and eight barrels of gunpowder; all that remained was too much damaged for use. Many of the natives, in the mean while, were busily engaged in stripping the upper works of their iron and knocking the hoops off the casks in the hold, iron being a most valuable commodity to them. During these operations, the ground tier of oil, the hoops being knocked off the casks, burst out and suffocated eight of the natives. In consequence of this great discharge of oil, the water in the hold was covered with it to the depth of two feet. Three other men were, at the same time, severely wounded by some butts bursting out on them while they were in the act of knocking off the hoops.

Finow observed one of the natives busily employed in cutting out the iron fid from the main-topgallant-mast, and as he was a low fellow, whom he did not choose should take such a liberty, he was resolved to put a stop to his work, so, speaking to a Sandwich Islander who was amusing himself on deck by firing off his musket, he bade him try to bring that man down from aloft. Without the least hesitation he levelled his piece and instantly brought the man down dead. The shot entered his body and the fall broke both thighs and fractured his skull. Finow laughed heartily and seemed mightily pleased at the facility with which it was done. When Mariner understood the language, he asked the king how he could be so cruel as to kill the poor man for so trifling a fault? His Majesty replied, that he was only a low, vulgar fellow (a cook) and that neither his life nor death was of any consequence to society.

On Tuesday, the 9th of December, it being spring-tides, the ship floated and was warped in to low-water mark and that evening they set fire to her in order to get more easily at the iron work. All the great guns on board were loaded and as they began to be heated by the general conflagration they went off, one after another, producing a terrible panic among all the natives. Mariner was at this time asleep at a house near the shore and being awakened by the noise of the guns, he saw several of the natives running into the house in great fright; they, no doubt, thinking everything was going to wreck and ruin. Seeing their distress, he gave them to understand by signs, that nothing was to be feared and that they might go to sleep in safety. After the guns had ceased firing, he went down to the beach and found the ship burnt to the water's edge.

The next day, as soon as it was daylight, the natives flocked to the beach and, by the direction and assistance of Mariner and some of the crew, got five of the carronades on shore by tying a rope round them and dragging them with the main strength of two or three hundred men. A few days afterwards, three more carronades were brought on shore and also four long guns.

About a week now elapsed without any material circumstance occurring, during which time Mariner kept, for the most part, within doors, by the advice of Finow, lest he should be injured by the wantonness or malice of the lower orders who took every opportunity of insulting him. On the 16th of December, Finow, having a mind to go to the Island of Whiha, for the recreation of shooting rats, invited Mariner to accompany him. The inhabitants of this island made great rejoicings on account of Finow's arrival. He remained there three or four days, spending the time principally in shooting rats and birds.

This ambitious chief, having procured the necessary materials of warfare, was now determined to conduct a campaign in the European manner. With the assistance of the survivors of the *Port au Prince,* he felt sanguine that he could vanquish his enemies and conquer the neighboring islands.

At the time when Captain Cook was at these islands, the habits of war were little known to the natives. The only quarrels in which they had at that time been engaged, were among the inhabitants of the Fiji Islands, about one hundred and twenty leagues to the westward; for, having been in the habit of visiting them for sandal-wood, &c., they occasionally assisted one or other of the warlike parties against the enemy. The bows and arrows which, before that period, had been in use among the people of Tonga, were of a weaker kind and fitted rather for sport than war, — for the purpose of shooting rats, birds, &c. From the fierce and warlike people of those islands, however, they speedily learned to construct bows and arrows of a much more martial and formidable nature and soon became acquainted with a better form of the spear and a superior method of holding and throwing that weapon. They also imitated them, by degrees, in the practice of painting their faces and the use of a peculiar dress in time of war, giving a fierce appearance, calculated to strike terror into the minds of their enemies. These martial improvements were in their progress at the time of Captain Cook's arrival but not in general practice.

Mariner, and those of his companions who were with him at the Island of Lefooga (four in number), received orders from the king to prepare for the usual annual attack upon the Island of Tonga and to get ready four 12 pound carronades. They immediately set to work to mount them upon new carriages, with high wheels made by the native carpenters under their directions. This being done, Finow expressed his opinion that the gun was an instrument not well fitted for their mode of warfare, which consisted in sudden attacks and retreats, according to circumstances, rather than in a steady engagement. He very readily entered into an acknowledgment of the advantages of a steady contest but was apprehensive that his men would not easily be brought to stand it. Mariner and his companions, however, promised that they and their countrymen (who were dispersed upon other islands) would remain in the front of the battle with their four guns, provided the Tonga people would agree to stand fast and support them. The king assented to this on the part of his men and a few days afterwards, when he reviewed them, he signified his wishes and they swore to fulfil their duty.

In the mean time, the Englishmen employed themselves in collecting the shot which the natives had brought from on board, but which they had thrown aside, not being able to shape them for any common purpose. They also cut up a quantity of sheet lead and made it up in rolls to be used as shot. During this time, every preparation was also making by the natives for the approaching war. They repaired the sails of their canoes, collected their arrows, spears and clubs; and the women employed themselves in packing up bales of gnatoo, mats, &c.

One day, while these preparations were going forward, the king asked Mariner whether he had a mother living and upon his replying in the affirmative, he appeared much grieved that he should be separated so far from her. It was a custom in the Tonga Islands, for men (and sometimes women) to adopt or choose a foster mother, even though they have their own natural mother living, with a view of being better provided with all necessaries and conveniences, as cloth, oil, food, &c. On this occasion, the king appointed one of his wives, Mafi Habe, to be Mariner's adopted mother, telling him that if there was any thing he wanted to make his situation more comfortable, he need only apply to Mafi Habe and as she was a woman of consequence, it was in her power to procure him anything that in reason he might require. This woman had afterwards as much real esteem and parental affection for him as she could possibly have for her own son.

All things being now prepared for the invasion of Tonga, the gods were invoked and the priests assured Finow of success. The large canoes of Lefooga, about fourteen in number, were then launched, which, with Toobó Nuha's fleet from Vavaoo, made together about fifty sail. Orders were sent by Finow to all the Hapai Islands to make the Island of Namooca the place of general rendezvous. These fifty sail, under the direction of Finow, four of the largest having each a carronade on board, proceeded towards the appointed place, but on account of contrary winds were obliged to put into Whiha. Here Finow took an opportunity to review his men, most of them being painted and dressed after the warlike manner of the Fiji Islands. They paraded up and down for some time, brandishing their clubs and spears and exhibiting a sort of sham fight. Finow sat, with several other chiefs, in the house on the *malái*. Each warrior of note ran singly close up to Finow and striking his club violently on the ground, cried out, "This is the club for ——," mentioning the name of some individual enemy whom he meant particularly to seek out and engage. Others, running up in the same way, exclaimed, "Fear not, Finow; no sooner shall we land at Tonga than here is the club with which I will kill any one who dares to oppose us."

Finow and the chiefs thanked them for their sentiments of love and loyalty and then he addressed them in a speech to the following purpose: "Be brave in battle; fear not death: it is far better to die in war than to live to be assassinated at home, or to perish by a lingering disease."

After remaining a day and a night at this island, they again put to sea with the additional force of six canoes, and made sail for Namooca where they arrived in a few hours. Here they had another review like the former, and after remaining two days, sailed with all the rest of the forces of the confederate islands, amounting in all to about one hundred and seventy canoes, direct for the Island of Tonga. Owing to the calmness of the weather they did not reach their destination the same evening in sufficient time to land, but went on shore at a small island close by called Pángaimótoo, where they passed the night.

Before morning, several presents were brought to Finow and his chiefs, by the people living at a consecrated place on the Island of Tonga, called Mafanga. Mafanga is a piece of ground about half a mile square, situated on the western part of the island. In this spot are the graves where the greatest chiefs from time immemorial have been buried and the place is therefore considered sacred. It would be a sacrilege to fight there and nobody can be prevented from landing. If the most inveterate enemies meet upon this ground they must look upon each other as friends, under penalty of the displeasure of the gods.

The next morning the whole fleet proceeded to a neighboring fortress called Nioocalofa, the strongest, though not the largest in the whole island. It was situated on the western coast of the island, about one hundred yards distant from the water's edge, occupying about four or five acres of ground. It consisted in the first place, of a strong wall or fencing of reeds, something like wicker-work, supported on the inside by upright posts, from six to nine inches in diameter, and situated a foot and a half distant from each other, to which the reed-work was firmly lashed by tough sinnet, made of the husk of the cocoa-nut. This fencing was about nine feet in height, the posts rising about a foot higher. It had four large entrances, as well as several small ones, secured on the inside by horizontal sliding-pieces made of the wood of the cocoa-nut tree. Over each door, as well as at other places, were erected platforms even with the top of the fencing, supported chiefly on the inside, but projecting forward to the extent of two or three feet. These platforms were about nine feet square and situated fifteen yards distant from each other; and, as they were intended for the men to stand on, to shoot arrows or throw down large stones, they were also defended in front and half way on each side, by a reed-work six feet high, with an opening in front, and others on either hand, for the greater convenience of throwing spears, &c. The lower fencing had also openings for a similar purpose. On the outside was a ditch of nearly twelve feet deep, and as much broad, which, at a little distance, was encompassed by another fencing, similar to the first, with platforms, &c., on the outside of which there was a second ditch. The earth dug out of these ditches formed a bank on each side, serving to deepen them. Opposite each large

doorway, there was no ditch. The inner and outer fenc-
ings were ornamented profusely with white shells.
Some of these fortifications were square, others round.
That of Nioocalofa was round.

Finow being arrived with the whole of his fleet, off
Nioocalofa, and having with him besides Mariner fifteen other Englishmen, eight of whom were armed
with muskets, he proceeded to land his troops under
cover of a fire of musketry, which speedily drove almost
all the enemy who had sallied forth back into the garrison. The first fire killed three and wounded several;
and a repetition of it threw them into such dismay that
in five minutes, only forty of the bravest remained to
molest them and these began to retire as the forces of
Finow increased on the beach. In the mean while, the
carronades were dismounted from their carriages, slung
on poles and conveyed over a shallow reef to the shore.
The whole army having landed and the guns again
mounted, the latter were drawn up before the garrison
and a regular fire was commenced. Finow took his station on the reef, seated in an English chair (from the
Port au Prince) for his chiefs would not allow him to
expose his person on shore. The fire of the carronades
was kept up for about an hour and as it did not appear
to do all the mischief to the exterior of the fortress, owing to the yielding nature of its materials, that the king
expected, he sent for Mariner and expressed his disappointment. The latter replied that no doubt there was
mischief enough done on the inside of the fort, wherever
there were resisting bodies such as canoes, the posts
and beams of houses, &c.; and that it was already very
evident the besieged had no reason to think slightly of

the effect of the artillery, seeing that they had already greatly slackened their exertions, not half the number of arrows being now discharged from the fort, arising, in all probability, from the number of the slain or of those who had fled up into the country.

It was now resolved to set fire to the place for which purpose a number of torches were prepared and lighted and an attack was made upon the outer fencing. It was found, however, but weakly defended and was soon taken, for the door-posts being shot away an easy entrance was obtained. A considerable portion of the inner fencing was now found undefended and towards this place a party rushed with lighted torches, while the enemy were kept in play elsewhere. The conflagration spread rapidly on every side and as the besieged endeavored to make their escape their brains were knocked out by a party of the besiegers stationed at the back of the fort for the purpose. During this time, the guns kept up a regular fire with blank cartridges, merely to intimidate the enemy. The conquerors, club in hand, entered the place in several quarters and killed all they met, — men, women and children. The scene was truly horrible. The war-whoop shouted by the combatants, the heart-rending screams of the women and children, the groans of the wounded, the number of the dead, and the fierceness of the conflagration, formed a picture, almost too distracting and awful for the mind steadily to contemplate. Every house that was not on fire was plundered of its contents and the conquerors made a considerable booty of bales of gnatoo, mats, &c.

In a few hours the fortress of Nioocalofa, which had

obstinately and bravely defended every attack for eleven years or more was completely destroyed. When Finow arrived at the place and saw several canoes which had been hauled up in the garrison, shattered to pieces by the shot; and discovered a number of legs and arms lying around and about three hundred and fifty bodies stretched upon the ground, he expressed his wonder and astonishment at the dreadful effect of the guns. He thanked his men for their bravery and Mariner and his companions, in particular, for the great assistance rendered by them.

The king having finished this affair, began to think of returning to Pángaimótoo. Mariner endeavored to persuade him to follow up the advantages of his victory by immediately laying siege to another fortress which, no doubt, would soon have fallen into their hands and the whole island, being struck with dismay, would readily have submitted to his government. But Finow was not yet the complete warrior or he thought, perhaps, that having such powerful weapons in his possession he could reduce the island at any future time.

Pángaimótoo is not more than three-quarters of a mile distant from the Island of Tonga, separated from it only by a long, narrow reef. To this place Finow returned with all his men, intending to go back to Tonga another day. As soon as they landed, they sat down to eat, not having taken any refreshment since morning, with the exception of some of the men, whose stomachs not being the most delicate, had partaken of some yams and plantains that they found roasting along with the bodies of the dead in the general conflagration at Nioocalofa.

A few days afterwards, a small party who went up into the country, according to their daily custom, for the purpose of gathering cocoa-nuts, were attacked by a larger party of the enemy, when one man was killed but the rest escaped back to the *colo*. Upon this, a body of two hundred set out (Mariner among them) in pursuit of the enemy. They found them and were kept at a running fight till they were decoyed beyond a place where another party lay concealed, who immediately rose, attacked them in the rear, and killed about thirty. The Hapai people now began to run and Mariner, with four of the natives who were engaged with another party, found it necessary to decamp also. In crossing a field of high grass, Mariner fell into a hole six feet deep, but his four faithful friends were resolved to save him and three defended the place with their spears, while one helped him out. One of the three was killed on the spot. Being extricated from his perilous situation and finding a large body of the enemy close upon them, they resolved to sell their lives to the utmost advantage. At this moment, their own party, looking round and seeing these four bravely make a stand, came up with all speed to their assistance and a general battle took place which was obstinately fought for some time and at length the enemy was completely put to the rout. While this was going forward, a Hapai chief at some distance from their friends met a Tonga chief under the same circumstances. They immediately engaged with their clubs, one, however, being soon disarmed and the other having broken his club, they fought a long time with their fists and when they were so weak that they could not strike, they grappled with each other and both fell to the ground exhausted with fatigue. The Tonga chief, incapable of injuring his antagonist in any other way, then got his opponent's fingers into his mouth and gnawed them dreadfully. After having thus lain for a long time looking at each other, they gathered a little fresh strength and by mutual agreement each crawled home to his respective fort.

The following day, some of the younger chiefs who had contracted the Fiji habits, proposed to kill the prisoners, lest they should make their escape, and then to roast and eat them. This proposal was readily agreed to, by some because they liked this sort of diet, and by others because they wanted to try it, thinking it a manly and warlike habit. There was also another motive, viz., a great scarcity of provisions; for some canoes which had been sent to the Hapai Islands in quest of provisions, were unaccountably detained and the garrison was already threatened with distress. Some of the prisoners were soon despatched; their flesh was cut up into small portions, washed with sea-water, wrapped up in plantain leaves, and roasted under hot stones. Two or three were emboweled and baked whole, the same as a pig. Mariner was not tempted to partake of this kind of diet, though the smell of it, when cooked, was exceedingly delicious. A few days now elapsed without any signs of the canoes from Hapai and the distress of those who did not choose to eat human flesh was very great. Mariner had been two days and a half without eating anything when, passing by a house where they were cooking something, he walked in with the pleasing hope of getting something that his stomach would bear, if it were only a piece of a rat. On inquiry, he was told they had some pork and a man offered him a piece of liver, which he eagerly accepted and was raising to his mouth, when he saw, by the smile on the countenance of the man, that it was human liver. Overcome by disgust, he threw it in the man's face, who only laughed and asked him if it were not better to eat good meat than die of hunger.

When Captain Cook visited these islands, cannibalism was scarcely thought of amongst them; but the Fiji people soon taught them this, as well as the art of war and a famine, which happened some time afterwards, rendered the expedient for a time almost necessary. On this occasion, they waylaid and murdered one another to supply themselves with food and they still tell an anecdote of four brothers, who, in this time of scarcity, invited their aunt to come and partake of a large yam which they said they had secretly procured. The poor woman, glad of the idea of getting something to eat and pleased with the kindness of her nephews, went to their house where they soon despatched her and she herself formed the materials of a repast.

Since that time, there was once a great scarcity at one of the fortresses on the Island of Tonga called Nookoo Nookoo and two daughters of a chief of this place agreed to play at the game of lafo against two young chiefs belonging to the same place, upon the following conditions: if the girls won the game they were to divide a yam which they had in their possession and give half to the young chiefs; but if, on the contrary, these won the game, they were still to have half the yam, but were to go out and kill a man and give half his body to the girls. The result was that the latter won the game and giving half their yam to the two chiefs they waited for the performance of the agreement. The two young men set out under cover of the darkness of the night and concealed themselves near an enemy's fortress. Early in the morning, a man came out of the fencing to fetch some salt water from the shore in cocoa-nut shells which he carried with him for the purpose. When he approached the place where the two lay concealed, they started out upon him, killed him with their clubs and at the risk of their lives, brought his body to Nookoo Nookoo where they divided it in halves, and faithfully performed their promise with the young women.

Having remained three weeks at Tonga in daily expectation of an attack from the enemy and seeing yet no signs of it, Finow and his warriors departed for the Hapai Islands. After arriving home he directed his attention against the Island of Vavaoo. But, at this time, there arrived from the Navigator's Islands, Finow's son and heir, after an absence of five years. With him came another great chief whose name was Voona and who had formerly been chief of Vavaoo. They and their retinue had sailed from Hamoa in six canoes, one of which, containing sixty persons and all the prince's treasure, was lost in a gale of wind. In their way they had touched at Vavaoo, not knowing the political state of the island, and were very near being forcibly detained; but observing something suspicious in the conduct of the people they put off to sea again and thus made their escape in time.

Their arrival at Lefooga occasioned great feasting and rejoicing, which lasted many days and served to divert the king from his warlike projects. Two daughters of chiefs had, for several years, been kept apart and reserved to be the wives of the young prince. He had, indeed, brought two wives with him, natives of that place; but finding that his friends at home had not been unmindful of him in this particular, he resolved to marry these young maidens also; and, partly to please his own humor and partly to afford a little amusement to the Hapai people, he resolved that the ceremony should be performed after the manner of the Navigator's Islands.

The ceremony and rejoicings being over, Finow again began to turn his attention towards Vavaoo. In the first place, he despatched canoes to the different Hapai Islands with orders to each that all the male inhabitants (excepting two of the oldest for each plantation, to keep them clear of weeds, &c., the yams being all planted) should assemble within ten days at Lefooga, armed with clubs and spears and supplied with a good store of provisions. Being all arrived within the time proposed, Finow issued orders to all his forces to prepare for a review. On the appointed day they assembled on a *malái,* to the amount of about six thousand, all armed and painted and dressed according to some warlike fancy. Finow then delivered a speech in which he declared his opinion that the Tonga mode of warfare had hitherto been upon a very bad principle; and that, instead of running forward and then retreating, accordingly as they met with advantages or disadvantages, they ought rather to remain together in a body and not to retreat on every trifling occasion, but to push forward with the most determined courage and thus dash terror into the minds of their enemies; or, by standing their ground with unconquerable steadiness, to strike them with astonishment at their fortitude and strength. Such, he had heard, was the way of fighting in England (meaning Europe at large) and it claimed his highest admiration. "And," he added, "if any man sees the point of a spear advancing upon his breast, he is not to run back like a coward, but push forward upon it and, at the risk of his life, deal destruction on his foe." This last sentence he bellowed forth in a tone and loudness of voice that made every one tremble, for in this particular he was very remarkable. When powerfully and passionately excited, the sound of his voice was like the roaring of a wild beast and might be heard at an incredible distance.

Having finished his speech, several of his warriors ran up to him, striking their clubs furiously on the ground, bidding him not to be afraid of his enemies for that, comparatively speaking, there were no real warriors in Vavaoo and that they would stand by him to the very last. The king then addressed them again, describing in a more particular manner how they were to proceed in their encounter with the enemy, on the approach of whom they were all to sit down on the ground and remain perfectly still, as if unconcerned in what was going forward; and, even though the enemy were to throw spears and discharge arrows, they were, nevertheless, to remain motionless till they received orders to rise and rush upon them in a body. This they were to do with ardor and impetuosity and he was quite certain, he said, that such a sudden and bold attack would put them completely to the rout. He then made them

View at Anamooka, Tonga Islands

From an engraving by W. Byrne, in Cook's *Voyages*, London, 1784

BOXING MATCH AT HAPAEE, TONGA ISLANDS
From an engraving by I. Taylor, in Cook's *Voyages*, London, 1784

practise this manœuvre several times. Lastly, he spirited them up with thoughts of glory and honor, telling them at the same time, that death was a thing to be despised, not to be feared, by a brave man whose name would still live with a lasting life, when his body was buried in the dust. He then dismissed them with orders that those belonging to the northern islands might immediately return home, but were shortly to proceed to Haano, the northernmost island of all the Hapais, and there to await the arrival of him and all his southern forces on their way to Vavaoo.

A few days afterwards, all affairs being settled in regard to the management of the plantations, the canoes were refitted and launched and early in the morning, the king and all the forces with him (about four thousand strong) proceeded to Haano, about three leagues to the north, to join those who, according to orders, were waiting for them. At Haano the king was received with customary feasting and rejoicing and on the following day the gods were consulted in regard to the expedition. The answer given by the priests was, that the king should proceed to Vavaoo with three canoes only, and offer terms of peace in the most friendly manner. Finow, having by this time had sufficient opportunity to reflect coolly and deliberately and therefore more wisely, upon this business, entered readily into the measure. Three canoes were got ready and Finow with some of the choicest fighting men, of such description as the oracle approved of, went on board. Mariner was in the king's canoe and two other Englishmen were on board one of the others, and they proceeded towards Vavaoo.

As they approached the shores of the island, they came up with several canoes belonging to it, endeavoring to make their escape, for they fancied these were only the head canoes of a large fleet drawing near to make an attack upon Vavaoo. The king, however, informed them that he was not coming with warlike intentions, but that his object was peace and he was paying them a visit for the sole purpose of adjusting matters amicably. He then dismissed them and they paddled away immediately for that part of the island where the great fortress was situated. As the expedition passed a point about five miles to the southward of the fort, a number of natives were seen on the beach, painted and dressed after the manner of war and armed with clubs and spears. They menaced the visitors with every martial gesture, furiously splashing up the water with their clubs and shouting the war-whoop loudly and repeatedly. When they had proceeded a little farther there came up to them a canoe from the garrison with a warrior who wore a turban on his head. He demanded the object of this visit and said he was ready to fight. Finow in answer told him the purpose of his coming, which was to make a peace; and whatever his enemies might think of him that was the object which was nearest his heart. No sooner did the Vavaoo warrior hear this unexpected declaration, than he pulled off his turban and taking a piece of cava root, went on board Finow's canoe and having presented the cava to the king he kissed his feet as a mark of respect. The king then dismissed him desiring him to relate to his chiefs the object of his coming and that he should, the same evening, if they would permit him, pass on to

Nëáfoo, to leave cava there and the following morning proceed to the fortress to adjust terms of peace.

As soon as the warrior departed with his message, Finow directed his course up an inlet to Nëáfoo where he arrived and landed without any opposition and having left cava with the usual ceremony, he returned on board and passed the night in another branch of the inlet leading up to the fortress towards which, early the following morning, he proceeded with the three canoes. At first, he intended to land in person and ascend the hill to address the garrison; but from this he was dissuaded by his chiefs. He then determined to go near to the shore in a small canoe which they had in tow, and be led along the shelf by his matabooles, wading through the water which was scarcely three feet deep. To this, also, his friends objected being apprehensive that if he left the large canoe in the way he proposed and approached too near the beach, his temper might be so worked into a rage by the insults of the natives as to induce him to rush on shore and run the risk of being killed. But Finow replied, by way of apology for not yielding to their advice, that it was the part of a brave man to keep himself perfectly cool and collected when insulted and that he was resolved to act up to this character. Matters being thus arranged, he went into the small canoe and was led along by the matabooles. As they drew near to the shore, many of the natives called out to them, saying a number of things in derision. One man threw them a piece of yam, another a piece of pork, telling them it was to be the last they should get from Vavaoo. Then they inquired whether they were not quite tired of living upon the scanty al-

lowance of the Hapai Islands. They next threw them a
piece of gnatoo, advising them in the most friendly
manner, to wear that instead of scrubbing their skins
with the coarse mats of Hapai and as this was all they
meant to give them, they were to tear it in small pieces
divide it among them and each wear a rag.

During all these insults, the king, contrary to the
expectation of every one (for he was of a very irritable
temper) kept himself perfectly cool and said nothing.
When he had arrived near enough to address them con-
veniently, he made a speech of about an hour's length.
He told them how much he loved and respected his
aunt (Tóë Oomoo) and nothing grieved him more, he
said, than that his best intentions should be thus regarded with suspicion; but he hoped that their candor
and liberality, upon a little cool reflection, would lead
them to place that confidence in him which his own
consciousness of upright intentions gave him reason to
expect and he trusted that they would submit to his
rule and government as formerly. To this some of the
Vavaoo chiefs replied that they should be willing enough
to acknowledge him king, as formerly, provided he
would reside altogether at Vavaoo and interdict all
communication with the Hapai people, among whom
there were many designing chiefs of whose treacherous
policy they had good reason to be afraid; or, if he did
not choose to remain altogether at Vavaoo, he might
reside at Hapai and they would send him annual tribute, as usual, upon condition that neither he nor his
chiefs nor any of the people of Hapai, would visit Vavaoo under any pretext whatsoever; for, as they were
quite tired of disturbances and insurrections, they

heartily wished to keep away all who were promoters of discord, all ambitious and discontented chiefs, all, in short, whose tempers were too fickle to love a peaceful and quiet life; and, as to the large fortress, they declared it had been constructed merely for the purpose of self-defence. Finow then took up the discourse, stating that he could not give his consent to terms which were inconsistent with his dignity as supreme governor both of Hapai and Vavaoo and that it was exceedingly hard he should suffer for the rashness and impolicy of others and that they should cease to put that confidence in his wisdom and justice which he hoped he had always merited. The king then ordered his matabooles to conduct him to his canoe, and, turning towards the Vavaoo people, said, "Live, then, among yourselves, in idleness, and we will return to Hapai."

During the time Finow was addressing the Vavaoo people, the matabooles and warriors that surrounded his canoe appeared much moved and several shed tears, for his powers of persuasion were such, that, in defending his own cause he seemed to be the most worthy, the most innocent, and the most unjustly used. On this account, the greater chiefs and old matabooles of Vavaoo remained in the fortress, fearing to listen to his arguments, lest, being drawn aside by the power of his eloquence, they might mistake that for true which was not and even lead the young and ardent warriors into an error by persuading them that what he said was reasonable and just.

The fortress, on the top of a steep, rising ground, as seen from the canoes, presented a most formidable and warlike appearance. Its extent seemed enormous and the tops of the white reeds, which were seen at a distance above the banks of red clay, the whole being strongly illuminated by the sun, represented to the imagination of Mariner the spears and javelins of ancient heroes drawn up in battle array. On the top of the banks, a number of warriors armed with clubs and spears, were running to and fro with fine light streamers, full thirteen feet long, attached to their heads and arms, which, floating in the wind, produced a most romantic effect.

The king and his matabooles having returned to their canoe, the expedition proceeded out of the inlet and arrived shortly at a small island on which they landed and stripped it of almost all its cava root. The three canoes afterwards proceeded a little farther onward and put in for the night at a small island called Hoonga, about two miles from Vavaoo. The next morning they resumed their voyage and arrived at Haano, the nearest of the Hapai Islands, in the afternoon.

The day after the return of the expedition, the gods were invoked in the usual way and the oracular answer was, to proceed immediately to war against Vavaoo. All things being in readiness, the following morning the king embarked with the whole of his forces, about five thousand men, besides one thousand women, in fifty large canoes with the four carronades, ammunition, and every thing necessary for a vigorous attack upon the strong fortress of Vavaoo. Towards evening the fleet arrived at Fonnooi-fooa (one of the small islands in the neighborhood of Vavaoo) from which Finow despatched four canoes manned with select warriors, up the inlet towards the fortress, with orders to kill whomsoever they could. They succeeded in killing three men and severely wounding a fourth, whom, with the three dead bodies, they brought to Finow. Killing these three men, in the first attempt upon the enemy, was by no means to be considered a trifling advantage; for it was supposed to augur the protection of the gods and great future successes.

Early in the morning, the Hapai fleet proceeded up the inlet to Nëáfoo, where they landed safely, leaving the women in the canoes. The four carronades were planted opposite the house of a neighboring *malái*, ready to be drawn up the following morning to the fortress, which was about three miles off. The day was spent in settling and arranging sundry matters.

Early the following morning, Finow divided his army into three grand divisions; the right wing was commanded by Toobó Tóa, the left by Lioofau, chief of Haano, and the centre by Finow himself; the guns were allotted, two to the centre and one to each flank, and were managed by seven Englishmen, besides Mariner and a black native of South America, taken by the *Port au Prince* in one of her prizes. Matters being thus arranged and Finow having repeated the orders he had formerly issued, viz., that his men should keep themselves perfectly steady and not attack the enemy till they were quite close to them, — the army began its march towards the garrison. After four or five hours' interrupted progress, owing chiefly to the weight of the guns and the badness of the road, they arrived before the fortress, on the banks of which a vast number of the

enemy were assembled. As they approached, a shower
of arrows was discharged upon them; but Finow ordered a mataboole to advance forward and request an
armistice that each party might take leave of what
friends and relations they might have among their op-
ponents; which being granted, a number came out of
the garrison to take a farewell of their relatives, — perhaps the last farewell of those who were about to fight
against them.

Here ensued a moving scene; many tears were shed
on both sides and many a last embrace exchanged.
This affecting spectacle had lasted about two hours,
when a circumstance accidentally occurred, unfortunate enough in its consequences, but which might have
turned out still more so. One of the enemy, upon the
outer bank of the fortress, wantonly shot an arrow at
Mariner, but which fortunately missed him and stuck
in a tree close at his elbow. He immediately turned
about and discovering the man who discharged it, levelled his musket on the impulse of the moment, and
shot him dead upon the spot. Instantly the enemy
sounded the war-whoop and all was uproar and confusion. The king, not understanding the cause, was in
a most violent rage with Mariner and would forthwith
have despatched him with his club had he been near
enough. His matabooles did all they could to calm his
temper but he was not easily pacified. He sent a man
to Mariner to demand his musket; but the latter, feeling himself aggrieved, peremptorily refused. Finow, by
this time becoming somewhat more calm and learning
the true cause of the disaster, was speedily reconciled.

In the mean time, the enemy conceiving this to be a

piece of treachery, returned to their intrenchments and assailed the besiegers with showers of arrows. The king now ordered the great guns to open a fire upon the fort; but they seemed to do little or no injury to the works owing to the height of the place and the strength of the embankment. Several, however, were killed who ventured outside of it. The firing had lasted, with occasional intermissions, during six or seven hours, when a considerable number of the enemy were perceived coming out of the fencing and sheltering themselves behind the banks with the evident intention of sallying forth. Upon this, the king ordered all his men to sit down and to remain perfectly quiet and steady, although the enemy should advance quite close to them, till they received his further orders to rise up and rush upon them. They accordingly sat down.

A party of fifteen or sixteen now came down from the fort and seven or eight of the Hapai people ran forward to skirmish with them. One of the advanced party of the enemy came up to within fifteen or sixteen yards of the carronade of which Mariner had the charge and there stood, brandishing his spear in a threatening attitude. Mariner immediately fired the gun at him, but the moment the match was applied the man fell flat on his face and the shot missed him. A moment after he sprang up again and advanced to within ten paces of the gun, dancing and making sundry warlike gesticulations. He then brandished and threw his spear intending it to enter the gun but it stuck against the muzzle Mariner, astonished at the boldness and presumption of this warrior, was determined to punish him for his rashness and accordingly levelled his musket, but just as he was pulling the trigger, an arrow struck the barrel of the piece and caused him to miss his aim. The warrior then shouted aloud and returned with all speed to the fortress.

The main body of the enemy was still stationed behind the banks, upon places cut for them to stand on, so that they were defended breast high and thus had an opportunity of discharging their arrows in abundance without much risk of receiving a shot in return. After a time, however, they came forth from their stronghold and assembled on the outside, forming themselves quickly into three divisions, the same as Finow's army. Having stationed themselves outside the bank the whole advanced slowly and steadily forward. Finow's men still remained seated on the ground, according to the orders that had been given them, except a few, who danced before them by way of showing their contempt for the enemy and of provoking them to hostilities.

When the enemy had advanced to within thirty paces they threw their spears and instantly the Hapai army, too eager to remain longer quiet, sprang up and rushing upon their foes, a close engagement commenced which was obstinately maintained for about an hour, when the enemy were repulsed and beaten completely back into their fortress. It was now twilight, but the Hapai warriors pursued them to their very doors. One chief in particular, Chioolooa, although he was wounded in the breast by a five-barbed spear, the shaft of which he had broken off, rushed even within the banks of their fortress and there knocked out a man's brains. In making his retreat, however, he was wounded in the back by another spear, which, not being barbed, he drew out and ran back to his own party; but the wound was mortal and he lingered till the next day.

Night was now set in but by Finow's orders, a firing was kept up, with stones, to avoid a waste of shot, because no good aim could be taken. This lasted for about an hour. The king's matabooles then made several speeches to the garrison, soliciting the Vavaoo chiefs to submit to the government of Finow; but they objected, under the apprehension that they should be afterwards killed by the treachery of the king. Finow then addressed them, threatening to remain there the whole night and the next day to set about building a fort opposite theirs and to keep up the war until they either yielded or were destroyed.

Shortly after this, however, he gave orders to his men to repair as silently and as speedily as possible to Nëáfoo. He deceived the enemy in this way to prevent them from proceeding by another road and cutting off his retreat. The guns were given in charge to some of the principal warriors, with men under their command to drag them along. The labor of doing this for three miles was by no means trifling, particularly as the road was very uneven. They swore heartily at all guns and all Englishmen for making them and wanted to know why they could not construct them a little lighter or, at least, as they had ingenuity enough to make the guns they ought to have, they said, the ingenuity also to make legs for them to walk with.

Having arrived at Nëáfoo, the king, his chiefs, matabooles, Mariner, and some of the Englishmen went on board the canoes to pass the night.

The next morning armed parties were sent out to cut reeds for the purpose of building a fortress at Nëáfoo. Finow and his principal chiefs remained to lay out the plan, while others were employed in digging a ditch about fourteen feet wide and ten feet deep. The spot on which this fortress was planned out, was so situated that one side was close upon the sea-shore, on a steep, rocky bank and therefore required no further defence for the enemy had no large canoes, having broken up all they had to make small ones and with these it would be imprudent to venture as far as Nëáfoo lest their retreat should be cut off by Finow's larger and swifter canoes. In the course of the day the fencing and ditch were tolerably well completed so that the following night the greater part of the army slept on shore; but they were not without alarm, for about midnight a small party of the enemy, having come down to reconnoitre, looked through the openings of some part of the fencing that was not quite finished and seeing several of the men sitting round a fire conversing together they threw several spears at them, which wounded many and struck all with a panic. The whole garrison was instantly in a state of confusion and a great number so far lost their presence of mind as to endeavor to make their escape on board the canoes. In this attempt, forgetting that it was low water, they leaped from off the banks and fell upon the shelf of rocks below, in consequence of which several of them had broken arms and legs and sundry contusions which, together with the fright, producing universal spasm (tetanus) in some of them, caused their death in a day or two afterwards.

In three days the fortress was completed and the guns

stationed one at each of the four entrances, of which there were two in front (on the inland side) and one on each of the other two sides. Finow then gave orders that a strong party should go forth early in the morning, towards the enemy's fortress, and destroy all the plantations they could come at, but in case of an attack they should make their retreat as speedily as possible. In the afternoon, they returned laden with yams, plantains, &c., but, having met with a sudden attack from the enemy, had lost several of their men. They brought intelligence that they had discovered a large field of fine yams nearly full grown, but it was so well defended that they could not with prudence make an attack upon it. Finow resolved to remain quiet the following night, lest the enemy should be lying in wait for him, but the night after that to proceed with a large and strong party to plunder and destroy this plantation.

Finow set off very early in the morning with the far larger part of his men, leaving the remainder, under the command of Lioofau, to take care of the *colo*. He proceeded towards the fortress of Felletoa, where the enemy finding themselves surrounded and seeing no other resource than to endeavor to force their way through, made the attempt and succeeded after a hard struggle, attended by great slaughter. Sixty of the enemy were killed and fourteen or fifteen of the Hapai people also fell. The enemy now retreated towards the field of yams to join these who were stationed there for its defence and Finow, thinking it hazardous to make a further attack retired back upon Nëáfoo taking with him the sixty dead bodies.

The king and his army being arrived at their fortress,

the sixty bodies were shared out to the different gods that had houses dedicated to them within the place. In performing this ceremony, the people formed a large circle on the ground with the king at the upper end. The bodies being placed in a row before Finow, a man rose and counting the bodies, declared aloud their number. The king then ordered that so many should be allotted to such a god and so many to such another and so of the rest. This being done the bodies were carried away and laid before the houses of the different gods to whom they were allotted, where, after they had remained three or four hours, those who had left relations among the garrison of Nëáfoo were carried away and buried; and the remainder, which were only nine or ten in number, were conveyed to the water side and there disposed of in different ways. Two or three were hung up on a tree; a couple were burnt; three were cut open from motives of curiosity, to see whether their insides were sound and entire, and to practise surgical operations upon; and lastly, two or three were cut up to be cooked and eaten, of which about forty men partook. This was the second instance of cannibalism that Mariner witnessed. The natives of these islands are not to be called cannibals on this account for it is generally held in abhorrence and when occasionally done, it is only by young warriors who do it in imitation of the Fiji Islanders, attaching to it an idea that there is something in it designating a fierce, warlike and manly spirit. When they returned to Nëáfoo, after their inhuman repast, most persons who knew it, particularly women, avoided them, saying, "Iá-whé moe ky-tangata," — Away! you are a man-eater.

For some time past several of Finow's men had been killed in different instances, by three or four of the enemy, under the command of a warrior named Moteitá, a most expert and daring fellow who often ventured by night and early in the morning, close up to the *colo* of Nëáfoo, to kill any stragglers they could meet with. One morning a party of Finow's men, twelve or fourteen in number, among whom was Mariner, being out on a little excursion, surprised four of the enemy who were busily employed digging *ma* in a pit. These they immediately laid hold of and dragged out to take them home prisoners. Imagining they had got Moteitá and his followers, who had so often committed depredations upon them, they resolved to make a signal example of their prisoners. A young chief, however, objected to this measure and proposed that it would be better to decapitate them at once and take their heads home. This plan was immediately assented to; but some one observing that they had no knives with them, another remarked there was something that would do as well; and taking up a shell from a neighboring spot where some persons had been eating large pearl oysters, he proposed to proceed to work with oyster-shells as substitutes for knives. This was immediately approved of and the four unfortunate victims were taken in hand.

It was in vain that they begged their lives protesting that they were not the persons they had taken them for. In vain did Mariner point out the cruelty of the act, urging them at least to kill them first speedily and cut off their heads afterwards. To this remonstrance they answered that their prisoners deserved to be severely punished for the many atrocities they had committed; and as to killing them first and cutting off their heads afterwards, they thought it unnecessary trouble. This horrible piece of cruelty was accordingly committed on the spot. They began the operation (after having stripped themselves to prevent their garments from getting bloody) by haggling at the back of the neck. They then cut gradually round the throat till they had got through every thing but the spine, which they divided by turning the head down and giving it a violent twist. This being done they washed themselves, resumed their *gnatoos* and proceeded with the four heads to the garrison. It was still early when they arrived, and they found the king sitting with his friends, on the *malái,* drinking cava. The four heads were brought to him by different men and placed in the middle of the circle, upright, with their faces towards Finow, who returned his thanks (as customary) to those who had killed them.

A fortnight now elapsed without any material circumstance occurring: almost every day, however, there was some little skirmish with the enemy, but which led to no particular result. At the end of this time, the canoes from Hapai not being yet returned, Finow began to turn his thoughts more seriously than ever towards the large field of yams before spoken of. He made preparations, therefore, for an attack upon it, hoping that, if he did not succeed in procuring some yams, he should, at least, be able to bring the enemy to a general engagement. In this he was successful for a party of his men dispatched to dig up the yams was able to do so at a time when few of the enemy were on guard. The main body warriors were sent for and as soon as they arrived and saw the field of yams completely despoiled they were greatly enraged and immediately in a body fell on Finow's guard which retreated, drawing them into an ambush with a general engagement which lasted for nearly an hour. The day was so rainy that no muskets could be used. During the affair, Mariner received an arrow in his foot, which passed quite through the broadest part of it. Luckily it was not a bearded arrrow; but the wound was, nevertheless, a very bad one; for, the weapon being made of a short, splintering wood, it broke in, and consequently he was afterwards disabled for several months, for the Tonga surgeons have not the best instruments in the world and the pieces of wood they took out from time to time, by no better means than cutting down upon them with sharp shells or bamboo, rendered the affair very tedious and painful.

About a week after the engagement, one of Finow's wives ran away from Nëáfoo. Being shortly missed by the rest of the women, in searching for her it was found that one of his son's wives had taken the same step and it was supposed they had gone together. When this was made known to the king, he left the fortress instantly accompanied by five or six men and directed his course along the main road leading to Felletoa, but without any success. He returned very much dejected and sent to his aunt, Tóë Oomoo (the chief of the enemy) requesting to have his wife returned, stating that it was a war between men and not women; but his remonstrances had no effect. These women both labored under the jealousy and tyrannic influence of Möonga Toobo, Finow's favorite wife. Partly to rid themselves of this and partly to visit and live with relations they had in the opposite garrison, they made their escape and took a by-road near the seashore. On the morning of their departure, Mariner was at some distance from Nëáfoo, gathering shaddocks in a thicket; for, although his wound did not allow him to use any active exertions, yet he now and then went abroad by the help of a stick which, no doubt, was one cause that rendered the cure very tedious. Being up in a tree, he heard a rustling noise in the bushes below and directing his attention to the spot, was surprised to see one of Finow's wives. Prompted by curiosity he came quickly down and seizing her by the arm inquired what caused her to stray so far from the fortress and to expose her person and her life to the insults and cruelty of the enemy. She replied, that she had only come out for a walk and was going shortly to return. To this account he objected that it was too far and too dangerous a walk for her to take alone with the risk of meeting Moteitá and his followers who often concealed themselves in those woods, and declared his suspicion that she intended to run away. She immediately fell on her knees, clasped her hands and begged and entreated most earnestly that he would not prevent her flight from the dominion of tyrany, to the bosom of her relations and appealed most pathetically to his own feelings and affections towards his mother or whatever relatives he might have in his own country, and represented how hard and cruelly severe it would be for any one to prevent him flying to them if it were otherwise in his power. Being moved by the earnestness of her manner and the unfortunate circumstances of her situation, he raised her up and promised not to interfere in her escape nor to divulge the matter to any one and gave her full liberty to proceed whichever way she thought proper.

Finow, for a long time past, had entertained the idea of seizing upon several of the enemy's women who were in the habit of assembling at a certain part of the inlet to gather shellfish; and now that his wife had run away, he was more than ever encouraged to do this by way of retaliation upon Tóë Ooomo for the detention of her. The place where they procured this sort of fish was upon a shelf of rocks (about a foot and a half deep at low water) that ran across the inlet at no great distance from Felletoa. Upon this shelf they were accustomed to fish every day, wading through the water. On these occasions, several men of their own party had frequently alarmed them by rushing out upon them, pretending to be the enemy and had repeated this so often that, at length, they only laughed at the joke and ridiculed the idea of running away. One evening, a party of Finow's men who had formed themselves for the express purpose of making an attack upon these women, set out in a canoe and sailed to a part of the island where they could land unobserved and proceed to the spot where the women were fishing, without any danger of discovery on account of the high bushes that were there in abundance. Having arrived on the spot, at an appointed signal they rushed out upon the women, who immediately set up a hearty laugh, taking them for their old friends so fond of a joke. But when they saw two or three knocked down with clubs, they ran away as fast as their strength and the resistance of the water would let them and the men after them in full pursuit.

There were thirty of them of which five were killed and thirteen taken prisoners; the other twelve escaping safe to the opposite shore. In this affair, the wife of Finow's son was very nearly retaken. She ran so exceedingly swift through the water, knee deep, and the young chief in pursuit of her exerted himself to much to overtake her, although he was near enough to knock her down with his club, that he actually fell through fatigue. It must, however, be said in favor of the chief, that the weight of his club was a great disadvantage, whereas his lovely fugitive ran without any encumbrance, for in her endeavor to quicken her pace, her gnatoo (dress) became loose and fell from her waist. This was the only time that she looked back, from a sense of modesty, to see if it was recoverable; but she was under the necessity of pursuing her flight without it.

The thirteen prisoners were conducted to Nëáfoo, though Finow had given orders that all taken should be killed on the spot. The captors saved their lives, however, partly from motives of humanity, and partly from those of profit (as they could employ them in making gnatoo, &c.). But when they arrived at Nëáfoo, there arose a dispute between relatives of the prisoners, and those who had taken them, the former arguing that they had a claim to the women, according to the old Tonga custom, which decreed, that all persons shall be in the service of their older and superior relations, if those relations think proper to employ them. The captors, on the other hand, grounded their claims on the right of conquest. The dispute ran very high, and they referred it to Finow, who at length, gave his opinion that the proper method would be, under the circumstances, to cut each woman in two and give one half to her relations and the other to the captors. The affair, however, was amicably settled without having recourse to such bloody measures, some being given up to their relatives and others retained upon terms mutually agreeable to all parties.

Finow already had grown tired of the war and soon he artfully negotiated a peace with his enemies and returned home.

Mariner relates that he saw no men at Tonga, nor did he hear of any, who made debauchery the business of their lives. On the contrary, they were wrestlers, racers, boxers, and club-fighters — strong, well-made men with fine swelling muscles. It must be understood, however, that no man was expected to be bound to conjugal fidelity; it was no reproach to intermix his amours, though a married man who did this to excess was thought inconsistent. The women of course occasionally showed jealousy, but it was seldom strongly expressed and rarely led to any fatal consequences.

With respect to the unmarried men, their conduct of course was free, but they seldom made any deliberate attempts upon the chastity of other men's wives. When a woman was taken a prisoner (in war) she generally had to submit; but that was a thing of course and considered neither an outrage nor a dishonor; the only dishonor was in being a prisoner and consequently a sort of servant to the conqueror.

In Tonga it was universally considered a positive duty in every married woman to remain true to her husband. A woman's marriage was frequently independent of her consent, she having been betrothed by her parents, at an early age. Perhaps about one-third were thus betrothed; the remaining two-thirds having married with their free consent. Every married woman must remain with her husband whether she chose or not, until he saw fit to divorce her. Mariner was of the opinion that about two-thirds of the women on the islands were married and of that number full half remained with their husbands until death separated them. The other half were soon divorced and remarried perhaps three, four or five times. The unmarried women lived principally at the mooa, or place where the chiefs lived, and were attendants upon them or their wives.

Mariner's opportunities to observe the social life in the chief's house, were unusual, for, being a foreigner, he was permitted to go into the houses of Finow's wives and converse freely with them, a liberty that no male native could take beside the husband, relations, or the cooks who carried in the victuals. From habit they became so much accustomed to his company and conversation as to think little more of his presence than of one of their own sex and consequently he had every favourable opportunity of becoming acquainted with their habits and their sentiments. He was decidedly of the opinion that infidelity among married women was comparatively rare. There was, moreover, great restriction upon the conduct of married women for they seldom went abroad unaccompanied by female attendants and servants, it not being thought decorous, particularly for the wife of a chief, to walk out by herself.

When a man divorced his wife, which was attended with no other ceremony than just telling her that she

might go, she became perfect mistress of her own conduct and she might marry again, which was often done
a few days afterwards, without the least disparagement
to her character. If she chose to admit a lover occasionally or even to remain at his house without being
considered his wife, she could do this without the least
reproach or need of secrecy. It was thought shameful,
however, for a woman to frequently change her lover.
As for those women who were not actually married,
they could bestow their favours upon whomsoever they
pleased, without any opprobrium. But it must not be
supposed that they were easily won.

Mariner having now nothing in particular in which
to employ himself, the war being at an end, begged of
the king to give up a plantation to him, that he might
amuse himself by seeing it properly cultivated and to
this the king, after a little hesitation, consented. He
was to regulate everything regarding it just as he
pleased and to consider it as his property, together with
all the persons who worked on it, consisting of thirteen
men and eight women. To these the king gave orders
they should pay the same attention and respect to Mariner as to himself or their former chief; he also informed the *matooa,* or overseer, that he had invested
Mariner with full power to despatch any of them with
the club who failed in their duty or neglected in any respect to show proper attention to their new master. As
soon as Mariner entered upon his new possessions, he
gave orders to get ready a large bale of gnatoo, which
he sent to Finow as a present.

About this time Mariner was very near being de-
voured by a shark. One of his servants, that worked

upon the plantation, had laid pots about four feet deep in the water for the purpose of catching cray-fish and Mariner, one afternoon, dived down to examine them in hope of finding fish. The spot was just upon the perpendicular declivity of a shelf of rocks. Having come up to take breath, with the intention of going down a second time, he saw the dorsal fin of a shark gliding swiftly along the surface of the water directly towards him. He instantly clambered upon the reef and sprang on one side and a moment after the shark rushed upon the shelf, in a foot and a half water, within a yard of him, and had some difficulty in getting off again.

Not long after this a ship arrived off the northwest coast of Vavaoo. She proved to be the *Hope,* Captain Chase, of New York. When Mariner heard of her arrival, he was with Finow at the small island of Ofoo, on the eastern coast of Vavaoo, and he immediately asked the king's leave to go on board, who very readily gave him permission. Several matabooles were with him, one of whom whispered something to the king, which Mariner imagining to be prejudicial to himself, endeavored to distract Finow's attention by repeatedly thanking him for his liberal conduct towards him, and expressing the grateful sense he entertained of his long-continued friendship and protection; assuring him that he had no other wish to leave the islands but what was prompted by the natural desire of returning to his native country and the bosom of his friends. In the mean time, he very distinctly heard the king say to the matabole, "But why should I keep him?" and, shortly after, his order to a fisherman to get ready instantly a certain canoe and paddle Mariner on board, removed from his mind a load of anxiety. He again and again thanked his benefactor and taking an affectionate leave of him, got into the canoe and pushed off from the beach. There were three men to paddle, who, after four or five hours' hard pulling, came up alongside the vessel. He saw upon the deck Jeremiah Higgins, John Parish, and Hugh Williams, and hailed the ship, when the captain, or the mate, looked over the quarter and said, "We can't take you, young man; we have more hands than we know what to do with."

Mariner could hardly believe the evidence of his senses. Not take him! when he saw three of his companions already on board! He began to expostulate. "It is no use, your saying any thing; we can't take you," replied the other. He then offered to procure whatever provisions the ship might want, but the unfeeling officer turned his back and gave no answer. Thus, in one minute, from the elevation of hope, his soul sank into despair. Besides suffering the acute pain of disappointment, he also found himself in a very awkward dilemma. If the natives knew that the captain had refused to take him, it would hurt his reputation in their esteem, as they would look upon him to be a low-born *tooa*, without friends or consideration in his own country. Fortunately, during this time, the men in the canoe were too much occupied in viewing the appearance of the ship to pay much attention to him. Having, at length, a little recovered himself he informed the men that, unfortunately, the ship was bound to a country as far from his as his was from Tonga; and, although the captain wished him to come on board, he had determined to remain at Vavaoo until some British ship should arrive. With feelings that almost choked his utterance, he then ordered them to return to Ofoo.

Everybody wondered to see him return. His story, however, was readily believed; but it seemed strange that he had brought them no presents from on board. "What a number of axes he has got for us!" said one, ironically. "And what a heap of looking-glasses!" said another. "Beads will now become quite common," said a third; "for Togi is going to give necklaces to all the girls in Vavaoo." These jokes were mortifying and nothing could be worse-timed; but he endeavored to laugh at their humor and, by way of apology for his neglect, he told them he was so disappointed at not finding the ship bound for his own country, that he had forgotten to ask for some presents; and, besides, that he knew she had very few of those things on board, as she came from a country where they were scarce. Finow endeavored to console him for his disappointment, assuring him, in the kindest manner, that he should go by the next ship bound to his own country.

About a month after this, there arrived from the Fiji islands, four canoes, bringing a Tonga mataboole (one who ranks next to a chief) named Cow Mooala, and his retinue, who had been absent from Tonga many years. He originally had gone to the Fiji islands with a number of young men, for the sake of an excursion and to mingle in the wars of those people; sometimes at one island, sometimes at another. After having been absent about two years, he set sail on his return home and having arrived within sight of Vavaoo, the wind became unfavorable to land and the sea running very high, he was obliged to change his course and make for Hamoa, one of the Navigator's islands;* but the wind soon increasing to a heavy gale, drifted him to the island of Fotoona,† situated to the northwest of Hamoa. As soon as the natives of this place observed his approach, a number of small canoes (for they were not in possession of sailing canoes) came from the shore to meet him, took possession of his canoe and all his property.

Cow Mooala's canoe was laden with sandal-wood, esteemed a very rich commodity at Tonga; but not one splinter of it was ever returned to him, although the natives of Fotoona could make no use of it, not having adopted the practice of oiling themselves. His canoe was dragged on shore, broken to pieces, and offered up to the gods; afterwards the planks were shared out among the chiefs, who devoted them to the purpose of building smaller canoes, one large canoe making four small ones.

Cow Mooala described their method of fighting which was conducted, according to his account, in two different modes; that is to say, with spears and with shark's teeth. When a man pierced his enemy with a pike, he endeavored to lift him up from the ground on one end of it, or, if opportunity allowed, he called some of his comrades to his assistance, who thrusting their pikes also into him, they lifted him high in the air and carried him in triumph. The mode of fighting with shark's teeth was as follows: The teeth being fixed, in three rows, on the palm and fingers of a species of glove made of the plaited bark of the *heábo,* and both hands being armed in this manner, every man endeavored to come to a close scuffle with his antagonist and to tear

*Samoa islands. †One of the Gilbert group.

open his bowels with these horrible weapons. The supreme chief, in Cow Mooala's time, was a man of remarkable bodily strength, and was always accustomed to fight with this sort of gauntlet, in preference to the pike, not, however, to tear open the bowels of his enemy, but merely to catch a firmer hold of him whilst he threw him on his face. He would then place his foot upon the small of his back and, seizing fast hold of the hair of his head, so bend his spine as to break it. With small men or boys he would not take so much trouble, but, laying them across his knee, as one would a stick, break their backs without further ceremony. By way of defence from the pikes of their adversaries, they wore, on the left side, a species of armor made of the husk of the cocoa-nut, plaited thick and stuffed and quilted on the inside with the loose husk, picked fine. This reached from the axilla down to the hip.

Cow Moola remained at Fotoona at least a twelvemonth, affording him time to build another large canoe fit for his voyage in which he again set sail, with presents of gnatoo, mats, &c., and a sufficient quantity of provisions for his voyage, and directed his course for the Fiji islands, for the purpose of laying in another cargo of sandal-wood. He had now on board thirty-five of his own people, including fourteen or fifteen Tonga women; besides whom he had four male natives of Fotoona, who begged to go with him that they might visit distant countries.

Owing to the wind, he deviated a little from his course, but at length arrived safe at Navihi Levoo, one of the Fiji islands, to the northwest. Here Cow Mooala took up his residence with the chief of the island, where he remained a considerable length of time, assisting in the war with other islands. The inhabitants of Navihi Levoo are not only more ferocious, but they are much better skilled in war than those of the other islands, and are therefore much dreaded by them. To give themselves a fiercer appearance, they bore a hole through the soft part of the septum of the nose, through which, in time of war, they stick a couple of feathers, nine or twelve inches long, which spread out over each side of the face, like immense mustaches, giving them a very formidable appearance. The worst feature of their barbarism is the practice of eating human flesh, which they carry to a greater extent than any of the other Fiji people. The chief of the island was reported to have a remarkable appetite in this way; for he was not in the habit of sacrificing his prisoners immediately, but of actually ordering them to be operated on, and put in such a state as to get both fat and tender and afterwards to be killed as he might want them. The hands and feet, particularly the latter, were considered the choicest parts.

Cow Mooala, after remaining a considerable time at Navihi Levoo, sailed with his people for Tacownove, which is a district on the western side of Pau, the largest of the Fiji islands. Pau was much resorted to by American vessels, and vessels from Port Jackson, for sandal-wood, which grows to perfection only at a certain part of the island, called Vooía. The principal market for this article was China; and the demand for it so great, in proportion to the smallness of the place which produced it, that it is now growing scarce and consequently, dearer. The chiefs of the Fiji islands very seldom oil themselves and, consequently, require very little of this wood, the principal use of it being to scent the oil. The natives of the Tonga islands, however, who require a considerable quantity of it for the above purpose, complain heavily of its scarcity and what renders the matter still worse for them, is, that the Fiji people, demanding a greater number of axes and chisels for a given quantity of the wood, these implements are growing very scarce at the Tonga islands, and plentiful at Fiji. Before the Tonga people acquired iron implements, they usually gave whale's teeth, gnatoo, mats for sails, and platt; but whale's teeth were exceedingly scarce, and the other articles too bulky for ready exportation. The *sting* of the fish called stingray, was also occasionally given, but these *stings*, which they used for the points of spears, were by no means plentiful. This fish is found in the greatest quantity at an island called Ooea, which lies about midway between Vavaoo and Hamoa. It has already been remarked that the sandal-wood tree will not bear to be transplanted to Tonga.

During the time Cow Mooala was at Pau, a vessel was wrecked on a reef off that island. All the crew, except a couple, perished. The wreck was taken possession of by the natives. They got out of her a number of dollars and a quantity of muslins, with some other East India commodities. From these circumstances it would appear that she was an American smuggler on her return from Peru, with part of her original cargo undisposed of. One of the men was afterwards killed in a quarrel with the other. Mariner could not learn the name of the vessel.

Shortly after Cow Mooala's arrival, Finow's younger daughter, about seven years of age, fell sick and died to the great grief of her father. Before the death of the child, Finow was unwell, but had partially recovered; and, after the funeral ceremonies were ended, he retired to a small house, near the *malái;* and there he grew worse very rapidly and soon breathed his last, with violent struggles.

The king was succeeded by his son, who also bore the name of Finow, and about a month or six weeks after the funeral ceremonies were finished, Finow, who had not broken his head (as they call it) at the grave of his father, because, perhaps, on a public occasion, it would have looked in him like an ostentatious display of what might have been thought *affected* feeling, resolved to perform this ceremony in a more private manner, accompanied only by a few of his warriors. Accordingly, one morning, he and his men began to prepare themselves for this affair, when, unfortunately, an accident happened, for Mariner, on entering the house, happened to sneeze! Immediately every one present threw down his club; for who would proceed on so important an expedition after so dire an omen? Finow's eyes flashed with the fire of rage and he cursed him with the most bitter curse and snatching up a club, he would have instantly despatched him if some of the men present had not pushed Mariner out of the house, while the rest held Finow. Shortly after, Finow, having consulted with his men upon the subject of Mariner's sneezing, resolved that, as he was a foreigner and had different gods, his sneezing was not to be considered of any consequence; they then proceeded to the grave to perform the ceremony of head-breaking, when Finow and all his men, inspired with enthusiasm, cut and bruised their heads in a shocking manner. Finow in particular, not contented with the usual instruments made use of a saw, the teeth of which he struck against his skull with such vehemence and good will that he staggered, as he went home, with loss of blood.

Mariner, having gone to his plantation, resolving to remain there and see how long Finow would be contented without his company.

In the evening (a few hours after reaching his plantation), a girl came with a message from his adopted mother, assuring him that he was perfectly safe, Finow having expressed his extreme sorrow for his own conduct. She advised him, however, not to return to the king till after several invitations, nor even till he came in person to request a renewal of his friendship. He accordingly took her advice, and remained at the plantation ten days, notwithstanding repeated messages from Finow and entreaties to return; and, at last, he so intimidated the messengers, by threatening to shoot them if they appeared again with that errand, that Finow at length resolved to fetch him himself and accordingly, one morning entered his house and, having awakened him, saluted him in the kindest and most affectionate manner, begged his pardon for his too hasty conduct and wept abundantly. After this they were inseparable friends.

In this time of peace, when Mariner had nothing in which to employ himself but recreation and amusement, sometimes with Finow or other chiefs, and sometimes by himself, he would frequently go out for two or

TONGA ISLAND GIRLS

From a photograph in the Peabody Museum of Archæology and Ethnology, Cambridge, Mass.

A Tonga Island House

From a photograph in the Peabody Museum of Archæology and Ethnology, Cambridge, Mass

three days together, among the neighboring small islands on a fishing excursion. One evening as he was returning homeward in his canoe, after having been out three days, he espied a sail in the westward horizon, just as the sun had descended below it, and pointing it out to the three men in the canoe with him (his servants, who worked on his plantation) desired them to paddle him on board, holding out to them what an advantageous opportunity now offered itself to enrich themselves with beads, axes, looking-glasses, &c. — an opportunity which they might never again meet with. To this they replied, that they had seen her before; but that their fear of his wishing to go on board prevented them from pointing her out to him, for they had often heard their chiefs say that they never meant to let him go, if they could help it; and hence they were apprehensive that their brains would be knocked out if they suffered him to escape. Mariner then promised them very rich rewards. After conversing together, and whispering between themselves, they told him they owed it as a duty to their chiefs to refuse his request and, upon this, they began to paddle towards the nearest shore. Mariner instantly took up his musket from behind him and struck the nearest man a violent blow or stab, near the loins, with the muzzle of the piece, exclaiming at the same time, "Strike your Hotooa! There's your death!" This lunge produced a dangerous wound for the musket, being a very old one, had grown quite sharp at the muzzle. The man immediately fell flat in the bottom of the canoe, senseless, and scarcely with a groan. Mariner instantly pulled his legs out straight and then presented his musket to the other two, who appeared panic-struck, and threatened to blow out their brains if they did not instantly obey his orders, and pull towards the vessel. They accordingly put about, and made towards her. The wounded man was a piece of a warrior, but the other two had never been in battle and supposed he could fire off his musket as often as he pleased, without loading it.

They did not come up with the vessel till about daylight next morning. During the whole night, the man in the bottom of the canoe lay perfectly still and showed no signs of life except a slight gurgling noise in his throat, which was heard now and then. As soon as the canoe pulled up alongside the brig, Mariner, without stopping to hail, jumped up into the main chains and was very near being knocked overboard by the sentinel who took him for a native, for his skin was grown very brown, his hair very long and tied up in a knot with a turban round the head, and an apron, of the leaves of the chi-tree was round his waist. This disguise would have warranted the conduct of the sentinel, but as soon as Mariner spoke English and told him he was an Englishman, he allowed him to come on deck, where the captain cordially shook hands with him. The latter had heard from the captain of a schooner, the whole unfortunate affair of the *Port au Prince,* for the schooner had brought away two men from one of these islands during the time that Mariner was in another quarter upon some business for Finow.

The captain presented him with a pair of trousers and a shirt and as the latter was neither very new nor very clean, he took pains to wash it and hang it up in the rigging to dry; but in the morning it had disappeared, at the honest instigation of somebody; so his whole stock of apparel consisted of the pair of trousers; nor did he get better provided until he arrived in China, about seven weeks afterwards.

The brig proved to be the *Favorite*, Captain Fisk, from Port Jackson, about 130 tons burden and had on board about 90 tons of mother-of-pearl shells procured from the Society islands. She intended to make up her voyage with sandal-wood from the Fiji islands and thence to proceed to China. Mariner requested the captain to give the men in the canoe, which brought him, some beads, as a reward for their trouble, and also an axe, as a present for Finow. The captain complied and the canoe left the ship with a message to the king, requesting him to come on board. By this time there were about two hundred small canoes near the vessel and several large ones, so that all the people of Vavaoo seemed to be assembled to view the brig, for the whole beach was also crowded. As the vessel was very short of provisions, a very brisk traffic was carried on with the natives for yams, hogs, &c.; hence orders were given to the crew not to purchase any more trinkets till they had procured plenty of provisions. About the middle of the day, Finow came alongside, with his sister and several of her female attendants, bringing off as a present for Mariner, five large hogs and forty large yams, each weighing not less than thirty pounds, and some of the largest sixty or seventy pounds. Notwithstanding repeated messages from the chiefs on shore to Finow, requesting him to return, he resolved to sleep on board that night, if the captain would allow him, which he readily did. The women, however, wished to return, not liking the thought of trusting their persons among a number of strange men, and Mariner found it very difficult to remove their scruples, by assuring them that they should not be molested. At length, however, they consented to remain, on his promise to take care of them and to roll them all up in a sail, in which state they lay the whole night, in the steerage, and, as they said, slept comfortably. As to Finow, he was very well contented with sleeping on a sail on the cabin deck. As the weather was remarkably fine, the brig did not come to an anchor but stood off and on during the whole of the night.

At daylight, canoes came alongside in great numbers; but from prudent motives, dictated by former disasters, no more than three of the natives were allowed to come on board at a time, six sentinels being kept constantly on deck for that purpose. In the canoes were several chiefs who came to request Finow to return on shore, as the people were greatly alarmed lest he should form a determination of going to *Papalangi* (land of white people). They brought off some cava for him, but which he declined drinking, saying that he had tasted some on board (wine) which was far preferable; indeed, he considered it so much superior that the thoughts of cava quite disgusted him. He made a hearty dinner at the captain's table, ate plenty of roast pork, with which he admired very much the flavor of the sage and onions; the fowls he cared very little about, but partook of some made dishes. The women also ate very heartily and Finow handled a knife and fork, though for the first time in his life, with great dexterity. Sometimes, indeed, his majesty forgot himself a little and laid hold of the meat with his fingers; but instantly recollecting that he was doing wrong, he would put it down again, exclaiming, *"Woé! gooa te gnalo!"* (Eh, I forgot myself!)

Mariner had on shore, in a concealed place, the journal of the *Port au Prince,* which he was now desirous of securing. To get it again into his possession, he obtained the captain's consent to detain Finow Fiji (the king's uncle) on board, till the journal was brought to him; and accordingly two natives were despatched with directions where to find it. They had orders at the same time, to bring back with them three Englishmen that were on shore, viz., James Waters, Thomas Brown and Thomas Dawson. In the mean while, Finow Fiji, on understanding that he was detained a prisoner, turned very pale and was evidently greatly alarmed; and even when Mariner explained to him the cause, he seemed still to think every thing was not right and expressed his apprehension that they were going to take him to England, to answer for the crime of the Hapai people in taking the *Port au Prince,* and murdering the crew. At length the canoe returned with the journal and the Englishmen. James Waters was not disposed, however, to return to England. He was an old man and had become infirm and he reflected that it would be a difficult matter for him to get his bread at home; and as he enjoyed, at Vavaoo, every convenience that he could desire, he chose to end his days there.

Finow's sister, a girl of about fifteen years of age, went on shore and brought on board several other women of rank, who were all greatly pleased that they were allowed to come into the ship and satisfy their curiosity. Finow's sister, who was a very beautiful, lively girl, proposed, in joke, to go to England and see the white women. She asked if they would allow her to wear the Tonga dress, "Though, perhaps," she said, "that would not do, in such a cold country, in the winter season. I don't know what I should do at that time; but Togi tells me that you have hot-houses for plants from warm climates, — so I should like to live all winter in a hot-house. Could I bathe there, two or three times a day, without being seen? I wonder whether I should stand a chance of getting a husband; but my skin is so brown, I suppose none of the young *Papalangi* men would have me; and it would be a great pity to leave so many handsome young chiefs at Vavaoo and go to England to live a single life. If I were to go to England, I would amass a great quantity of beads and then I should like to return to Tonga, because, in England, beads are so common that nobody would admire me for wearing them and I should not have the pleasure of being envied." She said, laughing, that either the white men must make very kind and good-tempered husbands, or else the white women must have very little spirit, for them to live so long together without parting. She thought the custom of having only one wife a very good one, provided the husband loved her; if not, it was a very bad one, because he would tyrannize over her the more; whereas, if his attention was divided between five or six, and he did not behave kindly towards them, it would be very easy to deceive him. These observations, of which Mariner was interpreter, afforded very great amusement. Finow and the late Tooitonga's son (about twelve years of age), together with the females, now commenced dancing and singing, at the request of the captain, which gave the ship's company much entertainment.

The ship now prepared to take her departure from Vavaoo and Mariner took leave of his Vavaoo friends, probably forever. The king again embraced him, in the most affectionate manner, made him repeat his promises to return, if possible, to Tonga and take him back to England that he might learn to read books of history, study astronomy and thus acquire a *Papalangi* mind. At the parting abundance of tears were shed on both sides. Finow returned to his canoe with a heavy heart and Mariner felt all the sweet bitterness of parting from much-loved friends. The canoe returned to the beach and the ship got under way and steered her course to the Hapai islands, leaving Vavaoo and all her flourishing plantations, lessening in the distance.

After two days' stay at the Hapai islands, Captain Fisk ordered the natives out of the vessel and directed his course to the Fiji islands to lay in a stock of sandal-wood for the China market. The *Favorite* arrived at the island of Pau, one of the Fiji Islands, and anchored off a place called Vooiha, famous for sandal-wood, for which the captain soon began to treat with the natives and before the ship's departure laid in several tons. There were several Englishmen or Americans at the island of Pau, but none of them wished to come away in the *Favorite,* except one. As Captain Fisk had already more hands on board than he wanted and as this man was not thrown accidentally (by shipwreck or otherwise) among these people, but had left his ship voluntarily, the captain did not choose to take him.

The *Favorite* having laid in her store of sandalwood, after five or six days' stay at Pau, weighed anchor and resumed her voyage and in about five weeks arrived at Macao. As Mariner had but little money in his possession, he resolved the first opportunity, to enter on board one of the East India Company's ships bound to England and work his passage home. It happened, however, luckily, that he fell in with the officers of the Company's cruiser the *Antelope,* who, taking an interest in his story, corroborated by the account of Captain Fisk, invited him on board the *Antelope,* where he remained for a couple of months till an opportunity offered of going to England on the Honorable East India Company's ship, the *Cuffnells,* which arrived at Gravesend, in June, 1811.

It may be of interest to know the fate of all the ship's company of the *Port au Prince.* Besides the eight natives of the Sandwich islands, there were belonging to the ship fifty-two persons. Twenty-six were on board at the time the ship was taken and of these twenty-six, there were twenty-two massacred on the spot. Of those who were on shore, three, besides Mr. Brown, the whaling master, were also murdered making in all twenty-six who lost their lives. The remaining twenty-six are correctly accounted for in the following list. The eight natives of the Sandwich islands, probably had a hint from their countryman Tooi Tooi, to keep themselves out of harm's way, which they effectually did.

JOHN SCOTLAND, gunner, JACOB MYERS, seaman, WILLIAM FORD, seaman, left Namooca in a small, paddling canoe and were never afterwards heard of;

supposed to have been lost, as a paddle belonging to that canoe was found, shortly afterwards, washed on shore at Namooca Igi.

JOHN HEARSEY, sail-maker, left the island of Tonga in an American vessel; but was accidentally drowned at the Fiji Islands, as reported by some Englishmen at Fiji.

WILLIAM TOWELL, captain's steward, ROBERT FITZGERALD, a boy, left Vavaoo in the *Mercury,* a Botany Bay schooner, at a time when Mariner was at the Hapai Islands. William Towell afterwards lived in Cross Street, Westmoreland Place, City Road.

HUGH WILLIAMS, seaman, JEREMIAH HIGGINS and JOHN PARISH, landsmen, escaped from Vavaoo thirteen months before Mariner, in the *Hope,* Captain Chase, of New York. This was the captain that refused to take Mariner on board, stating that he had hands enough! Jeremiah Higgins afterwards lived at Aylesbury.

JOHN WATSON, seaman, had gone to the Fiji Islands, with a Tonga chief; but Mariner did not hear anything of him there.

SAMUEL CARLTON, boatswain, GEORGE WOOD, carpenter's mate, WILLIAM SINGLETON, landsman, and ALEXANDER MACAY, a boy, were at the island of Tonga at the time the *Favorite* arrived at the Hapai Islands, and lost that opportunity of escape. Mariner afterwards heard that Samuel Carlton came away in another vessel.

JAMES WATERS, ordinary seaman, refused to leave Vavaoo on account of age and infirmities.

NICHOLAS BLAKE, seaman, WILLIAM BROWN, and THOMAS EVERSFIELD, boys, JOHN ROBERTS, a black, native of the island of Tortola, a boy, refused to leave the Hapai islands, under various pretences.

WILLIAM STEVENSON, a child of two years of age, native of the Sandwich Islands, the son of a Botany Bay convict, resident at Woahoo, whence the sailmaker had taken him in the *Port au Prince*, at the request of his father, that he might be brought to his relations in Scotland, to be educated. This child was adopted by the daughter of the late king (the widow of the late Tooi-tonga) and was much noticed. He probably remained at Vavaoo.

ROBERT BROWN, cooper, THOMAS DAWSON, seaman, THOMAS BROWN, landsman, MANUEL PEREZ, seaman and JOSEF, a black. These came away with Mariner in the *Favorite;* all but Thomas Brown were under the necessity of remaining in the East Indies. Thomas Brown got employment on board one of the homeward-bound vessels from China and came to England in the same fleet with Mariner. Thomas Dawson afterwards reached London.

A NARRATIVE OF EVENTS IN THE LIFE OF JOHN BARTLETT OF BOSTON, MASSACHUSETTS, IN THE YEARS 1790-1793, DURING VOYAGES TO CANTON AND THE NORTHWEST COAST OF NORTH AMERICA.

O N March 19th, 1790, I shipped on board the ship *Massachusetts*, Capt. Job Prince, commander, bound on a voyage to Canton in China. She had been built at Quincy, by Daniel Briggs, for the firm of Shaw & Randall, and when brought to Boston, under jury masts, she excited a considerable sensation for she was the largest merchant vessel built at that time in the United States and nearly eight hundred tons burthen. As the voyage to China was almost new to Americans at that time hundreds of persons made application for a station on board.

The *Massachusetts* was acknowledged by all to be a fine ship and as she lay at her wharf, the officers from several French men-of-war, then in the harbor, frequently came aboard to gratify their curiosity and express their admiration. On her arrival at Batavia and also at Canton, the commanders of various foreign vessels came aboard to examine her and admire her model. She undoubtedly was the handsomest vessel in the two ports. But when her lower hold was opened at Canton, for the first time since she left Boston, she was rotten. She was loaded principally with green masts and spars, taken on board in winter, directly out of the water, with ice and mud on them. The lower deck hatches were caulked down in Boston and when opened at Canton the air was so foul that a lighted candle was put out by it almost as soon as by water. We had four or five hundred barrels of beef in the lower hold placed in the broken stowage and when the fresh air was admitted so that men could live under the hatches, the beef was found almost boiled; the hoops were rotted and fallen off and the inside of the ship was covered with blue mould an inch thick.

It is of interest to remark that the ship had three full crews shipped before she sailed, due to a prediction made by an old woman fortune teller, Moll Pitcher of Lynn, that the ship would be lost on the voyage and every man on her.

We set sail from off Hancock's wharf on Sunday, the 28th of March, 1790, at 4 o'clock, P. M. When the anchor was hauled to the cathead and the block was brought up suddenly against the under side of it, the hook of the cat-block snapped short and the anchor ran to the bottom stopping the ship's way. This occurred before the eyes of a great crowd of spectators thronging the wharves, houses and stores. We fired a salute after getting under way a second time. We then proceeded down the harbor and came to anchor at Congress Road where we remained until the next day when we slipped our cable, leaving the pinnace to take it up, and with a fair breeze ran outside of the light house and hove to for the boat.

We sailed eastward, making some southing, until April 24th, and then set a course south by west along the coast of Barbary and Guinea in water that was discolored much of the time.

MAP OF THE NORTHWEST COAST OF NORTH AMERICA

From a Dutch map after the Vancouver survey, now in the Harvard College Library

PROSPECT OF BATAVIA, JAVA

From an engraving made in 1652 and now in the Macpherson Collection

On June 25th, we ran in for Cape Agulhas with steering sails below and aloft. Saw a large flock of birds. At 5 P. M. got soundings in eighty fathoms of water with soft, muddy bottom. Nothing of consequence took place during our passage across the Indian Ocean.

On July 21st, while scraping the ship's sides in order to paint and varnish, one of the stage ropes accidentally gave way and three men were thrown overboard. One other man caught hold of something alongside the ship but the others went astern. The second mate, with four hands, went to their assistance in the jolly boat. Two of the lads swam to the stage and were saved but Samuel Tripe of Portsmouth, N. H. was drowned, not being able to swim. This happened off Java Head.

Made the Island of Java on August 22d, being 140 days from Boston. Five days later spoke the ship *Laurient,* of London, bound for Canton. We gave her a salute of seven guns which she returned. The captain and merchant[1] went on board of her at four P. M. On the 30th we saw Pigeon Island and ran in for it and anchored. Just as we let go our anchor, Thomas French, midshipman, while handling our mainsail, lost his hold on a gasket that was slack and fell from the mainyard across the barracade or rail and was instantly killed. He was a fine young man and was much lamented by the ship's company.

On August the 31st we got under way at 8 A. M. and ran in for an island called "the henroost," which lays before Batavia town, and at one P. M. came to anchor in seven fathoms of water and saluted the fort with nine guns. We buried Mr. French on Pigeon Island.

When the captain and merchant went ashore they found that American trade was stopped in Batavia and so after wooding and watering we bought stock enough to last for our passage to China, and on September 8th got under way bound for Canton.

Batavia is built much after the manner of Amsterdam in Holland, with canals running through every street with a large one let in from the sea. The morning after sailing from Batavia, two strange men came on deck. They were called aft and examined and it was found by their discourse that they had run away from the hospital. One was named John Armstrong, an Irishman, and the other was John Vannable, an Englishman. September 11th saw a sail standing to the northward and westward which we supposed to be a Chinese junk.

We made the Grand Ladrone Island on October 7th and kept beating to windward all night. The next day we steered to the northward and eastward trying to find a passage through the islands as we could not get a pilot out of any of the China junks, of which there were two or three hundred in sight. Saw a ship standing towards us from the northward and hove our main and mizzen topsails to the mast to speak to her. She proved to be Captain Le Gray bound to Canton. We followed him through the islands towards Macao and came to anchor in Macao Roads on the 9th, where we found the *Washington* of Providence, Captain Donnison. The captain and merchant went ashore to get a pilot for Wampoo and at 12 meridian, he came in a lare boat called the *Venger,* belonging to Captain Kendrick[2] of the sloop *Lady Washington,* of Boston. Got under way that night with several East India ships (the *Sir Edward Huse, Royal Admiral, Belvidere* and *Abergavanna*) and the *Washington* of Rhode Island, all bound up to Wampoo. The next day we went through the Bocca or Tiger's Mouth, where there is a small fort kept up by the mandarins to board ships that go up the river to Wampoo.

Before we reached a landing the wind died away and some two hundred China boats that they called sampans, with many men, women and children in them, towed us up the river and at 6 P. M. we moored above all the rest of the shipping finding three American vessels there, — the *Nancy* of New York, the *Brothers* of Philadelphia, and the *Washington* of Rhode Island.

On October 25th, the captain representing the Danish Company, with an English Commodore and several other gentlemen came on board with the intention to buy our ship and our merchant went up to Canton with them to agree upon a price. While here our people began to grow sick daily. The ship was attended by a hopoo[3] boat that found us in vegetables. About this time the servants of the captain and the merchant died; one a black man named Charlestown and the other a mulatto called Isaac. Our ship was sold for $65,000 and all the men paid off. Some expected to be sent home; the English sailors[4] went on board of English ships; and I and eight others shipped on board the snow[5] *Gustavus*, Thomas Barnet, commander, bound to the Northwest Coast of North America. The other men were: Thomas Williamson, John Wall, John Harris, Thomas Lunt, Charles Treadwell, Joseph Grounard, Benjamin Head, and Malachi Foot. We preferred this to going home in an old Danish ship that had lost her masts and bowsprit in a gale of wind and was eleven months from Denmark to Wampoo. She had been bought by Captain Metcalf[6] to be sent to New York.

On November 5th I received my wages amounting to forty-nine dollars, and spent about thirty dollars for various articles to be sent home by Captain Prince who was returning in the ship *Washington.* At this time fifteen or sixteen of our old hands lay sick at the Bank's Hall. Those of us who belonged to the *Gustavus* went up to Canton, the next day, to the factory of our new owner, 'Squire Cox,[7] and received two months' advance pay, ten dollars of which went for our stores for the voyage. Most of us were sick at the time including myself. On the 11th, we went down to Wampoo and carried our chests and bedding on board the *Carnetic,* a country ship bound for Bombay, she having our stores on board, as our vessel lay at Lark's Bay, one of the Ladrone Islands, about twelve miles below Macao.

Two days later we went on board the *Gustavus*[8] and for some days were employed in fitting our vessel for sea. We were allowed salt beef and fresh pork which was hardly eatable on account of its fatness which is the fault of all Chinese pork. The animals generally weigh from one hundred and fifty to two hundred pounds and it is remarkable that they can live upon so little. A Chinese hog doesn't eat more than half as much as an American hog of the same weight and their fat is very disagreeable being more like hog lard than American pork. Their bellies hang down to the ground when they are on their feet. We had plenty of bread aboard that had been in China for more than eighteen months and was hardly fit for hogs to eat. This was the beginning of our voyage and only God knew how it would end.

November 14th, 1790, we got under way from Lark's Bay bound for the Northwest Coast of North America with thirty-one men on board, all in good health.

LIST OF MEN'S NAMES, RANK, AND NATIONALITY

Thomas Barnet	Captain	Englishman
Samuel Gray	Sailmaker	do
David Whitney	Second Mate	Irishman
William Gibson	Third Mate	do
William Emery	Seaman	do
John Wall	do	do
Henry Evans	Gunner	Welshman
William Howard	Carpenter	do
John McColaning	Chief Mate	do
Thomas Williamson	Seaman	do
Leonard Chapman	Boatswain	American
John Bartlett	Seaman	do
Thomas Lunt	do	do
Charles Treadwell	do	do
Joseph Grounard	Armourer	do
Benjamin Head	Seaman	do
Malachi Foot	do	do
John Harris	Captain of the Colors	Swede
Antony Jose King	Seaman	Portuguese
Manuel Antony	do	do
Manuel Decenter	Carpenter's Mate	do
Jose Antony	Seaman	do

Louis Antony	Seaman	Portuguese
Thomas Freer	do	do
John Mando	Cabin Steward	Manilla man
Antony Deaman	Cook	Goa
Angee		Chinese
Highee		do
Chinkqui		do
Archching		Native of O-why-hee

On December 19th we made the Island of Sanquin and came to anchor in Troner Bay close in shore in twenty-five fathoms of water and sent the long boat ashore for wood and water. The natives of this island are Malays and are governed by the Dutch. We found here one black Dutch sergeant who told us that our vessel was the first one that had been in the bay for three years. The natives were very shy and kept themselves armed during the entire time that we were in the bay. They behaved very civil to us but more from fear than for any other cause. They are a very deceitful people and when they laugh and play round you that is the time to be on guard against attack. The captain gave the sergeant a long coat and other small articles to buy some stock for the ship and he went ashore and did not return. After we were done watering, the third mate and four hands went ashore well armed to make trade with the natives who turned out to be well armed themselves and in less than two hours' time they loaded our boat as deep as she could swim with cocoa nuts, plantains, fowls, etc.

December 30th, we saw a small, low island not shown on our charts and about that time the native of O-why-hee died of scurvey. A week later we sighted a lot of driftwood and rock weeds and other signs of land to the windward, the wind to the E. S. E. Probably undiscovered land as the charts make no mention of land in that direction. Sounded several times but could get no bottom.

We made the Northwest Coast of America on March 5th, 1791, after a tedious passage of seventy days attended with gales and dirty weather most of the time, and ran into Bartlett's Sound,[9] coming to anchor with great difficulty as we could not find less than thirty fathoms of water a cable's length from the shore. The next day we came to anchor with a kedge under the lee of a small island where the canoes came off to us to trade with fish and furs. We soon parted from the kedge and not being able to find a good anchorage in this Sound we plied along shore in search of a safe harbor in which to overhaul and repair our rigging. This Sound takes it name from Captain Bartlett of the ship *Lourden* of Ostend, and lays in Latitude 48° 56″ North.

After sailing along shore for several days we at last found the harbor of Wickannish[10] which was pointed out to us by an Indian named Captain Hannah[11] who came on board not long before. Near the entrance was an island that had three trees on it that appear like a ship in stays and is called Ship Island. At four P. M. we saw the smoke at Wickannish. Captain Hannah had been in this harbor but once before but we steered according to his best judgement. Before long the natives on shore began to make signs to us to steer more to the northward which were not regarded by our captain and soon we ran on a ledge of rocks and came near

losing our vessel. We hove all sails back and fortunately she fell off the ledge into twelve fathoms of water.
A boat sent to sound for the channel soon discovered
the entrance between two islands and at five P. M. we
came abreast of Wickannish town or village[12] which
contained about two hundred houses or long huts of
square form built about twenty yards from the water.
We were soon honoured by a visit from their chief
whose name was Wickannish. He was a tall, raw boned
fellow who came attended by thirty or forty canoes
with fish and furs to sell. Several of them were bound
out a whaling with gear in the canoes. Their lances
and harpoons were very curious being made of bone
neatly polished. Their lines were made of animals'
hides and their drags were made of skins blown full of
wind in the form of a winter squash.

Early the next morning we weighed anchor and ran
up to Cox's Harbour with the boat sounding ahead of
us. The tide was running very strong at the entrance
of the harbour and we were swept in alongside of some
rocks and so near the shore as to rack the limbs of the
trees with our yards and very near being cast away a
second time. In this harbour we lay moored for several days as it was landlocked and a safe place in which
to overhaul our rigging. One day the boat went ashore
to kill geese which were very plentiful.

On Saturday, March 15th, the boat was sent with
the carpenter and Charles Treadwell to cut wood at a
point about a mile from the vessel and out of sight of
her. Late in the afternoon the boat went to get the
man and just as she went ashore three canoes put out
from where our men had been cutting wood. They had

stolen a large iron maul and threatened to pick out the carpenter's eyes with their arrows when our boat coming just at that time saved their lives. The next day, at 10 o'clock, our second mate died of the scurvey having been sick for some time. He was born in Cork and was twenty-eight years old. We did not bury him until the sun was down and it was so dark when our captain was reading prayers that he began to damn his eyes because he could not see the print plainly.

We remained at this village until the 26th when we got under way at four P. M. bound to the north on our trading voyage. In all we bought forty skins at this place. A week later we made Douglass Island[13] at the entrance of Queen Charlotte's Sound and saw Cape St. James.

On Thursday, April the 3d, we ran into a small bay and a great number of canoes came off with men, women and children in them. The dress of the men was made of three or four skins[14] sewed together which covered them from their shoulders down to their knees. They were ornamented with bird's feathers all over their heads and besmeared with grease and paint. On their heads there were a great number of tails or locks of hair which were full of lice and grease and made them look very frightful. We learned that whenever they kill a man in battle, they cut off his hair and mat it up in tails and tie it on their own heads. The women, when young, bore a hole in their under lips and run a piece of copper through it and as the girls grow up they put in bigger and bigger pieces of wire so that at the age of twelve or thirteen they can put in a small piece of wood of oval form, about the size of a half-crown piece. At the age of thirty, they can put in a piece as big as the palm of your hand. It hangs down below their chins.[15] The morning when we first came into the bay they clapped their hands over their mouths to hide their teeth when they laughed, for they seemed to know themselves to be frightful to all strangers. When they are better acquainted they put aside all modesty. The young women were well featured. We had them on board at from ten to twenty years of age. Their fathers would instruct them how to behave while our men had to do with them. We bought some dried halibut of these natives. They cure it without salt. They had no furs but wanted us to go into the bay to anchor. It had the appearance of being a fine harbour but our captain would not agree to it and stood off and on all night while the natives made fires as a sign for us to come in. Their chief's name was Huegur.[16]

While running alongshore, the next day, we fired one of our three pounders and five canoes came off with about seventy natives. Their chief was a young man who came on board and behaved very civil and made it his business to trade for the rest of the company. We bought eighty skins which brought up our total in the hold to about one hundred and twenty. At eight o'clock this morning (April 4th), Louis Anthony died of the scurvey. He was born at Lisbon and was about thirty-one years old. As there was an appearance of bad weather we stood off shore and made a good offing.

For the next three weeks we had dirty weather and spent most of the time laying to under a Bellamy tri-sail and Dungarvin reef in the fore-topmast staysail. Our people began to grow sickly on account of the short

allowance of one pound of beef and a pint of rice every
twenty-four hours. One day, six pounds of sugar was
served for a mess of six men and once a week, a pound
of pork and a pint of peas. On April 24th, the weather
became more moderate and we stood for land and the
next day saw land and ran close in and came to anchor
in twelve fathoms of water with a hawser run out on
each quarter and made fast to the limbs of trees ashore.
The place was called Cloak Bay[17] and their chief's
name was Connehow.[18] The natives came off with
plenty of large halibut and other fish. The carpenter's
mate, Charles Treadwell and I went ashore to cut wood
and the natives behaved very civil while we were at
work. There were thirty to forty there at a time, the
most of whom were women who kept up a continual
singing. The ship while here was surrounded by two or
three hundred canoes at a time with a plenty of furs.
The chief trade was iron, buttons and old clothes.

The next day, April the 26th, while trading with the
natives on the quarter deck, a large canoe came alongside having on board a great number of spears and bows
and arrows. The men began to flock on board in great
numbers and at the same time we noticed that they
were sending their women ashore which seemed to
show a bad design. They also were seen to put on their
shields and hand up their targets and pass their knives
from one to the other on the quarter deck there being
about one hundred and fifty of the natives there at the
time. Seeing this we manned our tops with blunder-
busses and the remainder of our men with small arms.
Charles and I were on shore at the time of the fray with
the natives on board. The women surrounded us on

shore singing their war song. We both took up our pistols, resolved to sell our lives as dearly as possible if they molested us. Soon the noise on board began to abate and the natives would not trade any more unless we would disarm our men. We did so as all was quiet. Their armed canoes went away and trade went on brisker than ever.

The next day the natives began to come in large numbers from all parts of the islands and the captain began to grow dubious of the appearance of things and at ten o'clock cast off at the stern and hove up the anchor to go out but we were prevented by a variable wind in the passage. Trade went on faster than ever when the natives saw that we intended to go out. There were about six hundred canoes alongside at the time. We bought about four hundred skins in this bay. The next morning we got under way bound southward with a great many canoes following us.

For several days we ran down the shore, part of the time bad weather holding us off. Our people who had been sick for the past month were now getting better daily. A few greens that we had picked up on shore[19] had been a great service. Thank God! I was not sick at any time though sometimes eight or nine were sick at a time.

On Monday, May 4th, we hauled in shore in Queen Charlotte's Sound, with a light wind and a great swell but being a considerable distance from the land no canoes came off and we proceeded on our course to double Cape St. James. At this time the people began to grow uneasy on account of the food, as we had nothing but rice and fish to live upon and since the 24th of

March all the fish had been purchased by the ship's company with their own clothes except the 3d of May, when the captain served out two strings of beads to a mess to buy fish. But the beads were of little service to us and of little value to the natives so that it was fair to say that three-quarters of the fish was bought by the ship's company with no other allowance but rice and salt. When there was any beef allowed at 12 o'clock, the boatswain was always damning and swearing for his share of the slush for the rigging and the captain's servant was bottling off the remainder to fry fish to save the captain's butter of which he had four firkins aboard at that time.

At six A. M., on May 5th, we saw a breaker a point off the lee bow and with difficulty got clear of it for there was little wind and a strong current and heavy swell setting us directly upon it, but fortunately a light breeze sprung up and we wore ship and soon left the breaker astern. We then stood into Queen Charlotte's Sound and at four o'clock a canoe came alongside with sixteen natives in her of whom we bought forty skins. Five prime skins could be bought here for a sheet of copper; one skin for about two feet of bar iron or for ten spikes. 180 beads were served out here to each six men. Cape St. James may be well known by the five islands that lay to the southward of it. The next day no natives came off notwithstanding we fired a gun.

No pork was allowed this day and the slush barrel being empty the captain passed word forward for us to buy train oil with which to fry our fish, which was miserable, indeed, there being on board at that time sixteen tierces of beef, four of pork and two of flour and two of split peas; four hogsheads of bread; five bags of sago; fifteen bags of rice and one cask of raisins.

On the morning of May 8th, we discovered an island in this Sound that the charts gave no account of.[20] It bore N. E. from us in Latitude 52° 33″ N. Saw a great number of whales — two or three hundred at a time. At 2 P. M. two canoes came off to us and soon there were a hundred canoes alongside. Their chief's name was Clutiver.[21] We bought a hundred skins here. At sunset the canoes went away. We lay offshore all night and the next morning four canoes came off having nothing but fish to sell. Continued steering alongshore to the northward and at 11 o'clock saw a smoke in-shore. Four canoes came off with their chief whose name was Comeeshier.[22] Bought seventy skins here bringing the whole number up to 775 now in the hold. The chief and his son remained on board all night. The next morning the tribe came off to the number of two hundred and fifty men, women and children and we bought 210 skins. The natives of this place were a very quiet set of people.[23] At 2 P. M. made sail along-shore, sounding all the way, in from thirty-five to five fathoms of water.

Continued steering to the northward and at 10 A. M. on Monday, May 11th, saw a smoke in shore in Lati-tude 53° 4″ N. and at 3 P. M. came abreast of a bay. Two canoes came off and said that their chief would come off the next morning. The captain bought a few salmon and served out two to each mess. The next morning we beat in shore with all sail set and at 2 P. M. brought up with the small bower in five fathoms of water. Several canoes came alongside and we bought

VIEW OF HABITATIONS IN NOOTKA SOUND

From an engraving by S. Smith, in Cook's *Voyages*, London, 1784

INTERIOR OF A HOUSE IN NOOTKA SOUND

From an engraving by W. Sharp, in Cook's *Voyages*, London, 1784

one hundred and fifty skins. Their chief's name was Skoitscut.[24] Got under way at 4 P. M. and stood off shore. From here may be seen at one view the main continent of America; the island on the west, the continent on the east, which forms Queen Charlotte's Sound. At 2 P. M. the water growing shoal we brought up with the small bower and soon several canoes came alongside. Bought one hundred and fifty skins here. At 4 P. M. got under way and stood offshore. One canoe lay astern all night and early the next morning we began trading. Several more canoes came off and we bought about fifty more skins which were cheaper here than at any other place that we had visited. A prime skin was bought for about ten inches of iron.

For several days we continued beating down the Sound and near Cape St. James. Several canoes came off and we bought a few skins and some dried fish. Our allowance between the sixth and the nineteenth of May was four small salmon, weighing about four pounds each, with rice and salt as usual. We expected to leave the coast about the first of August.[25]

On May 26th we ran in close to the land and sent the boat ashore twice for wood having little left on board. The boat's crew discovered two or three fine harbours that could not be seen at a mile's distance from the land. The coast was so bold that a ship of five hundred tons could come within twice her length of the rocks. They saw many wild berries — raspberries, mulberries and blackberries, and a great number of sea otters. The land had a very remarkable appearance. The mountains were nearly perpendicular and appeared to be an entire rock. We supposed them to be

three-quarters of a mile high.[26] That day we were cut
short four pints of rice and issued only sixteen pints for
twenty men and had had nothing but fish for six days
past. The next day began with dirty weather. Several
canoes came off from which we bought a few fish. At 7
P. M. bore away from the shore and proceeded on our
course to the northward for the latitude 59° under
close-reefed topsails.

On June 1st, 1791, in the latitude of 63° 6″ we saw a
remarkable high land[27] to the northward and westward, which was supposed to be about 160 miles off.
Saw several smokes on shore and fired a gun but no natives came off. We supposed that they were not much
acquainted with Europeans. The day ended with thick
weather. Still running along to the southward. The
next day at six A. M. came abreast of a sound that our
drafts gave no account of but the weather continuing
thick we kept beating off the entrance and the next day
continued our course southward. The land appeared
to be very high all along the coast. The tops of the
mountains appeared high up in the clouds.

We had several days of dirty weather and the supply
of wood and water began to be short. On June 6th several canoes came off to us, the first we had seen in that
part of the coast. The men wore whiskers and the females ornamented themselves with fish bones[28] and
wore one run through the division of their nostrils in
their noses. I bought a fresh seal and had it fryed for
breakfast. It proved to be a delicate meat and was the
first fresh meat we had had for nearly six months. The
next day a canoe came off with a chief from whom we
bought two beaver skins and some fish.

Nothing remarkable happened for several days but on the 10th four canoes came off with seventy natives. These were the stoutest men that we had seen on any part of the coast. They had no women with them and by their actions they seemed to have in mind an attempt on the vessel. At 11 o'clock they went away singing their war song and throwing their arms about them in a very savage manner. Bought nineteen skins of them which brought the total up to 1,218. They made signs for us to go into their harbour but our captain didn't think proper to go in and so we proceeded alongshore to the eastward. At 4 P. M., Samuel Gray died of the scurvey, aged about 32 years. He was born in the West of England. This was the fourth man that we had lost. Our ship was very crank owing to the greater part of the water being out.

June the 12th, we stood in for land and saw Mount Fairweather. This mountain was the highest land that we had seen on the Northwest Coast of America. The top of it appeared a vast height up in the clouds. Filled seventeen casks with salt water for the hold. Two days later we saw a sail astern. She soon came up with us and fired one of her lee guns and proved to be the brig *Grace,* of New York, Captain Douglass,[29] from Canton, six weeks out. She gave us our first intelligence of the Spanish War[30] and of five sail of English men-of-war going round Cape Horn.

On the 19th of June we finished wooding and watering in a very convenient harbour in Latitude 57° N. Here we tarred the rigging, blacked the masts and yards and painted and caulked the ship round. The natives were the most quiet and civil of any that we had seen.[31] The chief trade was in old clothes of any kind. We lay here until the 23d and then dropped down the Sound followed by the natives who pitched their huts on shore abreast of the vessel. The next day we got under way and directed our course for Queen Charlotte's Islands, bound for Cloak Bay, and two days later came to in 19 fathoms of water and ran a hawser ashore from each quarter and made fast to the limbs of trees to steady the ship. There were few natives here in comparison with the number here when we left it before. Most of them wore red jackets and we knew by this that Captain Douglass had been here. We did not get a single skin here.

Connehaw, their chief, came on board and informed us that most of his tribe had left their winter quarters and distributed themselves among the islands for the summer. They return to their winter houses about the end of August. The natives at this place use no bread nor do they at any other part of the coast. The most of their living is fish which they cook in baskets by first digging holes in the sand and making the sand hot; then setting the basket in it and feeding it with hot stones until the fish is boiled enough. We went ashore where one of their winter houses stood. The entrance was cut out of a large tree and carved all the way up and down.[32] The door was made like a man's head and the passage into the house was between his teeth and was built before they knew the use of iron. Our people were very uneasy and wished to proceed homewards on account of provisions being very short; bread in particular. Captain Douglass' assistance was inadvisedly refused as we were in need of bread and he of liquor of which we had a great plenty aboard. On the 3d of July, all hands went on the quarterdeck and told the captain that we could not live on our allowance of bread, it being three days between allowances. The captain said that it wouldn't do to eat up all at once and would not give us any more bread but allowed us caravansers one more meal per week and took away the allowance of flour — a fine exchange indeed, the flour being better than all the caravansers aboard. We told the captain that it wouldn't do for him and his officers, eleven in number with their servants, to have as much provisions as they could eat and keep fifteen hands before the mast upon a very short allowance and he had much to do to get the men to their duty again.

July 4th, the glorious day of America's independence, but our circumstances allowed us nothing to celebrate equal to our wishes. Unexpectedly the captain gave us an allowance of grog, extra, and the mates gave half a gallon of rack which was sufficient to last until night. In the morning we saw a brig bearing W. N. W. Several canoes came alongside and we bought twenty skins which brought up the number to about 1,683 in all. At 10 A. M. made all sail to speak the brig but could not come up with her. Supposed her to be Captain Kendrick from Lark's Bay.[33]

July 6th, we ran in close with the cape and a canoe came off with three natives who told us that their chief with all their tribe had gone to war with Skeitcutes who appeared to be the greatest chief in the Queen Charlotte Islands. Bought some halibut of them and continued on our course up the Sound.

Nothing very remarkable happened for several days

after this. We bought more skins bringing the number in the hold up to 1869 and on the 16th had a narrow escape from running on a reef in Norfolk Sound. Two days later we ran into Civility Harbour where we formerly were and moored the ship and began to paint her and tar the rigging. Here we lay for several days, the weather being dirty most of the time. On the 23d we unmoored and dropped down to the reef and the next morning sailed for Queen Charlotte's Island, which we saw on the 27th and here we left with pleasure the Northwest Coast of America, bound for the Island of O-why-hee where Captain Cook was killed. On the passage we ran into a gale that lasted for thirty-six hours the wind blowing all round the compass. It was called a "tuffune."[34] We were upon a short allowance of three pounds of bread per week and no beef, having nothing but our own salmon that we had bought with our clothes before we left the coast. At the Sandwich Islands we had expectations of getting a good supply of yams. The boatswain piped to dinner and turned the hands out as usual whether we had anything to eat or not. Our vessel also began to leak in her upper works.

On the 22d of August we began to see a great number of birds and much seaweed and early the next morning sighted land on the bow. It proved to be O-why-hee. At 10 A. M. several canoes came off with potatoes and hogs to trade. They craved nothing but iron in return. We bought their hogs at the rate of two spikes apiece. At 4 P. M. we came abreast of Kelaco-koo Bay[35] where Captain Cook was killed. Here we had upwards of three hundred double and single canoes alongside at a time with men, women and children aboard. Their chief's name was Tianner.[36] He would not come on board on account of his taking and killing Captain Metcalf's son in a schooner[37] and only left one man alive in her. This was done while young Metcalf's father lay in another bay only six leagues away. Captain Metcalf commanded the brig *Eleanore*, mounting 16 guns. About the same time that his son was killed he had his boat moored astern with one man in her to keep the natives from stealing her but they swam off in the night and killed the man and took the boat ashore. The next day they brought out some of the man's bones to sell. They had been scraped. This unfortunate man was a Portuguese. His name was Anthony. Seeing this man's bones put Captain Metcalf into such a rage that he ordered all his guns loaded with grape shot and the hinges of the ports greased and after he got his vessel all clear for action he got one of the chiefs to taboo one side of her so that he might have a good chance to fulfill his desire. Tabooing is an authority that the chiefs use over the lower sort of the people and is death if anyone of his class break it. The taboo on one side of Captain Metcalf's brig brought all the natives over on the opposite side. The captain then ordered all hands to heave beads overboard to draw the natives as near as possible to the vessel and when he had collected upwards of three hundred canoes alongside he called out "Anthony," the name of the man who was killed, as a signal for his men to fire. They did so and killed upwards of three hundred men, women and children. At the time he knew nothing of the death of his son.

All the next day we lay with the main-topsail to the mast and the courses held up, trading with the natives off Kelacokoo Bay. We bought a great number of hogs, potatoes, bread fruit, grass lines and tapper[38] which they make from the bark of trees and use for their clothing. It looks very much like calico but will not stand the water. We had upwards of one hundred girls on board at a time but not a man excepting one at a time. One of their chiefs came alongside with one of young Metcalf's muskets. He was one of the stoutest men that I ever saw. Our captain compared his hind quarters to that of a bullock and would not suffer him to come aboard. Afterwards the captain asked him for his musket and made signs for him to stand on the quarter bridge of our vessel and when he did so the captain gave him his musket and at the same time fired a musket over his head with made him jump overboard and swim ashore. At night every man took his girl and the rest jumped overboard to swim upwards of three miles for the shore.

Early on the morning of the 25th of August, we took our departure from the island of O-why-hee which is a very fine island with level land as far as we could see to the windward and with mountains on the lee shore with snow on them all the year round. At 10 A. M. saw the island of Moue. A great number of natives followed us from the island of O-why-hee. At six o'clock the next morning we saw the island of Worhoo and at 10 A. M. came to in twenty fathoms of water. A great many natives came alongside with plenty of hogs, potatoes, yams, bread fruit, grass lines, spears, mats, mother of pearl beads and a great number of curiosities. All hands were employed the next day in buying hogs and vegetables for a sea stock. During the morning the natives stole the buoy from our anchor and kept stealing and cutting all the hooks and thimbles they could get at.

The next day, Sunday, August 28th, the king, his brother and son, came on board and made the captain a present of three red feather caps and some tapper cloth. Our captain gave them a musket and some powder. This day they sent all the handsomest girls they had on board and gave every one their charge how to behave that night. When they gave a signal every one of them was to cling fast to the Europeans and to divert them while they cut our cable. At night every man in the ship took a girl and sent the remainder ashore. At 12 o'clock at night the watch perceived the ship adrift and at the same time every girl in the ship clung fast to her man in a very loving manner. All hands were called immediately. I had much to do to get clear of my loving mistress. The girls all tried to make their escape but were prevented by driving them all into the cabin. We found the cable cut about two fathoms from the hawse hole and made sail and stood off and on in the bay all night and the next morning ran in and came to with the best bower. Saw a number of canoes trying to weigh our anchor. Three of the girls jumped overboard and two canoes came and picked them up. We fired a musket at one of them and a native turned up his backsides at us. We fired three or four more times so they were glad to leave off and make for the shore.

The following morning a double war canoe came off

with the men singing their war song. They paddled
round our vessel and when abreast of the lee bow, seeing no anchor, they gave a shout and went on shore
again. At eight o'clock forty or fifty canoes came off to
trade but seemed shy of us. We bought some hogs and
potatoes and sent several messages on shore to the king
but could not get our anchor from him. At 12 meridian, the king sent a man off to dive for the anchor pretending they had not stolen it. The boat was manned
and two bars put in her as a reward for the native if he
found the anchor. He dived several times but did not
go to the bottom. He would stay under water longer
than any man we ever saw. We could see him lay with
his back against the bottom of the canoe for some minutes and then let himself sink down and come up again
about three or four yards from the canoe, pretending
that he had been to the bottom. Seeing this we were
fully convinced that they had our anchor ashore and
meant to keep it so we sent another message to the
king and told him if he didn't send the anchor aboard
that we should be obliged to fire on his town and lay it
in ashes.

The next day we could not get a canoe to come
alongside and could see natives running in from all
parts of the island to assist the king if we attempted to
land, which our mate was for doing but our captain
didn't approve of it and so at 11 o'clock we got under
way and fired four or five broadsides into the village.
We could see thousands of the natives running, one on
top of the other. On the beach were a number of canoes off the lee bow so we made for them and fired a
broadside that stove a great many of them and sent

THE SNOW "GUSTAVUS"

From the drawing in Bartlett's Journal, now in the possession of
Lawrence W. Jenkins

HOUSE AND TOTEM POLE OF THE HAIDA INDIANS

From the drawing in Bartlett's Journal, now in the possession of Lawrence
W. Jenkins. Supposed to be the earliest known representation of a Totem Pole

HAWAIIAN ISLAND GIRLS
From a photograph in the Peabody Museum, Salem, Mass.

the natives a swimming and diving under water. We ran by two men swimming and shot one of them through the shoulder and killed him. We also ran alongside of a canoe with a man in her. We stood by with ropes to heave to him to get him on board at the same time pointing six muskets at him if he refused to take hold of the rope. He layed hold of it and hauled himself aboard and let his canoe go adrift. We then hove about and came abreast of the village a second time when the natives on the beach fired a musket and kept running along with white flags flying in defiance for us to land. Seeing no possibility of our getting our anchor we bore away and ran out to about two miles from the shore where we gave the native on board six spikes and let him go to swim ashore. The seven girls on board we gave a number of beads and let them go likewise.

From here we set a course for the island of Otehy[39] where we were in expectation of getting a new supply of yams. At 6 A. M. saw the island bearing E. by N. and ran down the lee side. A great number of natives came alongside with articles to barter for iron. Several of their chiefs came aboard when we came abreast the watering place. One brought a letter to the captain the contents of which gave us warning of the bad intentions of the natives. It was written by Captain Ingraham of the brig *Hope* of Boston. He said the natives of that island were treacherous and deceitful and required good looking after. They informed us of an anchor lying in Anahoo Road. Whether it was cut away from some vessel or parted while trying to heave it we were not certain. We took this to be a deceitful story to decoy us into the bay. Their intentions were happily prevented by our taking our farewell of the Sandwich Islands at 3 P. M., September 1st, when we bore away for Canton with one of the natives on board. After all our trouble at these islands our captain bought but only three hundred weight of yams to last us on our passage. Of bread, we had but fifty pounds on board.

For the next three weeks nothing of importance happened. We were attended with clear and pleasant weather. But on the 23d the weather began to look black and stern. The next morning the topsails were sent down and the top-gallant yards and mast and we scudded under the foresail. The vessel began to make water fast so that it was necessary to keep one pump going all the time. The pump that was made in China, out of two pieces of wood, began to blow and would not work. At 12 o'clock at night we shipped a very heavy sea which broke in the main grating and the water kept pouring down the main hatchways until it was up to the lower deck. In this miserable condition our ship was so waterlogged that she would not steer. In about half an hour she broached to. The foresail being handed would not wear and we were under the disagreeable necessity of cutting away our mainmast. After the mast went she wore round before the wind and all hands were called to clear the wreck for the mast kept beating under the counter so that we had much ado to get clear of it. All hands then turned to the pump and sucked her in about four hours' time, to our great joy, as we were expecting every minute to go to the bottom. At 8 o'clock the next morning, a sea pooped and stove in all the dead-lights which kept the pump going continually. All hands then went to work and took the lower deck-hatches for dead-lights to keep the tops of the seas from beating in at the cabin windows and stove up the chest to nail over the main hatchways.

The next day at 4 P. M. the gale died away to a calm but the weather still looked black all round the compass and we went to work and stove up the long boat that lay in the lee scuppers and hove her overboard and lashed the small boat, bottom upwards, to the ring bolts. It was well that we did so for at 10 P. M. another gale sprang up which blew harder than the first. At one o'clock a sea pooped us which stove in all the hatches that we had for dead-lights and set us a bailing out of the after hatchway which wet one half of our cargo.

At eight o'clock in the evening of the next day, September 27th, we shipped a sea that struck us on the larboard quarter and stove the small boat into a thousand pieces. It also washed overboard three men and we could not give them any assistance. They were John Wall, Antony Frair and Jose Antony. At the same time all the spars broke adrift and broke two men's legs. The next morning the topmast was hanging over the bows and the wind blew to that degree that there was not a man on the ship that heard the topmast when it broke. The fore-yard also got loose and blew twenty or thirty yards from the vessel. All hands were obliged to lash themselves to the pumps and could but just keep her free by pumping and bailing all the time. All hands were beat out for want of victuals having had nothing to eat but half a biscuit and about an ounce of cheese since the 24th of the month. God only knows what kept us alive for the wind would take the tops of the seas and blow them continually over us. If our vessel had not had a high quarter deck we should all have perished from the top of the seas that blew over us so that we could not tell whether it rained or not. At 4 o'clock that afternoon, a sea pooped us that filled our cabin half-full of water, wet all the bread and upset the cogs of the wheel and broke it in two pieces and cut in two pieces the man's lip who was steering. In this pitiful condition our ship would not steer but lay in the trough of the seas. At the same time the pump got choked and all hands became discouraged expecting every minute to be the last. After much ado, however, we got the pump working and she sucked again in about five hours' time. At 10 P. M. the gale died away and one man was set to watch and the rest of the hands went to sleep.

The next day the wind abated and the water began to grow smooth and at 12 meridian, all hands were called to get up a jury mast and set the fore-topmast gallant sail upon the foremast to keep her steady. We cut a mortise in the stump of the mainmast to step the jurymast and at night the mast was all ready to get up in the morning. We also overhauled the hold and found all the water spoiled except two hogsheads and the liquor also spoiled as well as was all the bread on board, so there was nothing left but Sandwich Island pork and sago to last us the passage to China.

It was October 22d when we made the island of Formosa and ran alongshore, the natives making smokes as a sign for us to come in but none would venture off.

Four days later we saw about a hundred Chinese fishing boats but they all seemed very shy of us. After a great deal of trouble we got a pilot out of one of them who agreed to pilot us to Macao for nineteen dollars, and at four o'clock that afternoon we saw the Grand Ladrone Island,[40] and at six came to anchor at Macao Roads and heard the news of the death of our owner, 'Squire Cox. The next morning the boats came alongside with plenty of bread and eggs and fruit but the captain bought for himself and none for the ship's company. This day, the last of the water was used and as the captain would not get any in during the time we lay in the Road the ship's company bought their own water of the Chinese at the rate of two dollars for five gallons.

The Northwest men having been stopped from trading[41] at Canton, at 9 A. M. on the 28th, we got under way and ran down to Lark's Bay, intending to smuggle our skins. After mooring at 4 P. M. the captain called all hands aft and gave them notes to receive their wages at Macao from Mr. McIntire[42] and as we received our notes he sent us into the boat and would not suffer any to come aboard again for fear we should take skins out of the vessel. He also took care to search our chests before they went over the side for he well knew that we all had skins in the vessel and for that reason he took every advantage of us to try to wrong us out of our wages. The fear of losing them made us put up with more than we otherwise would have done. At 6 P. M. we put off for Macao leaving William Emery, my partner aboard, for the boat was overloaded and could not carry him. We landed at Macao at nine o'clock that night and the mandarins or custom house officers over-hauled our chests to see if we had any skins with us, for their laws were very strict so that if they found any skins in our possession the Governor could send us as slaves to Goa. If a Chinese was found with any it meant present death for him. We all went to lodgings at a Portuguese house where we paid at the rate of ten dollars per month.

October the 30th, I received my wages from Mr. McIntire, amounting to ninety dollars, and then hired a China boat and went down to Lark's Bay and went on board the *Gustavus* to see if there was any possibility of getting my skins. When I went aboard I told them I had turned a fisherman and hoped to carry passengers with my boat up and down from Lark's Bay to Macao. The captain commended me for it and said that I was an industrious man and would live where one half of the ship's company would die. I then went to my partner to see how we could manage to get our skins out of the vessel, for I was resolved to lose my life or to gain what I had so dearly earned. He told me there was a strict watch kept every night, with pistols and cutlasses, to keep boats from coming alongside and he believed that the captain mistrusted that I was coming aboard that night, knowing that I had skins in the vessel, for he had ordered all the arms to be loaded in case I should come on board. My partner and myself then laid the plan out so that I was to anchor my boat so that I might hear his signals and not be seen. I did so by anchoring my boat under the land. He was to have the twelve o'clock watch that night and they were all Portuguese in his watch. Their custom was to strike

MACAO, CHINA

From a Chinese painting in the Peabody Museum, Salem, Mass.

the bell before they rang her and he said he would bribe them with a skin and would strike the bell himself. The signal was to strike one bell over the number and I was then to come under the bows and take the skins from him. At twelve the signal was given and I went under the bows and got the skins safe in the boat. Just then one of the Chinese went and told the second mate that I was on board but the mate proved to be my friend and held the Chinese fast until I got clear with my skins — seventeen in number — which I sold the next day for six hundred dollars. So there was an end to my Northwest voyage.

On November 12th, 1791, I shipped on board the Portuguese ship *St. Cruiz*, Capt. Jose Francisco, commander, bound for Lisbon, at six dollars and a half per month wages. With me went Robert Lovis of Marblehead in Massachusetts. The captain gave us a note to the boatswain for he had command of the ship while she lay in the harbour. The captain told us if we wanted liberty to go on shore for a day, the boatswain would grant it, but if for a longer time, to come to him and we should have three or four days liberty if we desired it. The Portuguese were a very kind people to strangers and used both of us very well for they would call their own men out to work at four o'clock in the morning and let us lay in our hammocks until we pleased to turn out ourselves.

In a few days we were obliged, for some time, to keep ourselves armed on account of a Manilla man who had killed three Chinese. It appeared that this man and the Chinese were gambling together when the Manilla man found that the Chinese were cheating him. He immediately drew his knife and killed two of them on the spot and with the bloody knife in his hand he ran through the streets crying for all Christians to keep out of the way, and made his way to the waterside. To get across, he got into a boat but the man refused to put him over the water and he stuck his knife into the poor man's body and killed him. His knife broke of in the man's body which prevented him from killing any more. He then made off and was away three days before they caught him. The Chinese wanted three Christians in place of the three Chinese who were killed.

On December 25th, 1791, I shipped myself on board the *Lady Washington,* Captain Kendrick, commander, bound for the Northwest Coast of America,⁴³ then laying at Lark's Bay. This brig had been taken by the natives on the Northwest Coast on a previous voyage. They were lying at Coyours on the coast and the captain was in liquor one day and trusted more to the natives than did his own people and would suffer great numbers of them to come on board. His gunner went to the quarter deck and told him the natives would take the vessel and that it was dangerous to let so many come on board. The captain struck the gunner and pushed him off the quarter deck so that he had no time to take the keys out of the arm chest. When the natives saw this they took possession of the arm chest immediately and began to flock on board from the shore in great numbers and made a terrible noise with their war songs. They took the men's hats off their heads and laid their knives across their throats and threatened to kill them if they made the least resistance and then drove them all into the hold. They then went to

work and divided the copper that lay upon the deck and
kept running out on the bowsprit and yelling to their
women on shore to come aboard and assist them for it
seems that the women are more courageous than the
men. All this time Captain Kendrick was on the quarter deck with a piece of bar iron in his hand treating
with them. Twelve of the savages stood with knives
pointing at the captain's body to prevent him from going below. All this time he was conversing with his
men below, telling them to muster up all the arms that
they could find, which was only two pistols, one musket and two cutlasses, and be in readiness to make a
sally up on deck when he should give the watch word,
which was — *Follow me.* Coyour, the chief, knowing
that he had sufficient command of the deck, made a
spring below to see what force was below and Captain
Kendrick at once jumped down the hatch upon the
chief's back and at the same time called out *Follow me.*
At that, all the men made a sally and the chief seeing
this, was for making off with all his tribe. In less than
five minutes the ship's company had possession of the
deck and had broken open the arm chest and killed
forty of the natives on the spot without losing a man.

On January 16th, 1792, I shipped myself as gunner
on board the snow *Eleanore*,[44] Capt. Simon Metcalf,
commander, bound for the Isle of France. We sailed
the next day and on February 26th ran into Bantam
Roads, at the island of Java, and came to in twelve
fathoms of water. We were about three miles distant
from the fort and soon sent a boat ashore to buy a few
hogs and vegetables for our sea stock. At the landing
we were met by a Dutchman who conducted us to the

gates of the castle[45] and in about a half an hour a sergeant came out with a halbert and walked before us up
to the Governor's house. He received our officers kindly and gave us liberty to buy anything we pleased.
Here I fell in with an Irishman, one Robertson, that I
formerly knew at Amsterdam, and he showed me all
about the place except where the monument was erected over the people killed at the massacre of Bantam.

We arrived at Port Louis, on the Isle of France, on
March 12th and discharged our cargo of 2,500 chests
of tea and then began to repair our vessel; got in new
beams, fore and abaft and bought copper and iron and
other trade for a Northwest voyage. On May 9th, our
captain bought a small French brig, about 90 tons burthen, for $4,000. She was full of water at the time
which was the reason they sold her so cheap. She had
struck coming in and they thought she was bilged. We
hove her down and found her to be a good vessel. We
mounted ten guns on her and got her in readiness to go
with us on our Northwest voyage. I was sent on board
as gunner and had my wages raised. Young Robert
Metcalf, the captain's son, was appointed captain of
the brig which was named the *Ino*. Here I found Captain Low, an old shipmate of mine, lying sick in the
hospital. He had been there and at Bourbon for three
years and had sent his vessel home. The American
captains made a contribution and collected upwards of
four hundred dollars to pay his passage in the ship
Sally, Captain Kenneday. The ship sailed and left him
behind. When Captain Low heard of it he took opium
and put an end to his life.

By the middle of July we had taken in our copper

VIEW OF PORT LOUIS, ISLE OF FRANCE
From an engraving in the Macpherson Collection

VIEW OF CHRISTMAS HARBOR, KERGUELEN LAND

From an engraving by Newton, in Cook's *Voyages*, London, 1784

and iron for the trading voyage and also a great quantity of cordage and canvas for China, on our return there from the Northwest coast; but buying all this trade and also the brig *Ino,* and repairing the *Eleanore,* brought down our captain's purse so low that he was obliged to sell off all the trade that he had on board for the Coast and alter his voyage from the Northwest coast to that of an oil, and sealskin voyage to the island of Desolation or Munsair, Kerguelen, in the southern Indian Ocean. He had just enough money left to pay his men their advance and get his vessels out of port.

I received my wages on the *Eleanore,* to the amount of sixty dollars in paper, on September 9th, and ten days later we cast off our head fast and hung to stern moorings and at 12, meridian, the pilot came aboard and at 4 P. M. we dropped down to the buoys and came to anchor. At 12 o'clock at night we got under way with the *Eleanore* in company, bound for the island of Madagascar, to wood our vessels and buy rice and other things for a sea stock to last us the passage to Kurguelen. The first day we were out the *Eleanore* began to make water on account of her striking on an old rock when coming out of the Isle of France.

On September 23d, at 12, meridian, we came to anchor at Port Dauphin, Madagascar, in 12 fathoms of water with a rocky bottom, it being a very bad roadstead. Later we weighed anchor and beat up under the fort which was called the one-gun battery. The natives came down with white flags flying to direct us to the best anchorage and would have had us haul our stern close in to the landing place and make fast to a gun that the French had laid down for that use, but our captain paid but little attention to their signs and came to anchor in twenty-five fathoms, about half a musket-shot from the battery. Sent a boat ashore and found one white man here, a German, a renegade from the Isle of France, who had but little command over the natives. They met us at the landing armed with muskets, spears and knives and conducted us to the fort where the white man was who informed us that the king lived at a town four miles in the country and would be down the next day. He told us that we must make the king a present or we should not be able to get any rice. The next day the king came down with a large train of armed men and we sent him two muskets, a barrel of powder and a kittysol as a present and desired him to come on board; but he thought the present was not sufficient and would not come that night.

Early on the morning of the 25th, the king made his appearance again on the bank and the boat was sent ashore for him to come on board but he would not except that we left an officer on shore in his room. Mr. Cartright, the second mate of the *Eleanore,* agreed to stay on shore and accordingly the king came off with his queen. She had lived at the Isle of France for two years and understood the French tongue very well and served as an interpreter for the king. With them was an Arabian, a stout, savage-looking fellow who wanted as many presents from us as though we had come to slave instead of to wood and water. The king asked for a great number of things that took his fancy, particularly our muskets that he saw laying in the cabin. When he found that our captain would not give him any more presents he began to grit his teeth in a very savage manner, being about half drunk at the time, and soon went ashore grumbling, and knocked down two of our wood cutters. Seeing this our people all took to the boat and came aboard bringing Mr. Cartright with them. At the time, the *Eleanore* had five girls and three men aboard and wouldn't let them go on shore.

In the afternoon they began to fetch down the wood that we had cut and piled it up on the beach and made signals to us to come and fetch it. Accordingly we sent a boat ashore for it but by the time we got our boat half laden the king made a signal with his spear, from a hill near by, for his people to close upon our boat's crew and they flew upon our men and took two of them on their shoulders, viz., John Bradley and Francis de Mace, a Frenchman, and ran away like a parcel of deer. The rest of our men took to the boat and defended themselves with billets of wood for the natives ran into the surf and tried to drag the boat on shore. It was upwards of half an hour before they could get clear of them and the boat was no sooner out of the surf than they began to fire with muskets. One musket ball went through the stern of the boat and wounded the boatswain in the arm. By this time both vessels began to fire at them. Our vessel had a brass four pounder which I loaded with nearly half a nine pound cartridge, but the captain insisted upon having more powder put in and so I loaded her almost up to the muzzle and after elevating the gun for the shore, I took a long stick of fire, for with the common britchens the gun would fly round against the capstan, and for the same reason I went behind the capstan to fire her, to prevent her breaking my legs. But our cook, being about half drunk, ran with a brand of fire and fired her before I could do it myself and the gun burst and wounded the captain on his lip and the cook in his arm and knocked all the victuals out of the caboose. At the same time two men were killed on shore which soon put an end to their firing for before that they were firing from behind every bush on shore.

The next morning, at daylight, we saw the natives busily employed in digging a hole in the wall of the fort and at 8 A. M. they pointed a gun at us, but at 12, meridian, they sent a flag of truce down to the shore for our boat to come on shore and make an exchange of prisoners. We did so and got our two men on board but kept two of the natives still on board. The next day it blew a very heavy gale, right upon shore, so that we expected every minute to break adrift and drive ashore to be left to the mercy of the savages; but fortunately at four o'clock the wind died away and we got up the yards and topmasts.

The morning after began with clear and pleasant weather with light airs off land. At 6 A. M. both vessels got under way and ran out of the harbour and hove to while our boats went in and tried to find the anchor of the *Eleanore* which she lost while trying to weigh. They went in close under the fort and kept sweeping for the anchor and all the time the natives kept pointing their gun at us and threatening to fire if we did not send their two men ashore. Our captain told them if they fired at us he would hang them both at the yard arm and that prevented them from doing any mischief. At 4 P. M. we gave up looking for the anchor and ran alongshore to find another harbour, called Port Louis.

On the morning of September 28th, we came to anchor at Port Louis and their king came off and gave us liberty to wood and water. The captain gave him a small swivel and some liquor and he promised to supply us with rice. He seemed to be fully acquainted with what had happened at Fort Dauphin. We also bought a bullock. They behaved very civil to us but told a great many deceitful stories about the rice for in a day or two we found that they hadn't got any for themselves to eat, much less to trade to us.

October 1st, 1792, began with clear weather and all hands employed in getting everything clear for sea and at 10 A. M., seeing no prospect of getting any rice, we weighed anchor and got under sail eastbound for the islands of Kerguelen. Until the 25th, nothing remarkable happened save that the *Eleanore* continued making water so as to keep one pump going continually. That day she hoisted a signal for our boat to come on board and when coming away, Captain Metcalf gave to his son a small copper speaking trumpet to take on board with him, but Mr. Porter, the chief mate on the *Eleanore*, claimed the trumpet and said that it was his and refused to give it up. The captain then asked the armourer and found that his two mates had cut the top of the copper stove without orders, which put him into such a rage that he broke his two mates and made Mr. Williamson, the mate of the *Ino,* the mate of the *Eleanore*, in place of Mr. Porter, and made me mate of the *Ino,* in the place of Mr. Williamson.

November 29th began with clear and pleasant weather it being the first fair day that we had had for the past

ten days. Early in the morning we saw a great number
of penguins, divers, and rock weeds and other signs of
land. At 5 P. M. saw Mr. Blith's Cape,[46] distant about
four leagues, and several other barren rocks covered
all over with birds, after a tedious passage of fifty days
attended with dirty, rainy and blowing weather with
our decks covered with water most of the passage. At
7 P. M. we ran by Cape Francisco, which is a high, barren rock standing nearly perpendicular with penguins
covering it nearly one third of the way up. It makes
one side of Christmas Harbour. When we doubled the
cape we saw the *Eleanore* laying at anchor in Christmas Harbour and ran in and came to in twenty-five
fathoms of water about half a mile from the arch that
Captain Cook gives an account of in his voyage to this
place. We sent the boat on shore at the arch and found
it covered over with penguins. The boat's crew brought
off a great number of their eggs.

The next morning it blew very fresh out of the harbour and both vessels broke adrift and drifted out a
considerable ways and hove to in our cables and found
that each vessel had lost one fluke from its anchor.
Later in the morning we beat up into the harbour and
sent a boat ashore and went by the directions that Captain Cook gave and found the bottle[47] laying in a pile
of stones with a lead cap over it. Broke it open and
found the English two-penny piece and *Mons'r Kurguelen's* and Captain Cook's letters and also a letter of
Captain Durgin of the brig *Phœnix,* from Macao. Saw
a great number of sea elephants, sea lions, bears and
seals but very few of the seals were furred ones.

Seeing no prospect of getting any skins for China on

account of their being the wrong sort for that market, the next morning we weighed anchor bound southward in quest of a good harbour in which to load our vessels with oil for the Isle of France and to overhaul and repair our rigging and also to heave the *Eleanore* down to stop her leaks. Saw a great amount of kelp and rockweed with sunken rocks, their tops about two feet below the surface and very dangerous to shipping, for alongside these rocks will be found twenty-seven fathoms of water. At 4 P. M. came to anchor in a very fine bay and sent a boat ashore and found plenty of sea elephants, lions and seals. Moored both of vessels' sterns inshore and made fast to the rocks.

All hands went ashore the next morning to erect a couple of tents in which to boil our oil and at 6 P. M. all was completed and we killed eighteen or twenty lions and elephants and took the blubber from them and got our pots at work the evening. All hands were then put upon an allowance of flour — four pints for four men and no bread — so that our chief living was penguins and their eggs and a sort of wild cabbage that we picked up on the shore. It had a kind of peppery taste and was the only vegetable that grew on that barren land. During the next two weeks we were employed in making oil and fetching blubber from other parts of the island. On the 16th, we hove the *Eleanore* down to try to stop her leaks.

On January 1st, 1793, Captain Metcalf made or marked out the thirteen stripes and "U. S. A." on a sheet of copper and stuck it in a rock with an iron standard with braces of the same to prevent the wind from blowing it down and left a bottle with a letter in

it and named the place *Port Ino.* Twelve days later we
finished getting on board the oil — six hundred barrels
in all — and at 10 A. M. got under way bound for the
Isle of France. Hove to off Christmas Harbour to send
on shore the bottle with Captain Cook's letter, but the
wind blew so fresh that it was impossible for a boat to
land and we proceeded on our course. Made the islands of St. Paul and Amsterdam and ran close in towards Amsterdam which we could see was on fire in
several places.

I sailed from the Isle of France on March 17th, 1793,
in the ship *Pen,* a South Seaman belonging to Dunkirk, Capt. Obed Fitch, commander. This ship belonged to Mr. Rotch, an American merchant living at
Dunkirk.[48] At 6 P. M. ran by the island of Bourbon,
bound into Mosambique Channel to cruise for spermaceti whales and thence to Delegoa Bay to load our ship
with right whale oil for Dunkirk.

Saw large schools of spermaceti whales on April 5th
and the first and second mates' boats put off and gave
chase to them while the captain, with his boat's crew,
stayed on board to follow the boats with the ship until
they got fast to some of the whales. They rowed for
upwards of an hour when all the whales went down and
they lay on their oars and kept a good outlook for their
rising again. In about half an hour's time, a whale
came up and the chief mate got fast to her which soon
raised the rest of the school round her, for if you strike
a whale, and the rest of the school are at the bottom,
they will rise immediately and lay like so many logs
of wood on the water for some time. Then they will
draw up in straight lines and run to windward, side by

side, as if they were so many soldiers. When the captain saw that the chief mate had got fast, he put off with his boat. We met a whale coming with head towards the head of our boat so that we struck her head and head which hove the line out of the chocks of the boat and nearly swept every man out of her. The whale sounded and took the line abaft to the loggerhead of the boat and brought her stern down to the water.

Four days later we saw a school of whales and killed six of them and got four on board. They made sixty-two barrels of oil. On the 14th, while still cruising in the Mosambique Channel, early in the morning we saw a large school of spermaceties and loaded away all three boats. Our boat killed three, the chief mate two, and the second mate two. Got them all cabled safe alongside when the wind sprung up and blew very fresh and two of the ropes, that we had fast, broke and we lost two whales but saved the other five which made us forty-two barrels of oil.

On May 8th we killed two more whales and saw twelve or thirteen waterspouts which were broken up by a heavy clap of thunder. The next day, sent the mate's boat after a humpback, but it came back without her. On the 12th, saw a large school of spermaceties, killed seven and saved four. Began to cut in at 6 P. M. and finished cutting and got the try works under way at 6 o'clock the next morning. The body made us eighty barrels of oil and the head matter, ten barrels. We then had 255 barrels in the hold. During the rest of the month we killed five whales. On the 31st spoke the ship *Leveret,* Obed Bunker, commander, from Dunkirk bound into Delegoa Bay after a load of right whale oil. We agreed to mate our ships and to go as partners and at 6 P. M. we shaped our course for Delegoa Bay.

At 4 P. M. the next day we made Cape St. Mary's, which makes on side of Delegoa Bay, and ran into five fathoms of water and lay to that night with our heads off shore, about two leagues from the land. Two days later we sighted three ships laying in a small bay. One of them was trying out. On June 4th saw a right whale but could not make fast. Lost the fishhook overboard at 10 A. M. At meridian, Capts. Hess and Gardiner came on board and informed that the Portuguese governor had ordered the ship *Dolphin* out of the bay and not to kill any more whales. He said that he would send for a frigate to drive all the ships out of the bay. At 2 P. M. came to anchor in nine fathoms of water off Red Head. Found here three whaling ships, viz. the *Dolphin,* Capt. Aaron Gardiner, the *Niger,* Capt. Hess, belonging to Laurient, and the *Edward,* Capt. Cager Gardiner, from Dunkirk. Hove up the small bower and found it stranded about two fathoms from the clinch. Cut it off and shifted it end for end.

June 5th began clear and pleasant. At 4 P. M. called all hands out to get their breakfast before daylight to be in readiness to go in the boat, which is the rule of whalers. At 6 A. M. saw a whale and all the boats put off in chase. The second mate got fast to her and Mr. Hammond, Captain Bunker's chief mate, got fast to the calf. There were six boats on her. Hove three irons into her which made her spout blood. Gave her three lances and killed her. The killing place of a right whale is between the eye and the fin. At 12, meridian, the ship *Planter,* Capt. George Hale, arrived from London, and the ship *America,* Capt. *Thuten* Gardiner, commander, from Dunkirk, both whaling ships. The whale that we killed, Captain Bunker took; the next is for our ship. At 3 A. M. the next morning our ship broke adrift. We let go the small bower and brought her up again. At 9 A. M., hove short and our captain, being unacquainted in taking up anchors, would heave in both cables at once which brought the sheet cable across the small bower and put us to a great deal of trouble. We hove up the small bower, hooked the cat and brought the anchor to the opposite cat head, unbent the cable and cleared it of the other cable and then bent it again. At 4 P. M. we saw a cow whale with her calf and two boats went after her. She got galled and ran out of the bay, which put them to a great deal of trouble. At 6 P. M. they came aboard.

Mr. Whippey killed a porpoise on July 9th and that morning we saw the tarpaulin hoisted on board Captain Bunker's ship, for all captains to come on board and dine on roast pork. This afternoon our chief mate took a hand to moor the ship but made as bad a hand of it as the captain did. The next morning all the captains went on shore to the Portuguese fort to see if they could make any trade with the governor and also to buy some refreshment for their men. At the landing we were met by a great number of the natives, more civil than we expected. The governor gave us liberty to buy anything from the natives except ivory and we bought one bullock, a calf, a goat and some fowls, sweet potatoes and plantains. The governor set the natives to kill the bullock for us and they drove spears into him. When the beast found himself wounded he began to run at a great rate, with thirty or forty natives after him, until they had twenty-two or three spears in him which at last brought the beast to his knees. They then came up and soon killed him. The man that skinned him was to have his guts which made a great disturbance amongst them. In fighting for the guts one man cut another man's hand almost off. The natives took the guts as they came out of the bullock and ate them without cleaning and the dung would cling to each side of their mouths while they were eating. What spare guts were left they hung down their breasts to eat some other time. We were told the natives were descendants from the Hottentots who inhabit about the Cape of Good Hope. At 12 o'clock at night we got all safe on board.

The next day was Tuesday and at 6 A. M. all the mates from the ships went down to Cow Bay to look out for whales and all the captains went on board of Captain Bunker to divide the stock that had been bought at the fort. The mates came back at 4 P. M., not having sighted any whales. As they came down the river they cut some mangroves for iron poles. Saw a troup of sea horses and a man on shore fishing who made off as fast as possible as soon as he saw the boats. This day our people invited Captain Bunker's people on board to partake of a sea pie. We entertained them with a fiddle and had plenty of grog. At 7 P. M. they went on board. The most of them, and also our own people, were drunk as a result of the frolick.

June 12th, the mates put off in search of whales and late in the morning we saw a whale coming with eight

HOTTENTOTS DEVOURING THE ENTRAILS OF BULLOCK

From an engraving in Drake's *Collection of Voyages*, London, 1770, in the Library of Congress

or nine boats following close after her. She was coming with her head towards the head of our boat. When she was within twice the length of our boat we laid upon our oars by which means we lost our chance of her and the boats of the ship *America* killed her. This day the *Planter* killed one and the *Edward* one. The next morning three vessels arrived from Dunkirk, viz., the ship *Benjamin*, Capt. Isaac Hussey, the ship *Corjue*, Captain Swain, and the brig ————, Capt. James Whippey.

The next Saturday Mr. Whippey got fast to a whale which ran him a great way off and the sun going down and we being about seven leagues from our ship, with the wind and tide against us, we made a signal with a jacket upon an oar for Mr. Whippey to cut from the whale and to go aboard. We got on board at 12 o'clock at night after rowing nineteen hours against wind and tide the most of the time that day.

Tuesday, June 18th, 1793, at 6 A. M. our boat and one other went out to look for whales and found one drifted on the shore. It burst and made a report as loud as a three pounder. We cut the irons out. The *America* killed one today and the *Planter* one. The next day our captain went up the river to go on board of Captain Whippey's brig, to bury Christian Johnson in the earth for the scurvey in his legs.[49] Also went to make trade with John Eney, one of the head chiefs belonging to King Copall country but could not make any trade for bullocks. The next day we went on shore to the King Copall country and at the landing saw John Eney standing at high water mark, dressed in an old surtout coat and a small cocked hat. He made it his business to place all the natives on the grass as they came down to trade with us. When the captains advanced up the beach he came down to meet them and saluted them with a low bow.

*　*　*　*　*　*　*　*

Just at this interesting point the Bartlett journal comes to an abrupt ending and little else is now known of his after life and adventures save copies of two letters that appear at the end of his journal, showing that he had been pressed by some English man-of-war.[50] On Jan. 21, 1795 he was at "Brunswick," on board some ship shortly going to sea, and then in bad health and destitute condition. He had applied for a discharge to Lord Charles Fitzgerald and to the Port Admiral, Sir Peter Parker, but without success. Mr. Johnson, the United States consul, had laid his case before Mr. Thomas Pinckney, the American Minister, who had not been able to secure his release. He was hoping at that time to secure his "India note for wages" in order to obtain some necessaries and the letter to the unknown correspondent closes with the statement that he had never taken any bounty money or wages and that he never would and he was fully determined "never to take up arms for any but my own country, let the consequences be what it will." Amasa Delano, the second officer of the *Massachusetts,* on which Bartlett made his voyage to Canton, wrote a "Narrative" of his voyages and adventures which was published and in it he states that Bartlett was born in Boston and died at some time before 1816.

INDIAN VOCABULARY

In use from the Latitude of 52° North to the Southward about Charlotte's Island.

Iron	*Achyeach*
Coat	*Codats*
Cut	*Coo*
Chief	*Smoket*
Sing	*Cutoutluck*
Sleep	*Cude*
Ship	*Clue*
Skin	*Nicke*
Small	*Surmon*
Sun	*Luxstuckus*
Buttons	*Comalong*
Beads	*Cowet*
Long	*Eueone*
Look at anything	*King*
No	*Come*
Not good	*Pashack*
Knife	*Carth*
Woman	*Eno*
Water	*Hartle*
To go away	*Cluter*
Good	*Lux*
To ask the name of a thing	*Kisingtingtang*
Present	*Tingester*
To tread	*Wattele*
A tin pot	*Scutlong*
More	*Quan*
The Moon	*Cong*
Copper	*Cul*

NOTES ON BARTLETT'S NARRATIVE

By His Honour F. W. Howay, LL.B., F.R.S.C., of New Westminster, B. C.

1. Probably the purser, Nathaniel Shaw, a brother of the owner of the *Massachusetts*.

2. For a sketch of the life of Capt. John Kendrick who commanded the first trading venture sent to the Northwest Coast from Boston, see "Oregon Historical Quarterly," vol. xxiii, pp. 277-302.

3. A custom house boat which was usually placed near foreign vessels to prevent infractions of the strange Chinese regulations; these boats were always ready to supply provisions.

4. Of the sixty-one men on board the *Massachusetts*, twenty-three were British.

5. A snow was a two-masted, square-rigged vessel somewhat like a brig, but having the spanker on a gunter mast just abaft the mizzen mast. The terms "snow," "brig," and "brigantine" were used almost interchangeably on the Northwest Coast.

6. Very little is known concerning this man who was one of the earliest Americans to enter the Northwest trade. It is possible that he may have been there a season before the coming of the *Columbia* and the *Washington*, usually spoken of as the pioneer American vessels in this trade. Bartlett afterwards sailed with him to the Isle of France and thence a sealing.

7. 'Squire Cox, was John Henry Cox, well-known in the fur trade of the Northwest Coast.

8. *Gustavus III*, appears to have been her full name.

9. Barkley sound, the southernmost of the sounds on the west coast of Vancouver island, named for Capt. Charles William Barkley who traded here for furs in 1787, while in command of the *Imperial Eagle,* a British vessel, but sailing under the Austrian flag in order to evade the monopoly of the South Sea Company.

10. Port Cox, in Clayoquot sound, which lies west of Barkley sound and is about fifty miles distant. Wickananish was the chief of that region and his name, spelled in various ways, appears in all the accounts of early voyages.

11. This was chief Cleaskinah, but he exchanged names with Captain Hannah of the *Sea Otter* in 1786. The custom of exchanging names, in token of friendship, was quite common on the coast.

12. The Indian name of Wickananish's village or town was Opitsat. It is commonly called Clayoquot village at present and is situated on Meares' island in Clayoquot sound. Haswell calls it Opitsel'ah; Hoskins, Opitsitah; Boit, Opitsatah; Father Brabant, Opissat. It will be found on Meares' map of Port Cox, being the northerly one of the two villages there shown. It was destroyed by Capt. Robert Gray on Mar. 27, 1792. Boit says that it was half a mile in diameter and contained more than two hundred houses. "Every door you entered was in resemblance to an human and beast's head, besides which there was much more rude carved work about their dwellings, some of which was by no means inelegant." *See* "Oregon Historical Quarterly," vol. xxii, p. 303.

13. One of the Scott islands lying off the northwestern extremity of Vancouver island. No other trader seems to have given them this name. Hanna, in 1786, named them Lance's islands; Dixon, in 1787, named them Beresford's islands; but as Lowrie and Guise, who had preceeded Hanna in 1786, had called them Scott's islands, Vancouver placed that name on his chart and it has remained.

14. The cutsacks, or cotsacks as Meares calls them, of the traders, usually made of three sea otter skins.

15. This is called the labret or staie, and the custom prevailed on the Northwest Coast from Prince William sound in Alaska to Queen Charlotte sound.

16. Ucah, he was called by Ingraham. His principal village was at Skincuttle inlet on the east coast of Queen Charlotte islands.

17. Cloak Bay lies between North island and Graham island, the northerly of the two large islands of the Queen Charlotte group. It was discovered and named by Dixon in 1787 because of the number of sea-otter cloaks he obtained there.

18. This is the chief mentioned in Meares' voyage under the name of Blakow-Coneehaw, with whom Captain Douglas exchanged names in June, 1789.

19. Marchand (Voyages, London, 1801) found celery, parsley, purslain, water-cress, peas and vetches growing along the western shores of this island in August, 1791.

20. Probably Bonilla island, near Banks island, on the eastern side of Hecate strait. It is 550 feet high and was originally named Hatch's island by Captain Gray in 1791, for Charles Hatch, one of the owners of the *Columbia*. The charts of that time were mere fragments made by the traders. There was no real chart until Vancouver's was made.

21. No other trader mentions a chief by this name. He probably was Clue, a chief whose village, Tanu, was and is located about twenty miles south of Cumshewa, on the eastern coast of Queen Charlotte islands.

22. Cumshewa was a powerful chief whose village was on the northern side of Cumshewa inlet.

23. In 1793, Cumshewa and his tribe cut off the schooner used as a tender by the *Jefferson* of Boston, Captain Roberts, and massacred all the crew but one.

24. Skidegate, another prominent chief, described by Ingraham as a man of low stature and seemingly feeble constitution with a mild and agreeable countenance.

25. The *Gustavus* was making a successful voyage. The traders usually left the coast about the first of September.

26. The highest summit of the San Christobal range is 4,500 feet.

27. This latitude is clearly wrong for it places the *Gustavus* in the vicinity of Norton sound in Bering Sea, where the fur traders never went and, moreover, it would have been impossible for her to have covered the distance in the eleven days that had elapsed since she passed Cape St. James. The high land seen probably was Mount St. Elias, in latitude 60°, which is over 18,000 feet high.

28. At Prince William sound, Captain Cook found that some of the elderly men wore large, thick and straight beards. He also describes the perforation of the septum of the nose by the quill feathers of small birds.

29. The *Grace* was purchased from an American by a Mr. Douglas, a Scotchman, and placed under the protection of the American flag in order to avoid the monopoly of the South Sea Company. Douglas had been in command of the Meares' ship, the *Iphigenia*, when that vessel was seized by the Spaniards in 1789. Ingraham says that he died on this voyage, in 1791, between the Hawaiian islands and China.

30. The threatened war arising from the capture of Meares' vessels at Nootka sound in 1789, but which was settled by the Nootka Convention in 1790.

31. This was Norfolk sound, so named by Dixon in 1787, but now known as Sitka sound, Alaska.

32. This is one of the earliest references to the totem poles or heraldic columns of the Haida Indians. The first traders carried on trade off shore, as the ship lay to, and in consequence never saw the villages of the Indians.

33. Capt. John Kendrick, in command of the *Lady Washington,* usually called the *Washington,* had altered her rig from a sloop to a brig in 1790-1791 and in March, 1791, had sailed from Lark's Bay, sometimes called Dirty Butter Bay, three or four leagues from Macao, and arrived at Houston Stewart channel, near Cape St. James, on June 13th.

34. Typhoon. In strict usage this term is confined to the China Sea.

35. Now called Kealakekua Bay.

36. Kiana, a chief from Atooi, one of the Hawaiian Islands, whom Meares had taken to China in 1787 and returned the next year.

37. Vancouver says that it was Kameeiamoko who captured the vessel. The schooner *Fair American,* commanded by Captain Metcalf's son, a young man of eighteen, was captured in Toyahyah (Kawaihae) Bay, in March, 1790.

38. Tapa or kapa cloth, meaning *beaten.* It was thrown away when soiled.

39. Atooi (Kauai), discovered by Captain Cook.

40. Not to be confused with the Ladrone islands which lie to the northeastward of the Philippines. Probably the Grand Lema island, "a ruling mark" for the entrance to Macao Roads.

41. The Chinese were at war with Russia and had prohibited all trade in furs under the mistaken idea that all fur ships in some way were concerned with the Russians.

42. He was also the agent for the *Grace* and had resided at Macao for some years.

43. The *Lady Washington* did not, however, actually depart for the Northwest Coast until nine months later, in September, 1792.

44. The *Eleanore* was a New York vessel and was trading on the Northwest Coast in 1789 and perhaps the previous year. Captain Metcalf was killed by the natives of Queen Charlotte Islands in 1794 when they captured his brig and massacred all the crew except one man.

45. Fort Spielwyk, built by the Dutch in 1683. An English factory was established here in 1603 and continued until the massacre of the agents in 1677.

46. Blight's Cape, named for Lieutenant Bligh, the master of the *Discovery* and later famous in connection with the mutiny of the *Bounty*.

47. The bottle had been left by Monsieur de Kerguelen in December, 1773, when he took possession of the land for the King of France. Captain Cook found the bottle and wrote on the other side of the parchment left by de Kerguelen that the English vessels *Resolution* and *Discovery* had visited the spot in December, 1776.

48. These whalers hailed from Dunkirk and other French ports, because the French government offered inducements to Americans to emigrate and engage in the fishery.

49. The mere sight of land, the residence on land and the part-burial in the earth have all been found effective in the cure of scurvy. Bering was half-buried in the sand of Bering's Isle, in 1741, in an attempt to cure him of scurvy.

50. From a memorandum furnished by Prof. S. F. Bemis, it appears that Bartlett at one time secured his release from a Dutch ship at the Cape of Good Hope by declaring himself to be a British subject. On the general subject of impressments at that time, *see* "American Historical Review," vol. xxviii, pp. 228-247.

INDEX

Abercrombie, Sir Ralph, 162, 164.

Abergavanna *(ship)*, 291.

Aborn, Captain, 96.

Aboukir Bay, Battle of, 159.

Aitken, Captain, 143.

Ajax *(frigate)*, 162, 164.

Albatross eggs, 28, 34.

Albion *(whaler)*, 210.

Albrook, Joseph, 14, 22, 29, 47, 50, 57, 65, 75, 76.

Alexandria, Seige of, 163.

Amelia *(whaler)*, 144, 147, 151.

America *(whaler)*, 333, 335.

Anacan Islands, 3.

Anchor *(whaler)*, 119.

Ansel, Samuel, 14, 22, 29, 30, 32, 45, 47, 49, 50, 56, 58, 64.

Antelope *(ship)*, 284.

Antony, Jose, 293, 315.

Louis, 294, 298.

Manuel, 293.

Armstrong, John, 290.

Ascension Island, 199.

Asp *(whaler)*, 72.

Astraea *(Spanish frigate)*, 213.

Bailey, Capt. Samuel G., 89, 92, 96.

Baker, William, 220, 225.

Balcarras, William, 163.

Bantom Roads, Java, 321.

Barefoot, Captain, 151.

Barkley, Capt. Charles, 339.

Barkley Sound, 339.

Barnard, Capt. Charles H., sails from New York, 1; arrives at Falkland Islands, 2; discovers wreck of ship *Isabella*, 6; rescues the party, 13; is deserted by ship, 14; hardships suffered, 20; account of wild hogs, 24; captures large sea lion, 27; is deserted by his companions, 30; life while alone, 32; finds peat, 39; companions return, 46; goes after seal skins, 56; rescued by English whalers, 70; lands at Callao, 75; goes ashore on Massafuero Island, 77; taken off by ship *Millwood*, 90; visits Hawaiian Islands, 93; reaches Whampoa and takes passage for United States, 96; in severe storm off coast of Natal, 97; reaches Martha's Vineyard, 102.

Barnard, Valentine, 1, 103.

Barnet, Capt. Thomas, 291, 293.

Bartlett, Captain, 295.

Bartlett, John, sails from Boston in the *Massachusetts*, 287; reaches Wampoa, 291; ships on board the snow *Gustavus*, for a voyage to the Northwest Coast, 291; ship's list, 293; reaches Northwest Coast, 295; account of natives, 297; attacked by natives, 299; on short rations, 306; reaches

Hawaiian Islands, 308; natives attempt to capture the brig, 311; in severe storm, 314-316; saves his otter skins, 318; ships on board a Portuguese ship, 319; ships on board the *Lady Washington* for another Northwest Coast voyage but does not sail, 320; ships on board the snow *Eleanore* for Isle of France, 321; sails on sealing voyage to Kurguelen Land, 323; adventures with the natives at Madagascar, 323-327 sails from Isle of France on a Dunkirk whaler for the Mozambique Channel, 330; sees Hottentots kill a bullock, 334; is pressed on board an English man-of-war, 336.

Bartlett's Sound, 295.

Batavia, 289, 290.

Beaver *(ship)*, 129.

Beaver Island, Falkland Islands, 14, 15, 28, 42, 44, 58, 66.

Belvidere *(ship)*, 291.

Bemis, Prof. S. F., 343.

Bengal *(ship)*, 99.

Benjamin *(whaler)*, 335.

Bent, Robert, 215.

Bering, Captain, 343.

Blake, Nicholas, 286.

Bligh, Captain, 12.

    Lieutenant, 343.

Boit, ——, 339.

Bombay Castle *(man-of-war)*, 157.

Bond, Captain, 113.

Boston, Mass., 288.

Botany Bay, 10, 12.

Bradley, John, 325.

Briggs, Daniel, 287.

British Tar *(whaler)*, 214.

Brittania *(man-of-war)*, 156, 158.

Brittania *(whaler)*, 214.

Brooks, Captain, 8, 13.

Brothers *(vessel)*, 291.

Brown, ——, 216, 218, 221, 222, 224, 284.

    Robert, 286.

    Thomas, 281, 286.

    William, 286.

Buckle, Capt. William, 72, 74, 77.

Buenos Ayres, 12.

Bunker, Capt. Obed, 331-334.

Burgoyne, General, 108.

Butler, John, 129.

Callao, Peru, 75, 76.

Canton, 1, 96, 287, 291, 292, 317.

Cannibalism, 240.

Cape de Verd Islands, 2.

Cape Horn, 74.

Cape St. Vincent, Battle off, 155.

Carlton, Samuel, 285.

Carnetic *(ship)*, 292.

Cartright, ——, 324, 325.

Chapman, Leonard, 293.

Charlestown, ——, 291.

Chase, Captain, 268, 285.

    Capt. Obed, 3.

Chesapeake *(frigate)*, 73.

Chinese hogs, 292.
Clanding, ——, 94.
Cloak Bay, 340.
Cochrane, Capt. Alexander F., 162.
Cocos Islands, 215.
Cole, ——, 91, 92.
Collis, Lieutenant, 158.
Columbia (schooner), 94, 96.
Columbia (ship), 338, 340.
Conception, Chili, 210.
Convict ship, 136.
Cook, Capt. James, 121, 123, 137, 308, 328, 341, 343.
Cook's River, Northwest Coast of America, 124, 131.
Corjue (whaler), 335.
Corsica, 155.
Cottle, Capt. Obed, 212.
Cotton Planter (ship), 115.
Cow Mooala (Tonga chief), 270-275.
Cox, John Henry, 292, 317, 338.
Cozus, Samuel, 75.
Cuffnells (ship), 284.
Cyrus (whaler), 76.

Davis, George, 8.
Davy, Captain, 76.
Dawson, Thomas, 281, 286.
Day, Captain, 76.
Deaman, Antony, 294.
Decenter, Manuel, 293.
Delano, Amasa, 336.
Delegoa Bay, 330.
Dick, Sir John, 129.
Dickson, ——, 130.

Discovery (ship), 343.
Dixon, ——, 220-222.
Capt. George, 118, 131.
Dolphin (whaler), 332.
Donnison, Captain, 290.
Dorset, Sarah, 138.
Douglas, Captain, 305, 306, 340, 341.
Dublin, Ireland, 10.
Duck, Captain, 208, 216, 217, 223.
Duke de Chartres (man-of-war), 161.
Duncan, Admiral, 153.
Dunkin, William, 72.
Dunkirk, 343.
Durgin, Captain, 328.
Durie, Captain, 7, 10, 13.

Eagleston, Capt. John H., 184, 193.
Earl St. Vincent (whaler), 209.
East India Company's ships, 284.
Edgar, Lieutenant, 137.
Edgar (man-of-war), 153, 154.
Edinburgh, 165.
Edward (whaler), 332, 335.
Egypt, 164.
Eleanore (brig), 309.
Eleanore (snow), 321, 326-329, 343.
Eliza (whaler), 76, 77, 90.
Embargo law, 2.
Emery, ——, 194.
William, 293, 317.
Enterprise (ship), 95.
Essex (frigate), 73.

Evans, Henry, 293.
Everett, Captain, 95.
Eversfield, Thomas, 286.

Fair American (schooner),
   342.
Falkland Islands, 1-74, 119.
Fanning, Edmund, 1, 6.
Favorite (brig), 279, 283, 285,
   286.
Ferrel, Nance, 140.
Fiji Islands, 183-191, 193-198,
   270-274.
Fingal (ship), 99.
Fisk, Captain, 279, 283.
Fitch, Capt. Obed, 330.
Fitzgerald, Lord Charles, 336.
   Robert, 285.
Foley, Captain, 158.
Folger, Captain, 214.
Foot, Malachi, 291, 293.
Ford, William, 284.
Francisco, Capt. Jose, 319.
Freer, Thomas, 294, 315.
French, Thomas, 289.

Gallapagos Islands, 77, 90.
Gardiner, Capt. Aaron, 332.
   Capt. Cager, 332.
   Capt. Thuten, 333.
Geese, 67.
General Scott (ship), 97.
Gibralter, 162.
Gibson, William, 293.
Gilbert Islands, 271.
Gilchrist, Harry, 2.
Goa, 318.
Goats, 85.

Goliah (74 gun ship), 154,
   156-162.
Gore, Captain, 129.
Grace (brig), 305, 341, 342.
Granada, W. I., 115.
Gray, Captain Le, 290.
   Capt. Robert, 339, 340.
   Samuel, 293, 305.
Green, Jacob, 1, 14, 22, 29, 50,
   57, 65, 71.
Greenland, 113, 114.
Grounard, Joseph, 291, 293.
Guardian (ship), 136.
Gustavus (snow), 291, 292,
   318, 338, 341.

Hale, Capt. George, 333.
Halsey, Captain, 99.
Hammond, ——, 332.
Hannah, Captain, 339.
Harris, John, 291, 293.
Hatch, Charles, 340.
Havens, Tenant, 1, 6.
Hawaiian Islands, 93-95, 121-
   124, 130, 217, 308-314.
Hays, Sir Henry B., 10-13.
Head, Benjamin, 291, 293.
Hearsey, John, 285.
Herald (ship), 99.
Hess, Captain, 332.
Higgins, Jeremiah, 269, 285.
Higton, Capt. George, 8, 9, 12.
Hoay, James, 220, 225.
Hogs, account of wild, 24, 52,
   58.
Holt, General, 7, 9.
Hope, Admiral, 153.
Hope (brig), 313.

Hope *(ship)*, 3, 268, 285.
Hope *(whaler)*, 119.
Hottentots, 334.
Howard, William, 293.
Howay, Judge F. W., 338.
Hunt, Captain, 99.
Hunter, Thomas, 2.
Hussey, Capt. Isaac, 335.

Imperial Eagle *(ship)*, 339.
Impressment of sailors, 150.
Indian vocabulary, 337.
Indispensable *(whaler)*, 72, 76, 77.
Inflexible *(man-of-war)*, 154.
Ingham, Henry, 1.
Ingraham, Captain, 313.
Ino *(brig)*, 322, 327.
Iphigenia *(ship)*, 341.
Isabella *(ship)*, wreck of, 7, 47.
Isle of France, 322.

Jason *(privateer ship)*, 107, 108.
Jason Islands, 2.
Java Head, 289.
Jefferson *(sloop)*, 340.
Jennings, Captain, 94, 96.
Jervis, Sir John, 154.
Johnson, ——, 336.
    Christian, 335.
Jones, William, 117.
Julia *(brig-of-war)*, 100.

Kelly, James, 220, 225.
Kendrick, Capt. John, 290, 307, 320, 338, 342.

Kenneday, Captain, 322.
Kenny, Capt. John, 72, 73.
Kerwin, Mrs. Nelly, 139.
King, Antony Jose, 293.
King George *(ship)*, 118, 128, 131, 132.
Knights, Capt. John B., sails from Salem in the brig *Spy*, 168; reaches New Zealand, 170; account of the natives, 171-182; sails for the Fiji Islands, 182; narrowly escapes being cut off by the natives, 186; account of the natives, 188-190; returns to New Zealand and again sails for the Fijis, 191; life on the island of Rotumah, 194; discovers an island and names it New Salem, 200; is attacked by natives, 201; reaches Manilla and sells his vessel, 207.
Knowles, Capt. Charles H., 153, 157.
Knox, Tom, 93.
Kurguelen Land, 323, 328.

Ladrone Islands, 132.
Lady Julian *(ship)*, 136, 144.
Lady Washington *(sloop)*, 290, 320, 342.
L'Orient *(man-of-war)*, 160.
Lark *(vessel)*, 94.
Lark's Bay, China, 292, 317, 342.
Laurient *(ship)*, 289.
Lawrence, Joseph, 127.
Leveret *(whaler)*, 331.

Leviathan *(whaler)*, 113.

Lima, Peru, 75.

Lisbon, Portugal, 149.

Loan *(whaler)*, 171.

London, Lieutenant, 8, 13.

London, Eng., 106.

Lott, Andrew, 2.

Louder, James, 14, 29, 46, 49, 57, 64, 70, 75, 76.

Lourden *(ship)*, 295.

Lovis, Robert, 319.

Low, Captain, 322.

Luce, Capt. Jason, 171, 172.

Lucy *(privateer)*, 212, 214.

Lunt, Thomas, 291, 293.

Lush, ——, 96.

Macao, China, 284, 290, 317.

McAskill Island, 204.

Macay, Alexander, 285.

McColaning, John, 293.

McColliff, Captain, 204.

Mace, Francis de, 325.

M'Intire, ——, 317, 318.

Madagascar, 323-327.

Magoun, ——, 184.

Malcolm, Rear-Admiral, 100.

Malta, 161, 164.

Mando, John, 294.

Manley, Capt. John, 107, 108.

Marchand, ——, 340.

Mariner, Magnus, 215.

Mariner, William, sails from Gravesend in the privateer *Port au Prince,* bound for the South Seas, 208; captures prizes and fights a losing battle in the harbor of Conception, Chili, 210; has an engagement with a Spanish frigate, 213; reaches the Tonga Islands where his ship is captured by the natives, 218; is befriended by the King, 226; the ship is broken up, 228; is taken on an expedition against another chief, 230; is given a foster-mother, 232; takes part in an attack on a fortress, 235; narrowly escapes death, 239; cannibal feast, 240; a military review, 243; takes part in an expedition against another island, 245; the assault on the fortress and escape from death, 251; cruelty shown to prisoners, 259; adventure with one of the King's wives, 262; given a plantation, 267; arrival of ship *Hope,* 268; unfortunate sneeze, 275; escapes to brig *Favorite,* 278; preservation of ship's journal, 281.

Marshall, ——, 94.

Martha's Vineyard, 102.

Mason, Capt. Rishworth, 207.

Massachusetts *(ship)*, 287, 336, 338.

Massafuero Island, 77-90.

Mattison, ——, 9.

Meares, Capt. John, 129, 341.

Medcalf, Captain, 95.

Mercer, William, 148, 150.

Mercury *(schooner)*, 285.

Metcalf, ——, 342.

    Robert, 322, 327.

    Captain Simon, 292, 309, 321, 329, 343.

Millwood *(ship)*, 89, 90.
Minerva *(whaler)*, 212.
Missionaries, 175, 180.
Montague, Admiral, 107.
Moscow *(ship)*, 207.
Mozambique Channel, 330.
Murray & Son, John B., 1.
Myers, Jacob, 284.

Nancy *(vessel)*, 291.
Nanina *(brig)*, 1, 12, 103.
Neptune, Father, 2, 142.
Neutrality *(whaler)*, 214.
New Salem Island, 200.
New Zealand, 170-182, 191, 192.
Nicol, John, early life, 105; enters the navy and serves during the American Revolution, 107; ships on a Greenland whaler, 113; sails for the West Indies, 115; ships with Captain Portlock on a voyage to the Northwest Coast of North America, 118; reaches Hawaiian Islands, 121; life on the Northwest Coast, 125; reaches China, 132; sails for New South Wales in a convict ship, 136; ships on a South Sea whaler, 144; reaches London and escapes impressment, 150; sails on the *Nottingham* bound for China, 151; is pressed and serves on the *Venerable* and other ships, 153; in battle off Cape St. Vincent, 155; in battle of Aboukir Bay, 159; leaves the sea and marries his cousin, 165.

Niger *(whaler)*, 332.
Nimrod *(bark)*, 204.
Nimrod *(whaler)*, 76.
Nootka *(ship)*, 129.
Nootka Sound, 130, 131.
Northrup, Captain, 94, 99.
Northwest Coast of North America, 124-131, 295-308, 320.
Nottingham *(East India man)*, 151-153, 165.

O'Caen *(whaler)*, 217.
Owl, 36.

Parish, John, 269, 285.
Parker, George, 146.
    Sir Peter, 336.
Pease, Bazilla, 1.
Peat, 39.
Pedlar *(brig)*, 94, 99.
Pen *(whaler)*, 330.
Penguins, 40.
Perez, Manuel, 286.
Peru *(bark)*, 184.
Phillips, Stephen C., 168.
Phœnix *(brig)*, 328.
Pinckney, Thomas, 336.
Pitcher, Moll, 288.
Pitt, William, 139.
Planter *(whaler)*, 333, 335.
Port au Prince *(privateer)*, 208, 218, 284, 286.
Port Cox, 339.
Port Jackson, N. S. W., 7, 12, 142, 273.
Porter, ——, 327.
    Captain, 73.

Portlock, Capt. Nathaniel, 118, 121, 125, 126, 128, 130, 136.
Portuguese sailors, 147.
Power, William, 139.
Prince, Capt. Job, 287, 292.
Prince William's Sound, 124, 129, 341.
Proteus *(man-of-war)*, 107, 157.

Queen Charlotte *(ship)*, 118, 131.

Ramillies *(frigate)*, 162.
Reeves, Captain, 107.
Resolution *(ship)*, 343.
Rio Janeiro, 147.
Roberts, Captain, 340.
    John, 286.
Rogers, Captain, 151.
Rooks, 34, 37.
Rotch, ——, 330.
Rotumah Island, Life on, 194.
Roundy, Israel W., 168.
Royal Admiral *(ship)*, 291.
Royal William *(guardship)*, 162.

St. Cruiz *(ship)*, 319.
St. Helena, 85, 99, 100, 135.
St. Jago, Island of, 119.
St. Paul Island, 169.
Sally *(ship)*, 322.
Samoa Islands, 271.
San Benito Islands, 216.
San Pedro *(Spanish vessel)*, 214.
Sandal wood, 271, 273.

Sandwich Islands, 93-95, 121-124, 130, 217.
Sanguin Island, 294.
Santa Rosa del Calmo *(Spanish brig)*, 214.
Savage, Captain, 154.
Scotland, John, 284.
Scott's Islands, 339.
Scurvey, 343.
Sea lions, 146.
Sea Otter *(vessel)*, 339.
Sea pie and frolic, 334.
Seals, fur, 49, 60, 146.
Seaman, William, 2.
Shafford, Doctor, 94.
Shannon *(frigate)*, 73.
Sharks, 122.
Shark's teeth weapons, 271.
Shaw, Nathaniel, 338.
Shaw & Randall, 287.
Shiels, Captain, 144, 147.
Shute, ——, 96.
Singleton, William, 285.
Sir Edward Huse *(ship)*, 291.
Snakeroot, 131.
Snow, — type of vessel, 338.
South Sea Company, 339, 341.
Spear, John, 2.
Spencer, Mary Ann, 9, 13.
Spy *(brig)*, 168, 207.
Stevenson, William, 286.
Storms, Severe, 97, 168, 314-316.
Sunday Island, 183.
Surprise *(frigate)*, 107.
Surprise *(man-of-war)*, 157.
Swain, Captain, 335.
Swan Island, Falkland Is., 17.

Terrapin, 91.

Tigre *(74 gun ship)*, 161.

Tonga Islands, 218; natives capture the *Port au Prince* (privateer), 222; the ship is broken up, 228; account of an expedition against another chief, 230; the attack on the fortress, 235; cannibal feast, 240; military review, 243; the attack upon another island, 245; the assault on the fortress, 251; cruelty shown to prisoners, 259; capture of women, 263; condition of women on the islands, 265; death of the King, 275; breaking of heads, 275.

Tortoise, 91.

Tortoise shell, 200.

Towell, William, 285.

Treadwell, Charles, 291, 296, 299.

Tripe, Samuel, 289.

Trumbull *(ship)*, 96, 99.

Turner, William, 209, 210.

Tushook bogs, 42.

Vannable, John, 290.

Venerable *(man-of-war)*, 153.

Venger *(lare boat)*, 290.

Vibberts, Captain, 99.

Walker, Captain, 76-79, 90.

Wall, John, 291, 293, 315.

Washington *(sloop)*, 290, 291, 292, 338, 342.

Waters, James, 281, 285.

Watson, John, 285.

Whale ships, 3.

Whaling, 74, 75, 77, 114, 145, 216, 330-336.

Whampoa, 133, 291.

Whippey, ——, 333.

David, 186, 187.

Capt. James, 325.

Whitelam, Sarah, 140, 144, 151, 165.

Whitman, ——, 96.

Whitney, David, 293, 297.

Wickannish, 295.

Wilcox, ——, 96.

Wildman *(ship)*, 75.

Williams, Hugh, 269, 285.

Williamson, ——, 327.

Thomas, 291, 293.

Willis, George, 130.

Wines, John, 1.

Wood, George, 220, 285.

Women, Condition of Tonga Island, 265-267.

Wyld, Robert, 146.

Young, Captain, 115.

John, 94, 95.

Young Nanina *(shallop)*, 2.

A CATALOG OF SELECTED
DOVER BOOKS
IN ALL FIELDS OF INTEREST

A CATALOG OF SELECTED DOVER BOOKS IN ALL FIELDS OF INTEREST

100 BEST-LOVED POEMS, Edited by Philip Smith. "The Passionate Shepherd to His Love," "Shall I compare thee to a summer's day?" "Death, be not proud," "The Raven," "The Road Not Taken," plus works by Blake, Wordsworth, Byron, Shelley, Keats, many others. 96pp. $5\frac{3}{16}$ x $8\frac{1}{4}$. 0-486-28553-7

100 SMALL HOUSES OF THE THIRTIES, Brown-Blodgett Company. Exterior photographs and floor plans for 100 charming structures. Illustrations of models accompanied by descriptions of interiors, color schemes, closet space, and other amenities. 200 illustrations. 112pp. $8\frac{3}{8}$ x 11. 0-486-44131-8

1000 TURN-OF-THE-CENTURY HOUSES: With Illustrations and Floor Plans, Herbert C. Chivers. Reproduced from a rare edition, this showcase of homes ranges from cottages and bungalows to sprawling mansions. Each house is meticulously illustrated and accompanied by complete floor plans. 256pp. $9\frac{3}{8}$ x $12\frac{1}{4}$. 0-486-45596-3

101 GREAT AMERICAN POEMS, Edited by The American Poetry & Literacy Project. Rich treasury of verse from the 19th and 20th centuries includes works by Edgar Allan Poe, Robert Frost, Walt Whitman, Langston Hughes, Emily Dickinson, T. S. Eliot, other notables. 96pp. $5\frac{3}{16}$ x $8\frac{1}{4}$. 0-486-40158-8

101 GREAT SAMURAI PRINTS, Utagawa Kuniyoshi. Kuniyoshi was a master of the warrior woodblock print — and these 18th-century illustrations represent the pinnacle of his craft. Full-color portraits of renowned Japanese samurais pulse with movement, passion, and remarkably fine detail. 112pp. $8\frac{3}{8}$ x 11. 0-486-46523-3

ABC OF BALLET, Janet Grosser. Clearly worded, abundantly illustrated little guide defines basic ballet-related terms: arabesque, battement, pas de chat, relevé, sissonne, many others. Pronunciation guide included. Excellent primer. 48pp. $4\frac{3}{16}$ x $5\frac{3}{4}$. 0-486-40871-X

ACCESSORIES OF DRESS: An Illustrated Encyclopedia, Katherine Lester and Bess Viola Oerke. Illustrations of hats, veils, wigs, cravats, shawls, shoes, gloves, and other accessories enhance an engaging commentary that reveals the humor and charm of the many-sided story of accessorized apparel. 644 figures and 59 plates. 608pp. $6\frac{1}{8}$ x $9\frac{1}{4}$. 0-486-43378-1

ADVENTURES OF HUCKLEBERRY FINN, Mark Twain. Join Huck and Jim as their boyhood adventures along the Mississippi River lead them into a world of excitement, danger, and self-discovery. Humorous narrative, lyrical descriptions of the Mississippi valley, and memorable characters. 224pp. $5\frac{3}{16}$ x $8\frac{1}{4}$. 0-486-28061-6

ALICE STARMORE'S BOOK OF FAIR ISLE KNITTING, Alice Starmore. A noted designer from the region of Scotland's Fair Isle explores the history and techniques of this distinctive, stranded-color knitting style and provides copious illustrated instructions for 14 original knitwear designs. 208pp. $8\frac{3}{8}$ x $10\frac{7}{8}$. 0-486-47218-3

Browse over 9,000 books at www.doverpublications.com

ALICE'S ADVENTURES IN WONDERLAND, Lewis Carroll. Beloved classic about a little girl lost in a topsy-turvy land and her encounters with the White Rabbit, March Hare, Mad Hatter, Cheshire Cat, and other delightfully improbable characters. 42 illustrations by Sir John Tenniel. 96pp. 5¾₆ x 8¼. 0-486-27543-4

AMERICA'S LIGHTHOUSES: An Illustrated History, Francis Ross Holland. Profusely illustrated fact-filled survey of American lighthouses since 1716. Over 200 stations — East, Gulf, and West coasts, Great Lakes, Hawaii, Alaska, Puerto Rico, the Virgin Islands, and the Mississippi and St. Lawrence Rivers. 240pp. 8 x 10¾. 0-486-25576-X

AN ENCYCLOPEDIA OF THE VIOLIN, Alberto Bachmann. Translated by Frederick H. Martens. Introduction by Eugene Ysaye. First published in 1925, this renowned reference remains unsurpassed as a source of essential information, from construction and evolution to repertoire and technique. Includes a glossary and 73 illustrations. 496pp. 6⅛ x 9¼. 0-486-46618-3

ANIMALS: 1,419 Copyright-Free Illustrations of Mammals, Birds, Fish, Insects, etc., Selected by Jim Harter. Selected for its visual impact and ease of use, this outstanding collection of wood engravings presents over 1,000 species of animals in extremely lifelike poses. Includes mammals, birds, reptiles, amphibians, fish, insects, and other invertebrates. 284pp. 9 x 12. 0-486-23766-4

THE ANNALS, Tacitus. Translated by Alfred John Church and William Jackson Brodribb. This vital chronicle of Imperial Rome, written by the era's great historian, spans A.D. 14-68 and paints incisive psychological portraits of major figures, from Tiberius to Nero. 416pp. 5¾₆ x 8¼. 0-486-45236-0

ANTIGONE, Sophocles. Filled with passionate speeches and sensitive probing of moral and philosophical issues, this powerful and often-performed Greek drama reveals the grim fate that befalls the children of Oedipus. Footnotes. 64pp. 5¾₆ x 8 ¼. 0-486-27804-2

ART DECO DECORATIVE PATTERNS IN FULL COLOR, Christian Stoll. Reprinted from a rare 1910 portfolio, 160 sensuous and exotic images depict a breathtaking array of florals, geometrics, and abstracts — all elegant in their stark simplicity. 64pp. 8⅜ x 11. 0-486-44862-2

THE ARTHUR RACKHAM TREASURY: 86 Full-Color Illustrations, Arthur Rackham. Selected and Edited by Jeff A. Menges. A stunning treasury of 86 full-page plates span the famed English artist's career, from *Rip Van Winkle* (1905) to masterworks such as *Undine, A Midsummer Night's Dream,* and *Wind in the Willows* (1939). 96pp. 8⅜ x 11. 0-486-44685-9

THE AUTHENTIC GILBERT & SULLIVAN SONGBOOK, W. S. Gilbert and A. S. Sullivan. The most comprehensive collection available, this songbook includes selections from every one of Gilbert and Sullivan's light operas. Ninety-two numbers are presented uncut and unedited, and in their original keys. 410pp. 9 x 12. 0-486-23482-7

THE AWAKENING, Kate Chopin. First published in 1899, this controversial novel of a New Orleans wife's search for love outside a stifling marriage shocked readers. Today, it remains a first-rate narrative with superb characterization. New introductory Note. 128pp. 5¾₆ x 8¼. 0-486-27786-0

BASIC DRAWING, Louis Priscilla. Beginning with perspective, this commonsense manual progresses to the figure in movement, light and shade, anatomy, drapery, composition, trees and landscape, and outdoor sketching. Black-and-white illustrations throughout. 128pp. 8⅜ x 11. 0-486-45815-6

Browse over 9,000 books at www.doverpublications.com

THE BATTLES THAT CHANGED HISTORY, Fletcher Pratt. Historian profiles 16 crucial conflicts, ancient to modern, that changed the course of Western civilization. Gripping accounts of battles led by Alexander the Great, Joan of Arc, Ulysses S. Grant, other commanders. 27 maps. 352pp. 5⅜ x 8½. 0-486-41129-X

BEETHOVEN'S LETTERS, Ludwig van Beethoven. Edited by Dr. A. C. Kalischer. Features 457 letters to fellow musicians, friends, greats, patrons, and literary men. Reveals musical thoughts, quirks of personality, insights, and daily events. Includes 15 plates. 410pp. 5⅜ x 8½. 0-486-22769-3

BERNICE BOBS HER HAIR AND OTHER STORIES, F. Scott Fitzgerald. This brilliant anthology includes 6 of Fitzgerald's most popular stories: "The Diamond as Big as the Ritz," the title tale, "The Offshore Pirate," "The Ice Palace," "The Jelly Bean," and "May Day." 176pp. 5⅜ x 8½. 0-486-47049-0

BESLER'S BOOK OF FLOWERS AND PLANTS: 73 Full-Color Plates from Hortus Eystettensis, 1613, Basilius Besler. Here is a selection of magnificent plates from the *Hortus Eystettensis*, which vividly illustrated and identified the plants, flowers, and trees that thrived in the legendary German garden at Eichstätt. 80pp. 8⅜ x 11.
0-486-46005-3

THE BOOK OF KELLS, Edited by Blanche Cirker. Painstakingly reproduced from a rare facsimile edition, this volume contains full-page decorations, portraits, illustrations, plus a sampling of textual leaves with exquisite calligraphy and ornamentation. 32 full-color illustrations. 32pp. 9⅜ x 12¼. 0-486-24345-1

THE BOOK OF THE CROSSBOW: With an Additional Section on Catapults and Other Siege Engines, Ralph Payne-Gallwey. Fascinating study traces history and use of crossbow as military and sporting weapon, from Middle Ages to modern times. Also covers related weapons: balistas, catapults, Turkish bows, more. Over 240 illustrations. 400pp. 7¼ x 10⅛. 0-486-28720-3

THE BUNGALOW BOOK: Floor Plans and Photos of 112 Houses, 1910, Henry L. Wilson. Here are 112 of the most popular and economic blueprints of the early 20th century — plus an illustration or photograph of each completed house. A wonderful time capsule that still offers a wealth of valuable insights. 160pp. 8⅜ x 11.
0-486-45104-6

THE CALL OF THE WILD, Jack London. A classic novel of adventure, drawn from London's own experiences as a Klondike adventurer, relating the story of a heroic dog caught in the brutal life of the Alaska Gold Rush. Note. 64pp. 5³⁄₁₆ x 8¼.
0-486-26472-6

CANDIDE, Voltaire. Edited by Francois-Marie Arouet. One of the world's great satires since its first publication in 1759. Witty, caustic skewering of romance, science, philosophy, religion, government — nearly all human ideals and institutions. 112pp. 5³⁄₁₆ x 8¼. 0-486-26689-3

CELEBRATED IN THEIR TIME: Photographic Portraits from the George Grantham Bain Collection, Edited by Amy Pastan. With an Introduction by Michael Carlebach. Remarkable portrait gallery features 112 rare images of Albert Einstein, Charlie Chaplin, the Wright Brothers, Henry Ford, and other luminaries from the worlds of politics, art, entertainment, and industry. 128pp. 8⅜ x 11. 0-486-46754-6

CHARIOTS FOR APOLLO: The NASA History of Manned Lunar Spacecraft to 1969, Courtney G. Brooks, James M. Grimwood, and Loyd S. Swenson, Jr. This illustrated history by a trio of experts is the definitive reference on the Apollo spacecraft and lunar modules. It traces the vehicles' design, development, and operation in space. More than 100 photographs and illustrations. 576pp. 6¾ x 9¼. 0-486-46756-2

A CHRISTMAS CAROL, Charles Dickens. This engrossing tale relates Ebenezer Scrooge's ghostly journeys through Christmases past, present, and future and his ultimate transformation from a harsh and grasping old miser to a charitable and compassionate human being. 80pp. 5³⁄₁₆ x 8¼. 0-486-26865-9

COMMON SENSE, Thomas Paine. First published in January of 1776, this highly influential landmark document clearly and persuasively argued for American separation from Great Britain and paved the way for the Declaration of Independence. 64pp. 5³⁄₁₆ x 8¼. 0-486-29602-4

THE COMPLETE SHORT STORIES OF OSCAR WILDE, Oscar Wilde. Complete texts of "The Happy Prince and Other Tales," "A House of Pomegranates," "Lord Arthur Savile's Crime and Other Stories," "Poems in Prose," and "The Portrait of Mr. W. H." 208pp. 5³⁄₁₆ x 8¼. 0-486-45216-6

COMPLETE SONNETS, William Shakespeare. Over 150 exquisite poems deal with love, friendship, the tyranny of time, beauty's evanescence, death, and other themes in language of remarkable power, precision, and beauty. Glossary of archaic terms. 80pp. 5³⁄₁₆ x 8¼. 0-486-26686-9

THE COUNT OF MONTE CRISTO: Abridged Edition, Alexandre Dumas. Falsely accused of treason, Edmond Dantès is imprisoned in the bleak Chateau d'If. After a hair-raising escape, he launches an elaborate plot to extract a bitter revenge against those who betrayed him. 448pp. 5³⁄₁₆ x 8¼. 0-486-45643-9

CRAFTSMAN BUNGALOWS: Designs from the Pacific Northwest, Yoho & Merritt. This reprint of a rare catalog, showcasing the charming simplicity and cozy style of Craftsman bungalows, is filled with photos of completed homes, plus floor plans and estimated costs. An indispensable resource for architects, historians, and illustrators. 112pp. 10 x 7. 0-486-46875-5

CRAFTSMAN BUNGALOWS: 59 Homes from "The Craftsman," Edited by Gustav Stickley. Best and most attractive designs from Arts and Crafts Movement publication — 1903–1916 — includes sketches, photographs of homes, floor plans, descriptive text. 128pp. 8¼ x 11. 0-486-25829-7

CRIME AND PUNISHMENT, Fyodor Dostoyevsky. Translated by Constance Garnett. Supreme masterpiece tells the story of Raskolnikov, a student tormented by his own thoughts after he murders an old woman. Overwhelmed by guilt and terror, he confesses and goes to prison. 480pp. 5³⁄₁₆ x 8¼. 0-486-41587-2

THE DECLARATION OF INDEPENDENCE AND OTHER GREAT DOCUMENTS OF AMERICAN HISTORY: 1775-1865, Edited by John Grafton. Thirteen compelling and influential documents: Henry's "Give Me Liberty or Give Me Death," Declaration of Independence, The Constitution, Washington's First Inaugural Address, The Monroe Doctrine, The Emancipation Proclamation, Gettysburg Address, more. 64pp. 5³⁄₁₆ x 8¼. 0-486-41124-9

THE DESERT AND THE SOWN: Travels in Palestine and Syria, Gertrude Bell. "The female Lawrence of Arabia," Gertrude Bell wrote captivating, perceptive accounts of her travels in the Middle East. This intriguing narrative, accompanied by 160 photos, traces her 1905 sojourn in Lebanon, Syria, and Palestine. 368pp. 5⅜ x 8½. 0-486-46876-3

A DOLL'S HOUSE, Henrik Ibsen. Ibsen's best-known play displays his genius for realistic prose drama. An expression of women's rights, the play climaxes when the central character, Nora, rejects a smothering marriage and life in "a doll's house." 80pp. 5³⁄₁₆ x 8¼. 0-486-27062-9

DOOMED SHIPS: Great Ocean Liner Disasters, William H. Miller, Jr. Nearly 200 photographs, many from private collections, highlight tales of some of the vessels whose pleasure cruises ended in catastrophe: the *Morro Castle, Normandie, Andrea Doria, Europa,* and many others. 128pp. 8⅜ x 11¼.   0-486-45366-9

THE DORÉ BIBLE ILLUSTRATIONS, Gustave Doré. Detailed plates from the Bible: the Creation scenes, Adam and Eve, horrifying visions of the Flood, the battle sequences with their monumental crowds, depictions of the life of Jesus, 241 plates in all. 241pp. 9 x 12.   0-486-23004-X

DRAWING DRAPERY FROM HEAD TO TOE, Cliff Young. Expert guidance on how to draw shirts, pants, skirts, gloves, hats, and coats on the human figure, including folds in relation to the body, pull and crush, action folds, creases, more. Over 200 drawings. 48pp. 8¼ x 11.   0-486-45591-2

DUBLINERS, James Joyce. A fine and accessible introduction to the work of one of the 20th century's most influential writers, this collection features 15 tales, including a masterpiece of the short-story genre, "The Dead." 160pp. 5³⁄₁₆ x 8¼.
0-486-26870-5

EASY-TO-MAKE POP-UPS, Joan Irvine. Illustrated by Barbara Reid. Dozens of wonderful ideas for three-dimensional paper fun — from holiday greeting cards with moving parts to a pop-up menagerie. Easy-to-follow, illustrated instructions for more than 30 projects. 299 black-and-white illustrations. 96pp. 8⅜ x 11.
0-486-44622-0

EASY-TO-MAKE STORYBOOK DOLLS: A "Novel" Approach to Cloth Dollmaking, Sherralyn St. Clair. Favorite fictional characters come alive in this unique beginner's dollmaking guide. Includes patterns for Pollyanna, Dorothy from *The Wonderful Wizard of Oz,* Mary of *The Secret Garden,* plus easy-to-follow instructions, 263 black-and-white illustrations, and an 8-page color insert. 112pp. 8¼ x 11.   0-486-47360-0

EINSTEIN'S ESSAYS IN SCIENCE, Albert Einstein. Speeches and essays in accessible, everyday language profile influential physicists such as Niels Bohr and Isaac Newton. They also explore areas of physics to which the author made major contributions. 128pp. 5 x 8.   0-486-47011-3

EL DORADO: Further Adventures of the Scarlet Pimpernel, Baroness Orczy. A popular sequel to *The Scarlet Pimpernel,* this suspenseful story recounts the Pimpernel's attempts to rescue the Dauphin from imprisonment during the French Revolution. An irresistible blend of intrigue, period detail, and vibrant characterizations. 352pp. 5³⁄₁₆ x 8¼.   0-486-44026-5

ELEGANT SMALL HOMES OF THE TWENTIES: 99 Designs from a Competition, Chicago Tribune. Nearly 100 designs for five- and six-room houses feature New England and Southern colonials, Normandy cottages, stately Italianate dwellings, and other fascinating snapshots of American domestic architecture of the 1920s. 112pp. 9 x 12.   0-486-46910-7

THE ELEMENTS OF STYLE: The Original Edition, William Strunk, Jr. This is the book that generations of writers have relied upon for timeless advice on grammar, diction, syntax, and other essentials. In concise terms, it identifies the principal requirements of proper style and common errors. 64pp. 5⅜ x 8½.   0-486-44798-7

THE ELUSIVE PIMPERNEL, Baroness Orczy. Robespierre's revolutionaries find their wicked schemes thwarted by the heroic Pimpernel — Sir Percival Blakeney. In this thrilling sequel, Chauvelin devises a plot to eliminate the Pimpernel and his wife. 272pp. 5³⁄₁₆ x 8¼.   0-486-45464-9

Browse over 9,000 books at www.doverpublications.com

AN ENCYCLOPEDIA OF BATTLES: Accounts of Over 1,560 Battles from 1479 B.C. to the Present, David Eggenberger. Essential details of every major battle in recorded history from the first battle of Megiddo in 1479 B.C. to Grenada in 1984. List of battle maps. 99 illustrations. 544pp. 6½ x 9¼. 0-486-24913-1

ENCYCLOPEDIA OF EMBROIDERY STITCHES, INCLUDING CREWEL, Marion Nichols. Precise explanations and instructions, clearly illustrated, on how to work chain, back, cross, knotted, woven stitches, and many more — 178 in all, including Cable Outline, Whipped Satin, and Eyelet Buttonhole. Over 1400 illustrations. 219pp. 8⅜ x 11¼. 0-486-22929-7

ENTER JEEVES: 15 Early Stories, P. G. Wodehouse. Splendid collection contains first 8 stories featuring Bertie Wooster, the deliciously dim aristocrat and Jeeves, his brainy, imperturbable manservant. Also, the complete Reggie Pepper (Bertie's prototype) series. 288pp. 5⅜ x 8½. 0-486-29717-9

ERIC SLOANE'S AMERICA: Paintings in Oil, Michael Wigley. With a Foreword by Mimi Sloane. Eric Sloane's evocative oils of America's landscape and material culture shimmer with immense historical and nostalgic appeal. This original hardcover collection gathers nearly a hundred of his finest paintings, with subjects ranging from New England to the American Southwest. 128pp. 10⅝ x 9. 0-486-46525-X

ETHAN FROME, Edith Wharton. Classic story of wasted lives, set against a bleak New England background. Superbly delineated characters in a hauntingly grim tale of thwarted love. Considered by many to be Wharton's masterpiece. 96pp. 5$\frac{3}{16}$ x 8 ¼. 0-486-26690-7

THE EVERLASTING MAN, G. K. Chesterton. Chesterton's view of Christianity — as a blend of philosophy and mythology, satisfying intellect and spirit — applies to his brilliant book, which appeals to readers' heads as well as their hearts. 288pp. 5⅜ x 8½. 0-486-46036-3

THE FIELD AND FOREST HANDY BOOK, Daniel Beard. Written by a co-founder of the Boy Scouts, this appealing guide offers illustrated instructions for building kites, birdhouses, boats, igloos, and other fun projects, plus numerous helpful tips for campers. 448pp. 5$\frac{3}{16}$ x 8¼. 0-486-46191-2

FINDING YOUR WAY WITHOUT MAP OR COMPASS, Harold Gatty. Useful, instructive manual shows would-be explorers, hikers, bikers, scouts, sailors, and survivalists how to find their way outdoors by observing animals, weather patterns, shifting sands, and other elements of nature. 288pp. 5⅜ x 8½. 0-486-40613-X

FIRST FRENCH READER: A Beginner's Dual-Language Book, Edited and Translated by Stanley Appelbaum. This anthology introduces 50 legendary writers — Voltaire, Balzac, Baudelaire, Proust, more — through passages from *The Red and the Black, Les Misérables, Madame Bovary,* and other classics. Original French text plus English translation on facing pages. 240pp. 5⅜ x 8½. 0-486-46178-5

FIRST GERMAN READER: A Beginner's Dual-Language Book, Edited by Harry Steinhauer. Specially chosen for their power to evoke German life and culture, these short, simple readings include poems, stories, essays, and anecdotes by Goethe, Hesse, Heine, Schiller, and others. 224pp. 5⅜ x 8½. 0-486-46179-3

FIRST SPANISH READER: A Beginner's Dual-Language Book, Angel Flores. Delightful stories, other material based on works of Don Juan Manuel, Luis Taboada, Ricardo Palma, other noted writers. Complete faithful English translations on facing pages. Exercises. 176pp. 5⅜ x 8½. 0-486-25810-6

Browse over 9,000 books at www.doverpublications.com

FIVE ACRES AND INDEPENDENCE, Maurice G. Kains. Great back-to-the-land classic explains basics of self-sufficient farming. The one book to get. 95 illustrations. 397pp. 5⅜ x 8½. 0-486-20974-1

FLAGG'S SMALL HOUSES: Their Economic Design and Construction, 1922, Ernest Flagg. Although most famous for his skyscrapers, Flagg was also a proponent of the well-designed single-family dwelling. His classic treatise features innovations that save space, materials, and cost. 526 illustrations. 160pp. 9⅜ x 12¼. 0-486-45197-6

FLATLAND: A Romance of Many Dimensions, Edwin A. Abbott. Classic of science (and mathematical) fiction — charmingly illustrated by the author — describes the adventures of A. Square, a resident of Flatland, in Spaceland (three dimensions), Lineland (one dimension), and Pointland (no dimensions). 96pp. 5³⁄₁₆ x 8¼. 0-486-27263-X

FRANKENSTEIN, Mary Shelley. The story of Victor Frankenstein's monstrous creation and the havoc it caused has enthralled generations of readers and inspired countless writers of horror and suspense. With the author's own 1831 introduction. 176pp. 5³⁄₁₆ x 8¼. 0-486-28211-2

THE GARGOYLE BOOK: 572 Examples from Gothic Architecture, Lester Burbank Bridaham. Dispelling the conventional wisdom that French Gothic architectural flourishes were born of despair or gloom, Bridaham reveals the whimsical nature of these creations and the ingenious artisans who made them. 572 illustrations. 224pp. 8⅜ x 11. 0-486-44754-5

THE GIFT OF THE MAGI AND OTHER SHORT STORIES, O. Henry. Sixteen captivating stories by one of America's most popular storytellers. Included are such classics as "The Gift of the Magi," "The Last Leaf," and "The Ransom of Red Chief." Publisher's Note. 96pp. 5³⁄₁₆ x 8¼. 0-486-27061-0

THE GOETHE TREASURY: Selected Prose and Poetry, Johann Wolfgang von Goethe. Edited, Selected, and with an Introduction by Thomas Mann. In addition to his lyric poetry, Goethe wrote travel sketches, autobiographical studies, essays, letters, and proverbs in rhyme and prose. This collection presents outstanding examples from each genre. 368pp. 5⅜ x 8½. 0-486-44780-4

GREAT EXPECTATIONS, Charles Dickens. Orphaned Pip is apprenticed to the dirty work of the forge but dreams of becoming a gentleman — and one day finds himself in possession of "great expectations." Dickens' finest novel. 400pp. 5³⁄₁₆ x 8¼. 0-486-41586-4

GREAT WRITERS ON THE ART OF FICTION: From Mark Twain to Joyce Carol Oates, Edited by James Daley. An indispensable source of advice and inspiration, this anthology features essays by Henry James, Kate Chopin, Willa Cather, Sinclair Lewis, Jack London, Raymond Chandler, Raymond Carver, Eudora Welty, and Kurt Vonnegut, Jr. 192pp. 5⅜ x 8½. 0-486-45128-3

HAMLET, William Shakespeare. The quintessential Shakespearean tragedy, whose highly charged confrontations and anguished soliloquies probe depths of human feeling rarely sounded in any art. Reprinted from an authoritative British edition complete with illuminating footnotes. 128pp. 5³⁄₁₆ x 8¼. 0-486-27278-8

THE HAUNTED HOUSE, Charles Dickens. A Yuletide gathering in an eerie country retreat provides the backdrop for Dickens and his friends — including Elizabeth Gaskell and Wilkie Collins — who take turns spinning supernatural yarns. 144pp. 5⅜ x 8½. 0-486-46309-5

Browse over 9,000 books at www.doverpublications.com

HEART OF DARKNESS, Joseph Conrad. Dark allegory of a journey up the Congo River and the narrator's encounter with the mysterious Mr. Kurtz. Masterly blend of adventure, character study, psychological penetration. For many, Conrad's finest, most enigmatic story. 80pp. 5³⁄₁₆ x 8¼. 0-486-26464-5

HENSON AT THE NORTH POLE, Matthew A. Henson. This thrilling memoir by the heroic African-American who was Peary's companion through two decades of Arctic exploration recounts a tale of danger, courage, and determination. "Fascinating and exciting." — *Commonweal*. 128pp. 5⅜ x 8½. 0-486-45472-X

HISTORIC COSTUMES AND HOW TO MAKE THEM, Mary Fernald and E. Shenton. Practical, informative guidebook shows how to create everything from short tunics worn by Saxon men in the fifth century to a lady's bustle dress of the late 1800s. 81 illustrations. 176pp. 5⅜ x 8½. 0-486-44906-8

THE HOUND OF THE BASKERVILLES, Arthur Conan Doyle. A deadly curse in the form of a legendary ferocious beast continues to claim its victims from the Baskerville family until Holmes and Watson intervene. Often called the best detective story ever written. 128pp. 5³⁄₁₆ x 8¼. 0-486-28214-7

THE HOUSE BEHIND THE CEDARS, Charles W. Chesnutt. Originally published in 1900, this groundbreaking novel by a distinguished African-American author recounts the drama of a brother and sister who "pass for white" during the dangerous days of Reconstruction. 208pp. 5⅜ x 8½. 0-486-46144-0

THE HUMAN FIGURE IN MOTION, Eadweard Muybridge. The 4,789 photographs in this definitive selection show the human figure — models almost all undraped — engaged in over 160 different types of action: running, climbing stairs, etc. 390pp. 7⅞ x 10⅝. 0-486-20204-6

THE IMPORTANCE OF BEING EARNEST, Oscar Wilde. Wilde's witty and buoyant comedy of manners, filled with some of literature's most famous epigrams, reprinted from an authoritative British edition. Considered Wilde's most perfect work. 64pp. 5³⁄₁₆ x 8¼. 0-486-26478-5

THE INFERNO, Dante Alighieri. Translated and with notes by Henry Wadsworth Longfellow. The first stop on Dante's famous journey from Hell to Purgatory to Paradise, this 14th-century allegorical poem blends vivid and shocking imagery with graceful lyricism. Translated by the beloved 19th-century poet, Henry Wadsworth Longfellow. 256pp. 5³⁄₁₆ x 8¼. 0-486-44288-8

JANE EYRE, Charlotte Brontë. Written in 1847, *Jane Eyre* tells the tale of an orphan girl's progress from the custody of cruel relatives to an oppressive boarding school and its culmination in a troubled career as a governess. 448pp. 5³⁄₁₆ x 8¼.
0-486-42449-9

JAPANESE WOODBLOCK FLOWER PRINTS, Tanigami Kônan. Extraordinary collection of Japanese woodblock prints by a well-known artist features 120 plates in brilliant color. Realistic images from a rare edition include daffodils, tulips, and other familiar and unusual flowers. 128pp. 11 x 8¼. 0-486-46442-3

JEWELRY MAKING AND DESIGN, Augustus F. Rose and Antonio Cirino. Professional secrets of jewelry making are revealed in a thorough, practical guide. Over 200 illustrations. 306pp. 5⅜ x 8½. 0-486-21750-7

JULIUS CAESAR, William Shakespeare. Great tragedy based on Plutarch's account of the lives of Brutus, Julius Caesar and Mark Antony. Evil plotting, ringing oratory, high tragedy with Shakespeare's incomparable insight, dramatic power. Explanatory footnotes. 96pp. 5³⁄₁₆ x 8¼. 0-486-26876-4

Browse over 9,000 books at www.doverpublications.com

THE JUNGLE, Upton Sinclair. 1906 bestseller shockingly reveals intolerable labor practices and working conditions in the Chicago stockyards as it tells the grim story of a Slavic family that emigrates to America full of optimism but soon faces despair. 320pp. 5³⁄₁₆ x 8¼. 0-486-41923-1

THE KINGDOM OF GOD IS WITHIN YOU, Leo Tolstoy. The soul-searching book that inspired Gandhi to embrace the concept of passive resistance, Tolstoy's 1894 polemic clearly outlines a radical, well-reasoned revision of traditional Christian thinking. 352pp. 5³⁄₁₆ x 8¼. 0-486-45138-0

THE LADY OR THE TIGER?: and Other Logic Puzzles, Raymond M. Smullyan. Created by a renowned puzzle master, these whimsically themed challenges involve paradoxes about probability, time, and change; metapuzzles; and self-referentiality. Nineteen chapters advance in difficulty from relatively simple to highly complex. 1982 edition. 240pp. 5⅜ x 8½. 0-486-47027-X

LEAVES OF GRASS: The Original 1855 Edition, Walt Whitman. Whitman's immortal collection includes some of the greatest poems of modern times, including his masterpiece, "Song of Myself." Shattering standard conventions, it stands as an unabashed celebration of body and nature. 128pp. 5³⁄₁₆ x 8¼. 0-486-45676-5

LES MISÉRABLES, Victor Hugo. Translated by Charles E. Wilbour. Abridged by James K. Robinson. A convict's heroic struggle for justice and redemption plays out against a fiery backdrop of the Napoleonic wars. This edition features the excellent original translation and a sensitive abridgment. 304pp. 6⅛ x 9¼.
0-486-45789-3

LILITH: A Romance, George MacDonald. In this novel by the father of fantasy literature, a man travels through time to meet Adam and Eve and to explore humanity's fall from grace and ultimate redemption. 240pp. 5⅜ x 8½.
0-486-46818-6

THE LOST LANGUAGE OF SYMBOLISM, Harold Bayley. This remarkable book reveals the hidden meaning behind familiar images and words, from the origins of Santa Claus to the fleur-de-lys, drawing from mythology, folklore, religious texts, and fairy tales. 1,418 illustrations. 784pp. 5⅜ x 8½. 0-486-44787-1

MACBETH, William Shakespeare. A Scottish nobleman murders the king in order to succeed to the throne. Tortured by his conscience and fearful of discovery, he becomes tangled in a web of treachery and deceit that ultimately spells his doom. 96pp. 5³⁄₁₆ x 8¼. 0-486-27802-6

MAKING AUTHENTIC CRAFTSMAN FURNITURE: Instructions and Plans for 62 Projects, Gustav Stickley. Make authentic reproductions of handsome, functional, durable furniture: tables, chairs, wall cabinets, desks, a hall tree, and more. Construction plans with drawings, schematics, dimensions, and lumber specs reprinted from 1900s The Craftsman magazine. 128pp. 8⅛ x 11. 0-486-25000-8

MATHEMATICS FOR THE NONMATHEMATICIAN, Morris Kline. Erudite and entertaining overview follows development of mathematics from ancient Greeks to present. Topics include logic and mathematics, the fundamental concept, differential calculus, probability theory, much more. Exercises and problems. 641pp. 5⅜ x 8½. 0-486-24823-2

MEMOIRS OF AN ARABIAN PRINCESS FROM ZANZIBAR, Emily Ruete. This 19th-century autobiography offers a rare inside look at the society surrounding a sultan's palace. A real-life princess in exile recalls her vanished world of harems, slave trading, and court intrigues. 288pp. 5⅜ x 8½. 0-486-47121-7

Browse over 9,000 books at www.doverpublications.com

THE METAMORPHOSIS AND OTHER STORIES, Franz Kafka. Excellent new English translations of title story (considered by many critics Kafka's most perfect work), plus "The Judgment," "In the Penal Colony," "A Country Doctor," and "A Report to an Academy." Note. 96pp. 5³⁄₁₆ x 8¼.   0-486-29030-1

MICROSCOPIC ART FORMS FROM THE PLANT WORLD, R. Anheisser. From undulating curves to complex geometrics, a world of fascinating images abound in this classic, illustrated survey of microscopic plants. Features 400 detailed illustrations of nature's minute but magnificent handiwork. The accompanying CD-ROM includes all of the images in the book. 128pp. 9 x 9.   0-486-46013-4

A MIDSUMMER NIGHT'S DREAM, William Shakespeare. Among the most popular of Shakespeare's comedies, this enchanting play humorously celebrates the vagaries of love as it focuses upon the intertwined romances of several pairs of lovers. Explanatory footnotes. 80pp. 5³⁄₁₆ x 8¼.   0-486-27067-X

THE MONEY CHANGERS, Upton Sinclair. Originally published in 1908, this cautionary novel from the author of *The Jungle* explores corruption within the American system as a group of power brokers joins forces for personal gain, triggering a crash on Wall Street. 192pp. 5⅜ x 8½.   0-486-46917-4

THE MOST POPULAR HOMES OF THE TWENTIES, William A. Radford. With a New Introduction by Daniel D. Reiff. Based on a rare 1925 catalog, this architectural showcase features floor plans, construction details, and photos of 26 homes, plus articles on entrances, porches, garages, and more. 250 illustrations, 21 color plates. 176pp. 8⅜ x 11.   0-486-47028-8

MY 66 YEARS IN THE BIG LEAGUES, Connie Mack. With a New Introduction by Rich Westcott. A Founding Father of modern baseball, Mack holds the record for most wins — and losses — by a major league manager. Enhanced by 70 photographs, his warmhearted autobiography is populated by many legends of the game. 288pp. 5⅜ x 8½.   0-486-47184-5

NARRATIVE OF THE LIFE OF FREDERICK DOUGLASS, Frederick Douglass. Douglass's graphic depictions of slavery, harrowing escape to freedom, and life as a newspaper editor, eloquent orator, and impassioned abolitionist. 96pp. 5³⁄₁₆ x 8¼.   0-486-28499-9

THE NIGHTLESS CITY: Geisha and Courtesan Life in Old Tokyo, J. E. de Becker. This unsurpassed study from 100 years ago ventured into Tokyo's red-light district to survey geisha and courtesan life and offer meticulous descriptions of training, dress, social hierarchy, and erotic practices. 49 black-and-white illustrations; 2 maps. 496pp. 5⅜ x 8½.   0-486-45563-7

THE ODYSSEY, Homer. Excellent prose translation of ancient epic recounts adventures of the homeward-bound Odysseus. Fantastic cast of gods, giants, cannibals, sirens, other supernatural creatures — true classic of Western literature. 256pp. 5³⁄₁₆ x 8¼.   0-486-40654-7

OEDIPUS REX, Sophocles. Landmark of Western drama concerns the catastrophe that ensues when King Oedipus discovers he has inadvertently killed his father and married his mother. Masterly construction, dramatic irony. Explanatory footnotes. 64pp. 5³⁄₁₆ x 8¼.   0-486-26877-2

ONCE UPON A TIME: The Way America Was, Eric Sloane. Nostalgic text and drawings brim with gentle philosophies and descriptions of how we used to live — self-sufficiently — on the land, in homes, and among the things built by hand. 44 line illustrations. 64pp. 8⅜ x 11.   0-486-44411-2

ONE OF OURS, Willa Cather. The Pulitzer Prize–winning novel about a young Nebraskan looking for something to believe in. Alienated from his parents, rejected by his wife, he finds his destiny on the bloody battlefields of World War I. 352pp. 5³⁄₁₆ x 8¼. 0-486-45599-8

ORIGAMI YOU CAN USE: 27 Practical Projects, Rick Beech. Origami models can be more than decorative, and this unique volume shows how! The 27 practical projects include a CD case, frame, napkin ring, and dish. Easy instructions feature 400 two-color illustrations. 96pp. 8¼ x 11. 0-486-47057-1

OTHELLO, William Shakespeare. Towering tragedy tells the story of a Moorish general who earns the enmity of his ensign Iago when he passes him over for a promotion. Masterly portrait of an archvillain. Explanatory footnotes. 112pp. 5³⁄₁₆ x 8¼. 0-486-29097-2

PARADISE LOST, John Milton. Notes by John A. Himes. First published in 1667, *Paradise Lost* ranks among the greatest of English literature's epic poems. It's a sublime retelling of Adam and Eve's fall from grace and expulsion from Eden. Notes by John A. Himes. 480pp. 5³⁄₁₆ x 8¼. 0-486-44287-X

PASSING, Nella Larsen. Married to a successful physician and prominently ensconced in society, Irene Redfield leads a charmed existence — until a chance encounter with a childhood friend who has been "passing for white." 112pp. 5⅜ x 8½. 0-486-43713-2

PERSPECTIVE DRAWING FOR BEGINNERS, Len A. Doust. Doust carefully explains the roles of lines, boxes, and circles, and shows how visualizing shapes and forms can be used in accurate depictions of perspective. One of the most concise introductions available. 33 illustrations. 64pp. 5⅜ x 8½. 0-486-45149-6

PERSPECTIVE MADE EASY, Ernest R. Norling. Perspective is easy; yet, surprisingly few artists know the simple rules that make it so. Remedy that situation with this simple, step-by-step book, the first devoted entirely to the topic. 256 illustrations. 224pp. 5⅜ x 8½. 0-486-40473-0

THE PICTURE OF DORIAN GRAY, Oscar Wilde. Celebrated novel involves a handsome young Londoner who sinks into a life of depravity. His body retains perfect youth and vigor while his recent portrait reflects the ravages of his crime and sensuality. 176pp. 5³⁄₁₆ x 8¼. 0-486-27807-7

PRIDE AND PREJUDICE, Jane Austen. One of the most universally loved and admired English novels, an effervescent tale of rural romance transformed by Jane Austen's art into a witty, shrewdly observed satire of English country life. 272pp. 5³⁄₁₆ x 8¼. 0-486-28473-5

THE PRINCE, Niccolò Machiavelli. Classic, Renaissance-era guide to acquiring and maintaining political power. Today, nearly 500 years after it was written, this calculating prescription for autocratic rule continues to be much read and studied. 80pp. 5³⁄₁₆ x 8¼. 0-486-27274-5

QUICK SKETCHING, Carl Cheek. A perfect introduction to the technique of "quick sketching." Drawing upon an artist's immediate emotional responses, this is an extremely effective means of capturing the essential form and features of a subject. More than 100 black-and-white illustrations throughout. 48pp. 11 x 8¼. 0-486-46608-6

RANCH LIFE AND THE HUNTING TRAIL, Theodore Roosevelt. Illustrated by Frederic Remington. Beautifully illustrated by Remington, Roosevelt's celebration of the Old West recounts his adventures in the Dakota Badlands of the 1880s, from roundups to Indian encounters to hunting bighorn sheep. 208pp. 6¼ x 9¼. 0-486-47340-6

Browse over 9,000 books at www.doverpublications.com

CATALOG OF DOVER BOOKS

THE RED BADGE OF COURAGE, Stephen Crane. Amid the nightmarish chaos of a Civil War battle, a young soldier discovers courage, humility, and, perhaps, wisdom. Uncanny re-creation of actual combat. Enduring landmark of American fiction. 112pp. 5³⁄₁₆ x 8¼. 0-486-26465-3

RELATIVITY SIMPLY EXPLAINED, Martin Gardner. One of the subject's clearest, most entertaining introductions offers lucid explanations of special and general theories of relativity, gravity, and spacetime, models of the universe, and more. 100 illustrations. 224pp. 5⅜ x 8½. 0-486-29315-7

REMBRANDT DRAWINGS: 116 Masterpieces in Original Color, Rembrandt van Rijn. This deluxe hardcover edition features drawings from throughout the Dutch master's prolific career. Informative captions accompany these beautifully reproduced landscapes, biblical vignettes, figure studies, animal sketches, and portraits. 128pp. 8⅜ x 11. 0-486-46149-1

THE ROAD NOT TAKEN AND OTHER POEMS, Robert Frost. A treasury of Frost's most expressive verse. In addition to the title poem: "An Old Man's Winter Night," "In the Home Stretch," "Meeting and Passing," "Putting in the Seed," many more. All complete and unabridged. 64pp. 5³⁄₁₆ x 8¼. 0-486-27550-7

ROMEO AND JULIET, William Shakespeare. Tragic tale of star-crossed lovers, feuding families and timeless passion contains some of Shakespeare's most beautiful and lyrical love poetry. Complete, unabridged text with explanatory footnotes. 96pp. 5³⁄₁₆ x 8¼. 0-486-27557-1

SANDITON AND THE WATSONS: Austen's Unfinished Novels, Jane Austen. Two tantalizing incomplete stories revisit Austen's customary milieu of courtship and venture into new territory, amid guests at a seaside resort. Both are worth reading for pleasure and study. 112pp. 5⅜ x 8½. 0-486-45793-1

THE SCARLET LETTER, Nathaniel Hawthorne. With stark power and emotional depth, Hawthorne's masterpiece explores sin, guilt, and redemption in a story of adultery in the early days of the Massachusetts Colony. 192pp. 5³⁄₁₆ x 8¼.
0-486-28048-9

THE SEASONS OF AMERICA PAST, Eric Sloane. Seventy-five illustrations depict cider mills and presses, sleds, pumps, stump-pulling equipment, plows, and other elements of America's rural heritage. A section of old recipes and household hints adds additional color. 160pp. 8⅜ x 11. 0-486-44220-9

SELECTED CANTERBURY TALES, Geoffrey Chaucer. Delightful collection includes the General Prologue plus three of the most popular tales: "The Knight's Tale," "The Miller's Prologue and Tale," and "The Wife of Bath's Prologue and Tale." In modern English. 144pp. 5³⁄₁₆ x 8¼. 0-486-28241-4

SELECTED POEMS, Emily Dickinson. Over 100 best-known, best-loved poems by one of America's foremost poets, reprinted from authoritative early editions. No comparable edition at this price. Index of first lines. 64pp. 5³⁄₁₆ x 8¼. 0-486-26466-1

SIDDHARTHA, Hermann Hesse. Classic novel that has inspired generations of seekers. Blending Eastern mysticism and psychoanalysis, Hesse presents a strikingly original view of man and culture and the arduous process of self-discovery, reconciliation, harmony, and peace. 112pp. 5³⁄₁₆ x 8¼. 0-486-40653-9

SKETCHING OUTDOORS, Leonard Richmond. This guide offers beginners step-by-step demonstrations of how to depict clouds, trees, buildings, and other outdoor sights. Explanations of a variety of techniques include shading and constructional drawing. 48pp. 11 x 8¼. 0-486-46922-0

Browse over 9,000 books at www.doverpublications.com

SMALL HOUSES OF THE FORTIES: With Illustrations and Floor Plans, Harold E. Group. 56 floor plans and elevations of houses that originally cost less than $15,000 to build. Recommended by financial institutions of the era, they range from Colonials to Cape Cods. 144pp. 8⅜ x 11. 0-486-45598-X

SOME CHINESE GHOSTS, Lafcadio Hearn. Rooted in ancient Chinese legends, these richly atmospheric supernatural tales are recounted by an expert in Oriental lore. Their originality, power, and literary charm will captivate readers of all ages. 96pp. 5⅜ x 8½. 0-486-46306-0

SONGS FOR THE OPEN ROAD: Poems of Travel and Adventure, Edited by The American Poetry & Literacy Project. More than 80 poems by 50 American and British masters celebrate real and metaphorical journeys. Poems by Whitman, Byron, Millay, Sandburg, Langston Hughes, Emily Dickinson, Robert Frost, Shelley, Tennyson, Yeats, many others. Note. 80pp. 5³⁄₁₆ x 8¼. 0-486-40646-6

SPOON RIVER ANTHOLOGY, Edgar Lee Masters. An American poetry classic, in which former citizens of a mythical midwestern town speak touchingly from the grave of the thwarted hopes and dreams of their lives. 144pp. 5³⁄₁₆ x 8¼.
0-486-27275-3

STAR LORE: Myths, Legends, and Facts, William Tyler Olcott. Captivating retellings of the origins and histories of ancient star groups include Pegasus, Ursa Major, Pleiades, signs of the zodiac, and other constellations. "Classic." — *Sky & Telescope.* 58 illustrations. 544pp. 5⅜ x 8½. 0-486-43581-4

THE STRANGE CASE OF DR. JEKYLL AND MR. HYDE, Robert Louis Stevenson. This intriguing novel, both fantasy thriller and moral allegory, depicts the struggle of two opposing personalities — one essentially good, the other evil — for the soul of one man. 64pp. 5³⁄₁₆ x 8¼. 0-486-26688-5

SURVIVAL HANDBOOK: The Official U.S. Army Guide, Department of the Army. This special edition of the Army field manual is geared toward civilians. An essential companion for campers and all lovers of the outdoors, it constitutes the most authoritative wilderness guide. 288pp. 5³⁄₁₆ x 8¼. 0-486-46184-X

A TALE OF TWO CITIES, Charles Dickens. Against the backdrop of the French Revolution, Dickens unfolds his masterpiece of drama, adventure, and romance about a man falsely accused of treason. Excitement and derring-do in the shadow of the guillotine. 304pp. 5³⁄₁₆ x 8¼. 0-486-40651-2

TEN PLAYS, Anton Chekhov. *The Sea Gull, Uncle Vanya, The Three Sisters, The Cherry Orchard,* and *Ivanov,* plus 5 one-act comedies: *The Anniversary, An Unwilling Martyr, The Wedding, The Bear,* and *The Proposal.* 336pp. 5³⁄₁₆ x 8¼. 0-486-46560-8

THE FLYING INN, G. K. Chesterton. Hilarious romp in which pub owner Humphrey Hump and friend take to the road in a donkey cart filled with rum and cheese, inveighing against Prohibition and other "oppressive forms of modernity." 320pp. 5⅜ x 8½. 0-486-41910-X

THIRTY YEARS THAT SHOOK PHYSICS: The Story of Quantum Theory, George Gamow. Lucid, accessible introduction to the influential theory of energy and matter features careful explanations of Dirac's anti-particles, Bohr's model of the atom, and much more. Numerous drawings. 1966 edition. 240pp. 5⅜ x 8½. 0-486-24895-X

TREASURE ISLAND, Robert Louis Stevenson. Classic adventure story of a perilous sea journey, a mutiny led by the infamous Long John Silver, and a lethal scramble for buried treasure — seen through the eyes of cabin boy Jim Hawkins. 160pp. 5³⁄₁₆ x 8¼.
0-486-27559-0

THE TRIAL, Franz Kafka. Translated by David Wyllie. From its gripping first sentence onward, this novel exemplifies the term "Kafkaesque." Its darkly humorous narrative recounts a bank clerk's entrapment in a bureaucratic maze, based on an undisclosed charge. 176pp. 5³⁄₁₆ x 8¼. 0-486-47061-X

THE TURN OF THE SCREW, Henry James. Gripping ghost story by great novelist depicts the sinister transformation of 2 innocent children into flagrant liars and hypocrites. An elegantly told tale of unspoken horror and psychological terror. 96pp. 5³⁄₁₆ x 8¼. 0-486-26684-2

UP FROM SLAVERY, Booker T. Washington. Washington (1856-1915) rose to become the most influential spokesman for African-Americans of his day. In this eloquently written book, he describes events in a remarkable life that began in bondage and culminated in worldwide recognition. 160pp. 5³⁄₁₆ x 8¼. 0-486-28738-6

VICTORIAN HOUSE DESIGNS IN AUTHENTIC FULL COLOR: 75 Plates from the "Scientific American – Architects and Builders Edition," 1885-1894, Edited by Blanche Cirker. Exquisitely detailed, exceptionally handsome designs for an enormous variety of attractive city dwellings, spacious suburban and country homes, charming "cottages" and other structures — all accompanied by perspective views and floor plans. 80pp. 9¼ x 12¼. 0-486-29438-2

VILLETTE, Charlotte Brontë. Acclaimed by Virginia Woolf as "Brontë's finest novel," this moving psychological study features a remarkably modern heroine who abandons her native England for a new life as a schoolteacher in Belgium. 480pp. 5³⁄₁₆ x 8¼. 0-486-45557-2

THE VOYAGE OUT, Virginia Woolf. A moving depiction of the thrills and confusion of youth, Woolf's acclaimed first novel traces a shipboard journey to South America for a captivating exploration of a woman's growing self-awareness. 288pp. 5³⁄₁₆ x 8¼. 0-486-45005-8

WALDEN; OR, LIFE IN THE WOODS, Henry David Thoreau. Accounts of Thoreau's daily life on the shores of Walden Pond outside Concord, Massachusetts, are interwoven with musings on the virtues of self-reliance and individual freedom, on society, government, and other topics. 224pp. 5³⁄₁₆ x 8¼. 0-486-28495-6

WILD PILGRIMAGE: A Novel in Woodcuts, Lynd Ward. Through startling engravings shaded in black and red, Ward wordlessly tells the story of a man trapped in an industrial world, struggling between the grim reality around him and the fantasies his imagination creates. 112pp. 6⅛ x 9¼. 0-486-46583-7

WILLY POGÁNY REDISCOVERED, Willy Pogány. Selected and Edited by Jeff A. Menges. More than 100 color and black-and-white Art Nouveau–style illustrations from fairy tales and adventure stories include scenes from Wagner's "Ring" cycle, *The Rime of the Ancient Mariner, Gulliver's Travels,* and *Faust.* 144pp. 8⅜ x 11. 0-486-47046-6

WOOLLY THOUGHTS: Unlock Your Creative Genius with Modular Knitting, Pat Ashforth and Steve Plummer. Here's the revolutionary way to knit — easy, fun, and foolproof! Beginners and experienced knitters need only master a single stitch to create their own designs with patchwork squares. More than 100 illustrations. 128pp. 6½ x 9¼. 0-486-46084-3

WUTHERING HEIGHTS, Emily Brontë. Somber tale of consuming passions and vengeance — played out amid the lonely English moors — recounts the turbulent and tempestuous love story of Cathy and Heathcliff. Poignant and compelling. 256pp. 5³⁄₁₆ x 8¼. 0-486-29256-8

Browse over 9,000 books at www.doverpublications.com